ABOUT MOURNING
Support and Guidance
for the Bereaved

ABOUT MOURNING

Support and Guidance for the Bereaved

Savine Gross Weizman, Ph.D.
and
Phyllis Kamm

HUMAN SCIENCES PRESS, INC.
72 FIFTH AVENUE
NEW YORK, N.Y. 10011

Paperback edition copyright © 1987 by Human Sciences Press
Original hardcover edition copyright © 1985 by Human Sciences Press
72 Fifth Avenue, New York, New York 10011

Printed in the United States of America.

Library of Congress Cataloging in Publication Data

Weizman, Savine Gross.
   About mourning.
   Support and Guidance for the Bereaved

   Bibliography: p. 233
   Includes index.
   1. Death—Psychological aspects. 2. Bereavement—Psychological aspects.
   3. Psychology—Mourning
I. Kamm, Phyllis. II. Title.
BF789.D4W38 1985   155.9'37   83-12669
ISBN 0-89885-136-X
   0-89885-309-5 (Paperback)

IN MEMORY OF ALVIN A. WEIZMAN

This book is dedicated to those who have suffered a loss and have shared their experience for the comfort and support of others

ACKNOWLEDGEMENTS

I want to acknowledge my gratitude to my husband, Herb Kamm, a reporter, writer and editor for nearly fifty years, who wielded a sharp pencil to hone and clarify my writing.

I also want to thank the late Sam Levenson for his encouragement and permission to reprint his ethical will, and Danny Siegel for permission to reprint "Death of a Righteous One, Expiation and Irony," from his collection of poetry, *And God Braided Eve's Hair,* published in 1976 by United Synagogue of America.

Phyllis Kamm

CONTENTS

FOREWORD

Dr. Savine Gross Weizman and Phyllis Kamm have written a very moving book which is a guide for the bereaved, taking the reader through the mourning process. The need for such a book stems from the fact that while mourning is very much a part of the human condition, rarely are any of us prepared for the emotional pain and disruption that follows the death of a loved one. Most of us do not know how to mourn. There are a number of reasons for this. Among them are the inexperience we have with death. Most of us will grow into adulthood without having faced a death. Another reason for difficulty emerges from the embarrassment we feel when faced with extreme feelings and pain. When asked, "How are you?" we are conditioned to say, "Fine." We do not know how to accept in ourselves or others the pain and emptiness that follows a death without talking about these feelings as symptoms of an illness or as part of a deviant condition.

When we do think of mourning, we think of it as a process that relates only to the expression of the strong feelings of grief associated with weeping and sadness. Not only the mourner, but those friends and family who share the grief often assume that these feelings are temporary with a short life span that with time will go away completely. "Time heals" is the expression that is often used. It is true that the pain will be tempered with time as it loses its intensity, but the feelings of sadness do not go away. Mourners need to learn to accept these feelings. They will not be cured of grief, for it is not an illness; they will be changed by it. The readers are guided through this process, helping them sort out what can be realistically expected during the mourning period.

The mourner who has successfully coped with the issues and realities of a death is more sensitive to others and is more self-reliant with a new sense of self. People who have grieved appropriately are more accepting of the life cycle where death and mourning have their place and the readers may come to recognize the mourning period as a time for growth, for developing new skills to deal with change. It is a time when a good deal of learning must take place.

If people need to learn to mourn, in what way can they be taught? Our personal experience can be informed by trial and error. A good deal of learning does indeed take place this way. Most of us, however, learn more from watching others around us, from sharing with others who are having a similar experience. This kind of mutual aid takes place in self-help organizations, informal helping exchanges, in support groups, and most importantly, with friends, neighbors, and family. My own work at Harvard Medical School with widows has shown the value of learning from others who have been bereaved. Other widows have experience from which to draw, they are more patient and more tolerant of the despair and sadness that the bereaved feel, they understand how long it can take to make an accommodation, and they know what resources or help may be available. The newly bereaved in turn have also reported that it is easier to learn from a peer, to absorb information about the experience, and to feel genuinely cared about. When they see their feelings and experience reflected in others, the bereaved feel less alone and come to appreciate that they are typical, not deviant, because their reactions seemed to be very unusual. There is a growing consumer movement that recognizes and appreciates the help people offer each other. This is a move, beyond professionalism, which focuses on what people can do for each other, not because of their training but because of their successful experience in coping. Where mutual help programs for the bereaved are available, the mourning process has been facilitated and eased for those who affiliate and as a result, have learned how to cope.

Still another way for many people to learn is through self-study. The literature grows daily as people write about the broad range of human experience; they share with the reader their experiences in coping and giving some direction. Books can be a comfort and a support. Dr. Weizman and Mrs. Kamm have written such a book for the bereaved. They provide the reader with a clear statement of how to understand their feelings and what a range of appropriate reactions can be. This book is not just for people who are mourning, but for all of us. It contains important information about living that all of us need to negotiate our lives (and relationships) with greater awareness and competency.

While we cannot prevent the pain, we can promote our ability to cope competently with it, to respond appropriately to it when we see grief in others, and as a result to grow and develop as we move through the life cycle.

Phyllis R. Silverman, Ph.D.
Massachusetts General Hospital
Boston, MA

INTRODUCTION

This is not a book about death. It is a book about life, about the emotional life of one who has suffered the death of a loved one. It is about what it is like to go through an aversive experience, to endure emotional pain, and to heal painful memories.

Rather than an expert on death, I think of myself as an expert on living after experiencing a deep loss. I feel I have some understanding, knowledge, and experience that may help others to endure the emotional pain of one's own debilitating illness and death or that of a loved one.

It is hard to make sense out of what seems to be a senseless circumstance. The way for me to make sense out of it is in the opportunity it provides for personal growth, as well as an opportunity to help others. Experiencing and integrating the death of a significant person can add to one's maturity. While reading this book there will be times you may be moved, comforted, and helped to attain some freedom from past ties.

It is my sincere hope that this book will be of comfort to those in the throes of grief and give understanding to those who comfort the bereaved, in addition to helping all prepare for their own inevitable losses.

I want to express my deep appreciation to Rosemary Moroney and Charlotte Forster who contributed generously to the completion of this book and to my family for their help and endurance.

Savine Gross Weizman, Ph.D.

1

DEATH OF A LOVED ONE

The Inevitable Human Experience

There is an inevitable experience in human existence that touches everyone. Sometimes it occurs in adulthood, sometimes it reaches out to the small child. We speak of it in hushed tones. The death of a loved one or our own death is the profound experience none of us can evade. It is a shattering event that shakes us to the roots of our being. It presents a crisis that is difficult to endure.

This book is offered as a guide, support and comfort to those who are bereaved, and for those having close contact with the bereaved. It is written for everyone because eventually we will all be touched by the death of a significant person. Although there is little emotional preparation for the death of a loved one, understanding the mourning process can serve as a preparation and support for mourning. Understanding the natural process of mourning and the normalcy of feelings experienced is in itself supportive and reassuring.

Although there is no way to get beneath the skin of a grieving person and experience *exactly* the enveloping emotions, there are common and universal feelings. Recognizing this will decrease feelings of isolation and help you to feel connected to others who have had a similar experience. Many persons' feelings have been generously shared within the following pages for the purpose of helping other mourners.

The expression of feelings during this critical time is essential to the maintenance of good mental health. *Grief, the emotional suffering experienced after a loss, begs to be put into words, to be expressed and shared.* With sufficient and appropriate expression of your feelings, relief will come.

It is hoped that this book will aid you in coping with your grief and will help you know what is normal for mourning. A woman whose daughter died said: "I don't understand how I'm feeling. I'm not myself. The way I'm acting is not normal." She was reassured that what she was experiencing was normal for a person in mourning and normal after the death of a child. The mother responded, "Well, how do I know what is normal for grief? I have never gone through this before. I don't have a book to look in to tell me what is normal for mourning." This book contains explanations and personal experiences that are normal for the process of mourning. It is helpful for mourners, family, and friends to know what to expect, to be aware of feelings and symptoms that are a normal part of the process, and to understand how feelings will affect behavior. It is important to avoid unrealistic expectations for yourself and others. You will be helped to discover what you can do for yourself and how family and friends can be supportive through this difficult experience. Knowledge and understanding can dispel myths and combat misleading social messages for the bereaved and for the extended family and friends within the support system of the bereaved.

The emphasis of this book is on the family and the impact of the death of a family member on the individuals and on the family structure itself. No one mourns in a vacuum. When someone dies whether a parent, spouse or child, sibling or grandparent, relatives and dear friends are left to grieve. The family is a natural group and can be a significant support system. Everyone shares the loss of the same person and has similar emotions even though each may experience them at different times or with different intensity.

A death in the family thrusts unusual stress on each individual and on family relationships. At the same time, it offers an opportunity for strengthening the ties within the family. If each mourner recognizes and acknowledges openly the pain that afflicts each of them and is willing to give permission to share feelings, the death can augment family ties. It is within this context, the family and extended family, that guidance is needed to help each individual understand and support the others and also get support for oneself. It is a reciprocal process.

Crises causing grief occur at some time in all families. Families can take out insurance for coping with the unexpected difficulties by building their own support system, by teaching all members of the family how to talk about emotions, how to help, and how to accept help. Often families are brought together by a tragedy and someone will remark: "We have to stick together now. We need each other." They are welded together by the immediate event, but when the critical period is over sometimes the words are forgotten.

This book is about sharing and supporting, helping and being helped, permitting yourself and others to mourn. The lessons learned for coping with grief can enrich your life if they become a part of your life.

It is impossible to be totally prepared emotionally for an event of such magnitude as death, whether it strikes suddenly because of a heart attack or accident or as the finale to a long and debilitating illness. You may have fears and fantasies about your own death or the death of a loved one, but the intensity and depth of pain are beyond imagination. The lasting quality of the discomfort is something you cannot anticipate.

In these pages you will find many examples for the expression of grief, and you will read about many persons who have not only survived but recovered. You will read about the normal and common feelings during the mourning period for persons of all ages and how these feelings affect relationships within the family. If the process of mourning is understood, this in itself will be supportive and reassuring, and it will generate the patience necessary for enduring painful times.

There are various ways for dealing with a tragedy, and you will have your own style which fits your personality and the relationship that has ended. Not all the experiences you will read about will have relevance for you. Although there may be similarities to which you may relate, there will also be differences. Each person is unique, each relationship is unique, and each person's experience has a unique aspect to it. Take out of this book what fits for you; whatever makes you feel reassured.

Although uninvited, loss and mourning present an *opportunity for growth and maturation,* an opportunity to develop a deeper aspect of self. It is an opportunity to reach into untapped reserves and resources and to use them to grow in many dimensions. Many persons become strengthened through this experience.

Death can illuminate the importance of life. One of the major things we learn from death is that life is very precious. Understanding death and mourning is of major importance in helping us to understand and galvanize our daily lives, reorder our priorities, and focus our energy on issues and persons that are truly significant.

AVOIDANCE OF DEATH

Death and dying are difficult subjects to think and talk about. Despite the inevitability we shun discussion. Personal factors, as well as social, cultural and political factors contribute to this avoidance. We are often anxious, embarrassed, and inhibited by death and dying and this leads to avoidance of the subject and dealing with the event. The word "dead" is reated as if it were a dirty word, to be avoided like other four-letter rities. We shield ourselves from the reality by using euphemisms such as "passed away, gone, no longer with us, expired, with God, in Heaven." The fear of death and its accompanying denial are natural and present in everyone to some degree. The positive aspect of this fear is that it is one of the principal dynamics that motivates man and is connected to self-preservation. It is behind the need to stand out, to be of value, and to make life meaningful.[1]

If we were constantly aware of the fear of death, it would be distracting and interfere with our functioning. The widespread violence and crime in the world that is brought to us blatantly on television makes death real in one sense, but desensitizes us at the same time. The fear of total annihilation through nuclear warfare is a pervasive threat to mankind. To react with appropriate emotion to these horrors and dangers would overload our system and would keep the awareness of death unbearably prominent. The fear is of such magnitude that it increases our denial. It is normal and constructive to maintain a balance in the awareness of death so that it can serve as a positive force, not be denied, but not occupy a dominant distracting position.[2]

When death strikes where we live, it is impossible to ignore. The process of shutting out feelings about death may have become ingrained. As a result, our feelings may not be available to us when expression is necessary to maintain mental health.

There are times when our awareness of death, our own or of a loved one, comes to the surface. If we are confronted with death through the diagnosis of an illness, a soldier engaged in battle, or when a loved one dies, it is no longer possible to ignore. A heightened awareness of dying and death continually become prominent for the individual. This is precisely what happens during the mourning process and is the reason it is such a consuming emotional experience. Obviously, there are times when the acute awareness of death and dying is appropriate and the expression of feelings is necessary. Maintaining a posture of denial will inhibit the expression of grief when it is appropriate and can be a deterrent to the mourner.

ACKNOWLEDGEMENT OF DEATH

The opposite of the denial of death is the acknowledgement of death. Try as we do to avoid it, on some level we know full well it is real. There are those in every generation who are courageous and confront this reality. Great thinkers, poets, and writers have been struggling for centuries in an attempt to understand death and grief. There has been an increasing consciousness that the bereaved need understanding and that grief must have expression. That growing realization is apparent in the number of books and articles being written and the seminars and sermons being scheduled by clergy, psychologists, teachers, hospitals, morticians, and by family and health agencies.

It is intended that this book contribute to the cultural reorientation toward the acknowledgement of death and mourning. Some preparation for death and dying is possible by confronting death and being on speaking terms with it. Preparation involves more than making out a will and choosing a burial plot. It involves acknowledging your feelings and permitting others to acknowledge theirs. It means deciding what is truly important in your life and paying attention to those issues and those persons. It involves declaring your values and acting on them. It involves having the courage to feel and to put those feelings into words.

ORGANIZATION OF BOOK

The mourning process is similar as a result of different kinds of loss: death, divorce, separation, birth of a handicapped child, chronic or terminal illness, loss of a limb or eyesight, loss of a home or a job. This book is primarily an examination of the natural process of mourning after the death of a significant person. The loss of a specific relationship is presented within the context of the family and the family loss.

"Death of a loved one" is used repeatedly. The use of this phrase does not imply that any relationship is without conflict. Every important relationship generates a full range of feelings from love, affection, and devotion to anger, disappointment, and resentment. Some relationships have considerable conflict, but this does not minimize the importance of the relationship, the strength of the attachment, and the grief felt at its ending. "Death of a loved one" is synonymous with *significant person* or *important relationship*.

SOURCES OF INFORMATION

The contents of this book are drawn from Dr. Savine Gross Weizman's psychological training and clinical experience, ongoing clinical studies with individuals and families, groups and workshops conducted for the terminally ill and the bereaved, and teaching seminars for professionals who provide physical and mental health care. In addition, Dr. Weizman and Phyllis Kamm have reviewed the existing literature on grief and mourning, conducted face-to-face interviews, and drawn upon their own personal experiences of loss. Case examples have been selected to exemplify the various aspects of the mourning process.

Interviewing the bereaved is a delicate matter. They feel vulnerable and exposed, and it seems imposing to intrude on such an intimate experience. In spite of these factors, with few exceptions, those approached were pleased to be part of this undertaking. Permission for interviews and for the inclusion of the material was generously granted by those interviewed as it was seen as an opportunity to help other mourners. They also welcomed the chance to talk about their loss and found the interview itself helpful and often therapeutic. The interviews were conducted by Dr. Savine Gross Weizman, a psychotherapist, and Phyllis Kamm under Dr. Weizman's guidance. In order to encourage the participants to express their feelings, the interviews were conducted in an open-ended conversational encounter. The interviewing schedule was designed by Dr. Weizman, and the topics and content in this book reflect the subjects and results of the interviews. Consistent with other crisis research, subjects experiencing the life event were selected for this study from those who were available.[3,4,5] Some were persons or families in grief therapy; some were friends and acquaintances in mourning or who had experienced the death of a significant person in the past; some volunteered when they learned of the research project. Many more persons than appear as examples were involved in contributing to the observations and conclusions reported here. The same patterns and phenomena appeared again and again in interviews, consultations, and grief work with adults, children, and families. Several subjects and families are interwoven throughout the book to illustrate the phases and progression of mourning and to make the process itself more apparent and comprehensive. You may want to trace the progress of Ruth and her children and Sally Robbins and her children throughout the phases of their experience.

The case histories represent interviews with families and individuals stricken by the loss of a mate, parent, sibling, child and, in a few instances, another relative or friend. Men and women, black and white, blue-collar and white-collar workers, people in all types of work, businesses, and professions are included. They include Catholics, Protestants, Jews, and atheists. Incomes vary from lower income to upper and middle-income levels. Ages range from four to eighty-five years of age. All names were changed to conceal the identity and protect the privacy of the persons involved. An exception is found in the chapter concerning ethical wills and also where the writers of poems desired their actual names used.

SEQUENCE OF CHAPTERS

The next chapter will explain the purpose of funeral and memorial rituals and feelings connected with the initial impact of the death. The normal process of mourning is then described and discussed. Included are the many difficulties encountered during this period with guidelines and support for the healthy expression of feelings. Language is given to an experience that is difficult to put into words. There are many life examples to which you may respond, "That's just the way I feel. I'm glad to know someone else feels that way, too."

Following this is an explanation of the impact of a death within the context of the family and the effect on the family system. The loss of a particular relationship, spouse, parent and child, is described. The ethical will, a legacy for loved ones, and how others can help are also covered.

You will find an interweaving of ideas, feelings, and experiences from one chapter to another as the underlying form of the mourning process is revealed. It fits together into a pattern as the same concepts apply in the loss of different relationships. You will see how the process moves toward the healing of painful memories. It is hoped that the purpose of this book will be realized; that you will find comfort and support in the pages that follow to help you surmount your grief.

2

THE FUNERAL

Ritualized Mourning

Many emotional needs are served by the funeral, in addition to the practical and legislated necessity of taking leave of the physical being. It is the first step in the long process of mourning and important for the acknowledgement of the reality of the death of your loved one. The funeral is a ritualized way of saying goodbye and is one of the first of many emotional goodbyes to the significant person. As an ad hoc gathering of those who cared for the deceased and who care about the bereaved, it is also a way for a community to recognize and celebrate the meaning of the life of this person.

Rituals and traditions are helpful in the crisis presented by a death in the family. They provide a model for behavior and a structure to carry you through the *initial period of mourning*. Social and religious traditions supply guidelines for the mourners and for those assisting them such as family, friends, clergy, and funeral directors.

BACKGROUND OF FUNERAL PRACTICES

The event of a death evokes a pattern of action that has been recorded historically. A study of 78 societies in Europe, America, Japan, Africa, and the Pacific Islands confirmed that there are similar reactions to death in all cultures.[1] There is archeological evidence that ceremonial rituals have been used to commemorate the dead for at least 60,000 years.[2] The Mayan civilization, during its peak between the third and ninth centuries, had a highly ritualized way of dealing with death, impending death, and the bereaved. Prescribed expectations exerted

23

social control over the bereaved but also provided support and structure during a potentially devastating period. The Mayan community's loss and pain were expressed in pitiful cries and wails.[3]

The high-pitched keening and wailing heard at Arab, Greek, and Gaelic funerals is derived from the practice of Abyssinians during the time of the Queen of Sheba. These groups held *mourning bees* where the people would gather in a circle, start with a low moan and gradually work themselves into a frenzied exhibition of their grief.[4]

The Irish wake is a relic of ancient superstition. It was intended to prevent the soul of the dead from wandering around the house. Wailing and crying were encouraged not only to deter the ephemeral soul but also to release the tensions of the bereaved. In later times it was believed further release of pressure would be encouraged if the house were filled with convivial eating, drinking, dancing, and music. *The anguished wailing was the therapeutic aspect of these communal gatherings.* This emotionalism was also present in Eastern European cultural groups early in this century.

Throughout the centuries and among diverse cultures considerable activity centered around getting rid of lingering or evil spirits as an expression of the fear of death. The attempt to ward off death spirits with merrymaking is still evident. Implicit in the partying and celebration is an element of denial but also the recognition that life continues for the survivors. It is a time for friends and relatives to rally together for strength. The custom of the communal gathering has persisted throughout the ages. There was also a recognition of the need for a period of mourning and the need for protection and help for the mourners. Temporary withdrawal from social activity is almost a universal custom today as it was with the ancient Greeks, Romans, and Jews. The length of time for the abstinence depends upon the individual and the religious customs followed. This is an acknowledgement of grief, and that time is needed for expression and healing.

CHANGE IN RITUALS

While some old customs have carried over to the present, particularly the initial community response, we have given up the rituals which sanctioned the full expression of grief. During the last half-century people have become more controlled across all cultural groups. This conduct denies mourners the opportunity for catharsis of their grief and minimizes communal participation and permission for this expression. We know that open and spontaneous expression of grief promotes psychological health, but we do not provide an acceptance or structure for this expression as did the older cultures.[5]

The belief that overt, ritualized mourning can be therapeutic is confirmed by a study of bereaved persons in England and Scotland by Gorer.[5] It has also been pointed out that some of the problems resulting from bereavement are attributed to a lack of mourning rituals and the lack of guidance and models.[6,7]

Rituals and structure are necessary and supportive for the bereaved. It is helpful to have precedents to move you along. One problem is that most of the rituals and practices that remain are time limited, according to a prescribed schedule, while grief is not.[8] *The need for help and support outlasts the social and religious guidelines currently provided. The first year is a time of considerable suffering, and the need for comfort, and permission from others for emotional expression is great.* These needs continue even beyond the first year although grief is not so consuming.

Many modern rituals, secular and religious, cover the first few days, a week, or a month, and only a few last a year or provide anniversary commemorations. Often the bereaved person interprets this closure of ritual as a sign that he or she is not permitted to grieve openly. It seems that if there is no ritual, then there is no mourning. Thus, the mourning process may become aborted before it is fully underway. This may cause confusion to you, the bereaved person, because you do not feel better after a specified time has elapsed, even though you have gotten the mistaken idea that you "should." You continue to feel miserable, and heaped upon these feelings is the fear that you are not normal because you are unable to heed the admonition to "get over it." A message comes through in our society that allows expression of feeling up to a point, but once you have spoken and cried, the community says: "That's enough, it is time to be done with it and go on living."[9] *Life goes on for the community but mourning goes on for the mourner.* Unless you have been allowed and helped to feel all your pain no matter how often it recurs or how long it lasts, and also to express it through tears and words, mourning will not run its natural course.

VERIFYING THE DEATH: VIEWING THE BODY

It is important for the bereaved to make contact with the deceased by staying with the loved one for a while after the death or viewing the body. It is an important first step toward the intellectual and eventual emotional acceptance of the death. At least you *know* that it is true, even if you are reluctant to believe it. When death is sudden, because of heart attack, accident, suicide, or other unexpected circumstances, it is extremely important for the bereaved person to see and stay with the body in order to reinforce the reality and to counteract the shock and disbelief. Many people like to stay with their loved one who has been ill until expiration, and for a while thereafter. It is a special time, and reassuring, although very sad. For most people it is not frightening or aversive. Even though one might think it would be more difficult to take in the fact of the death when touching and caressing the warm body, that is not actually so. It is a way of taking your leave and beginning to absorb the reality.

Following are some testimonies from women who were allowed to stay with their loved ones.

> There is a recognition of "dead" about the person. It was a spiritual experience for me. I don't believe in the mystical yet I had this unusual feeling—especially when he was just on the brink of death. I can't say on the brink of life, it was on the brink of death. I wonder what happens to the part of the person that is "the person." Something must happen to it. It was almost like not being alone. He filled the room as if the air hung with his presence. It was a powerful experience.
>
> When I saw him a couple of days later (in the funeral home), he was unmistakably a corpse and I didn't have any of those feelings. I knew for certain, intellectually that is, that he was dead. It verified "dead" for me in the following months when I struggled with my disbelief and wished it to be untrue.

Sally Robbins, whose husband had been ill for several weeks, told about her leave-taking.

> I touched him and I held his hand. It was cool, not cold, but cool. Some parts of his body were a strange blue color. He looked peaceful, as if he were back together again, out of his misery. I was relieved that he didn't have to suffer any more. There was a strange peaceful feeling in the room, as if the whole room was filled with him. He was not in the body, but I was still very aware of his being there. It was strangely comforting. He was with me. Like a great intangible being—as if this life force was hanging there. I felt that I took him with me when I walked out of the room.

The two women followed their own inclinations in staying with their deceased loved ones. It was a profound experience for each of them and *the first step in their mourning*. They were fortunate there were medical personnel in attendance who understood the importance of allowing them time alone with the deceased.

Inability to View the Body

Not being able to see the body can be traumatic. When a soldier is missing in action, or killed and buried overseas, when someone disappears, or is drowned and the body not recovered, or any similar circumstances, it is more difficult to accept the reality of the loss. In these instances there is a little corner of the mind that says "it's not true." That vestige of doubt and denial is a barrier to integrating the loss and there may remain an unfinished aspect to the mourning.

Accidents

If the family is not present when death occurs or if the person dies as the result of an accident, viewing the body carries strong import. It is helpful to be able to convince yourself that the deceased is actually *your* loved one, so that doubt is eliminated.

Nine-year-old Lanny Hickock had been killed instantly when hit by a vehicle that ran a red light. Neither her mother nor father was permitted to view the body which had been identified by a friend. During those first agonizing minutes at the hospital, Nancy, the mother had begged to see Lanny.

> I wanted to see her. Everybody said: "No, you don't want to." That scared me. If she was hurt so badly does that mean I am not to have that last memory of her? I haven't satisfied myself with that yet. I do remember thinking months later, "Dummy, why didn't you at least get a lock of her hair." But I thought of these things too late.

The mother was left with a sense of confusion, self-reproach, and a feeling of something unfinished.

Mixed Feelings

People often have mixed feelings about viewing the deceased. Some may say, "I want to remember her alive." This may be resistance to facing "the truth." There may be an aversion to looking or touching because this will confirm the fact. As one woman said: "I didn't want to touch him because then I would have known he was dead."

Sometimes that last look on the features of the deceased does stay in one's memory for a while and recurs like a flashback. It is this image which verifies the death. After a time the image fades and the person is remembered and envisioned as he or she was known when alive and a vital human being.

Even for children from about ten years of age who might view the body, happy recollections eventually erase the overwhelming sight of the deceased. This matter should be discussed with the children. Certainly no one should insist they view the body, but they can be given the opportunity to do so. *If children are going to see the body, they must be prepared for what they will see. They must have the presence of an understanding and loving adult to give them explanation, support, and comfort.*

Use Your Judgment

No rule can be made that will apply in all situations. The special circumstances should always be taken into consideration and the good judgement of the responsible adult relied upon. Catherine's husband had been killed in an industrial accident. He was burned over 95 percent of his body and his face was completely disfigured. Catherine spent the final agonizing hours with her husband, but she made the firm decision that their two teen-aged daughters should not see him. In this instance the decision was correct. The extent of the disfigurement and the horror of the situation far outweighed any benefit the children would have gained by seeing their father in that state.

Generalizations are difficult to make and sometimes misleading. Although viewing the body is generally supportive to the mourning process, each case is unique. The decision of whether or not to look at the deceased depends upon the circumstances of the death and the stability and age of the family members involved. Each individual case must be resolved with good judgement and sensitivity to the existing circumstances. You should do what feels "right" to you.

Visitation, Viewing and Wake

The wake provides the setting for the verification of the death as well as an opportunity to say goodbye to the deceased. It is also a gathering of friends and relatives to show they care.

Margery gave a description of her father's wake.

> My father was probably one of the last ever waked at home. All night long different members of the family took turns "watching" the body. The coffin was left open all that time. I remember putting my hand on his hand, on his sleeve. We would go in and talk to him. I did that too. Talk about good old Irish wakes! There was eating and drinking but the purpose was to talk about him, the things he had done, remembering the things we did together, remembering the times we had with him.

Aaron told about his grandfather's wake at the funeral home. Each one came up to the casket, knelt by him, prayed, talked to him, touched him, cried over him. The actuality of his death seemed clear to each one. It was a healthy way to begin the process of mourning.

Occasionally, when a person has been embalmed, so much make-up has been applied that the deceased may at first appear "asleep" rather than dead. A young man sixteen years old said, "It is like looking at a picture of the person." This may interfere with acknowledging the death. People often remark that the deceased "looks good." Make-up or not, there is a dramatic difference between asleep and dead, and this is readily observable. Natalie's reaction to her friend proved this point. "Bobby didn't look like Bobby," Natalie said. "I hardly could look at her. I'd never seen her totally unanimated." That is the bottom line of being dead, "totally unanimated." Viewing the body confirmed Bobby's death.

THE FUNERAL

The funeral is a ceremony to acknowledge the death and pay tribute to the loved one. It is also a ritual which supports the mourning process. At the time of death a pattern of behavior is set into motion for family and helpers. Unwanted and unpleasant as it is, making the necessary arrangements forces one to deal with the reality of the death.

The deceased may have left directions for the funeral which are usually helpful but occasionally cause conflict. When the request previously made by the deceased is negative for the mourners, the request needs to be reconsidered in light of what would be supportive and comforting for the bereaved. Often the idea of cremation or donation of the body for research purposes produces aversive images for the family and adds to the pain of the death. Therefore directions and requests may need to be modified so they can meet the needs of the mourners.

Memorial Service, Homily and Eulogy: A Ritualized Farewell

The funeral service is the time of the most concentrated gathering of the family network and friends of the deceased and the bereaved. It is a commemoration to the person who has died, and a public farewell. The purpose of the service is also to comfort the bereaved through the testimony of one's presence. Such testimony says in action "I care about you, I grieve with you, I will miss the deceased."

Most religions include prayers in the service which reaffirm faith in God. In Christian religions this brief sermon is called the homily. In some religious services the emphasis is on the hereafter and the soul of the deceased or the souls in the congregation. Although raised in a religion and familiar with the practices, some bereaved persons find this is not comforting. They want to feel the service is for the deceased person and for them.

Claire Thomas said the clergyman was so busy "saving" people at Gerald's funeral he did not even talk about the man he was burying. He spent most of the time exhorting people to join the congregation or they would not go to heaven when they die.

Claire was sensitive and vulnerable and found no comfort in the service. She was especially hurt since the minister knew Gerald so well, as he had devoted years of service to the church.

The eulogy summarizes the significance of the deceased's life, highlights the person's qualities and important relationships, and acknowledges the sadness felt by the mourners. Although the clergyperson traditionally delivers the eulogy, it is sometimes offered by a close friend or relative. An unusual eulogy is the following poem a son wrote for his father. It symbolically captures the father's qualities and relationships and the son's sadness. It was read at the memorial service.

"What's wrong?" said the dog with a wondering eye,
"Why are the clouds blocking the breathing blue sky?"

A builder by trade—yes—a creator at heart.
A tree from the ground, a house from a tree,
Most of all, he created "three."

His wisdom was subtle, but yet so profound,
He was a blossoming crocus in a field of orchids.
"Think before you do" and "Do what you think"
Yes, he was and is part of all that he met.

He and his Love had a knot like the Sun,
So warm, so vibrant, so shining, so everlasting—
so near to perfect.

In the vivid shadows on the dining room table,
Stand five yellow roses,
Bound with a chain of iron.

David
Age 15

There are many ways to say goodbye. It is important that the memorial service fit the deceased and be comforting to the surviving family.

Burial Service

If the decision is made for a traditional burial, the survivors participate in the funeral service and at the gravesite. Sometimes, as a way of trying to protect the family, the coffin is not lowered into the ground until the group has left the site. The intent is to be considerate and not evoke painful feelings. Actually, the procedure then is incomplete and leaves you with an unfinished feeling. Seeing the coffin lowered into the ground completes the ritual. Recently there has been a revival of an old Greek, Egyptian and Jewish custom of throwing earth on the coffin after it is lowered into the ground. Inherent in this custom is the confrontation with the reality of the meaning of "dead."
Sarah described the burials of her aunt and father.

> As I stood at my aunt's grave holding up my mother and father, I felt no emotion. She was not that important in my life. Nothing to cry about, I thought. As I saw my cousins shoveling the dirt on her coffin, I finally cried. I realized I had been blocking my tears.
> When my father was buried, my brother and I and the grandchildren participated in throwing the earth over his coffin. As we did this we cried. It felt natural and appropriate. The women and the men all cried without embarrassment.

The physical participation in this procedure provides an acknowledgment of the fact and a natural outlet for emotions. Although this truth is painful it is also merciful, as you cannot evade the reality and cannot avoid your emotions. There is also a feeling of completion, of the person being "laid to rest."

Cremation

Some people prefer cremation for personal, financial, or philosophical reasons. It is customary to have a memorial service and some will hold a visitation also. When cremation has been chosen, it is important that the ashes be buried or put in a columbarium, which is a vault for urns containing the ashes of the deceased. The burial place or columbarium provides for the completion of the rituals. People are left feeling in limbo when the burial of the ashes is omitted. Families also need a place to visit the remains of their loved one.

It is paradoxical that cremation destroys so quickly, yet many people hold onto the ashes and are unable to take the next step in the separation process. Often, the ashes are kept at home in a drawer or closet. The burial of the ashes can be in a cemetery plot or any other designated spot, so that it is identifiable and has meaning for the survivors.

Following is a description of the way a family handled this situation.

> Sally and her three children decided that their father's ashes would be buried at home. They decided to plant a tree in the front yard and bury his ashes beneath it. That way, if they ever sold the house, they could still visit his remains without disturbing the new owner. They planted a tulip tree which was a favorite of Bob's.

Following through in this way provided a sense of completion.

Meal of Condolence And Other Mourning Rituals

The ritual of joining together and partaking of a meal is centuries old and observed in many cultures. The Irish, Amish, Jewish, European ethnic groups and many other Americans observe this custom today. *The true purpose of the meal of condolence is to symbolize the continuation of living and the life cycle itself. The gathering is to help the bereaved people to feel they are supported and cared about and to give them an opportunity to talk about their loved one and vent their grief.*

The Jewish religion offers the most prolonged ritualized support in Western cultures and includes many symbolic gestures.[5] These rituals are psychological supports for the bereaved and acknowledge mourning as a continuous process. They carry the mourner through the first year of bereavement, as well as through anniversaries of the death. There are four holidays during the year on which a memorial prayer is recited, and special prayers are said at the grave which is visited at least once a year at the time of the high holy days.[10] The Catholic religion includes mass on the anniversary, or other special days, and prayers to be recited at the grave. *Each ritual provides a way to deal with the reality of "dead" and a chance to perform another piece of the work of mourning.*

VISITING THE CEMETERY

Many people find comfort in regular visits to the cemetery during the first year after the death and special times thereafter. There is variance in the personal preference as to these visits. It is something you can *do* physically, with your whole body and is therefore a valuable form of expression. Visiting the grave of your loved one helps to reinforce the finality of the situation. It is also a symbolic way of having contact with the deceased. This activity stirs up memories and feelings and gives you another chance to express those feelings. The cemetery is important as a specific and socially acceptable place to mourn openly.

You usually see people approaching the grave, bending down, cleaning off the stone, brushing away the little blades of dried grass and pulling out weeds. This activity is an orientation to being there. Many people bring flowers or say prayers or psalms at the graveside. People cry unashamedly and embrace each other for comfort. It is an old custom to leave a pebble or stone on the tombstone. This is a symbolic way of having some contact with the deceased and a way of saying, "I was here."

Visiting the grave makes denial difficult. When you see the name of your loved one engraved in the stone, it strikes you sharply that he or she will not return, that the death is real. When you see something in writing, you tend to believe it. As Margery, a mother, said, "The first time I went to the cemetery after my son's burial I was in a state of shock again. I looked and I thought, oh God! This really can't be so, but it is because it is chiseled in marble."

Avoidance of Visiting the Grave

Many people avoid going to the cemetery and visiting the grave. They say, "Why should I go? My loved one isn't there." Of course that is true and that is one of the reasons for going to the cemetery—because your loved one is not there or anywhere, except in spirit. The avoidance of visiting the cemetery may be an indication of inhibited grief. Children often put up resistance to going to the cemetery. Nancy's children are an example of this.

> Although I like going to my daughter's graveside, the children are not comfortable going there. They think it is ghastly. "She's not here, why are we coming here?" they ask me. I tell them I understand she isn't here but we come because we honor and acknowledge her resting place and her physical body is here. The children did not even react visibly to the stone. They act as if she's taken her place in heaven; that she's happy, and that's that.

What is actually ghastly is the manner of their sister's death, her young age of nine, and that she is in fact dead. It is not the cemetery that is ghastly. The children's resistance indicates their difficulty in dealing with the reality and their attempt to avoid the painful feelings stirred up by visiting the cemetery. This is a difficult situation because their excuses *seem* so logical. "She's not here (in the cemetery)" or "We don't need to go to the grave to remember her. We always think of her." Those statements are true in a way, but not reasons to avoid occasional visits to the grave, especially on special dates. It is necessary for adults to be clear about these matters so they can provide guidance to children and help them with their mourning.

Visiting the grave of a loved one helps you to get in touch with feelings that have been suppressed. In a case of delayed grief, visiting the cemetery helps to release feelings that have been locked up. Ginny, a young woman of thirty, related her experience.

> The first time I visited my mother's grave I was very frightened. I had postponed the experience for 10 years and so it had taken on a monumental significance. I went over to the grave and was immediately shocked and extremely dismayed and angry because weeds had totally overgrown the marker. I pulled the weeds away (that felt good) and began crying. It was so hard to see my mother's name and dates on the plate. I felt an anger and frustration and a feeling that even this concrete evidence couldn't make me believe that she was really dead. I told her I just don't understand why she had to die. Then I became angry and started saying "How could you have done this to me?" That went on for a while and then I began to talk to her about myself, saying that all things considered, I was pretty good at taking care of myself.
>
> Then I thought about when I was little and how close we had been and how that was really the best time of all.
>
> I felt that I had cried about all that I could and that I couldn't stay there any longer, so I said goodbye to her and left. It was a beautiful day outside and the cemetery was a pretty one, and I was at least glad for that.

Ginny's experience points up the importance of visits to the grave in stimulating and allowing expression of feelings of sadness, longing, and anger. Although painful, it made the death more real. It also made her mother's life more real and enabled Ginny to remember good things and good times. She needed to get back in touch with those memories which supported her through mourning. It was also important that she focused on appraising her present situation and her happiness in spite of the tragedy.

LOOKING FOR COMFORT

At the time of the death, at the visitation, or the funeral, friends will say things to the mourners, or often the mourners themselves will say things that they have heard in the past that seem to be soothing. People are looking for ways to make the incomprehensible event understandable or tolerable. They say things like: "It was meant to be. It was fate; It is God's will. Don't be sad, he is with God now; he is happy!"

Sometimes others will recite these platitudes out of their own helplessness and their wish to be of comfort to the mourner. Sometimes we say things that are hard to believe ourselves, but we tell others and our children things to try to help them. Many of the phrases are *verbal rituals*. They are customary ways of expressing sympathy when everyone feels helpless and the "right" words are hard to find. There really are no words to remove the pain.

People get support from their religious beliefs in different ways. Some people are comforted by belief in an afterlife, or in the conviction that they will be reunited with their loved one some day. Some people believe that their loved one is a protection for them, watching over them from above.

Although it is hard to find comfort, many different phrases, religious beliefs, and ideas do bring comfort to the bereaved. You may relieve the burden of your grief in any way you can, providing your belief does not interfere with the mourning process or thwart acceptance of the reality of the death. You are still left to deal with the social separation and should not allow your beliefs to provide the basis for denial. You will experience feelings resulting from the separation, and you need to be careful not to avoid dealing with them. The deceased *may* be peaceful and happy, but *your* life has been upset and you have your anguish and sadness with which to deal. After the death of his mother, an eight year-old boy was told, "God wanted her." An understanding neighbor responded when he repeated this, by saying, "We wanted her too."

Support from Religious Institutions

Some people find solace by attendance at church or synagogue. This provides structure, familiarity, and a sense of community. It is a source of support to the mourning process and eventual integration of the loss.

We depend on the clergy and our religious institutions to offer us help at the time of a crisis. The clergy respond in a ritualized way according to the guidelines of the particular religion and help through the initial period of mourning. Occasionally clergy will continue contact with the mourners after the initial rituals are completed. However, it is unrealistic to expect a clergyperson to offer the continuing and frequent support that is needed throughout the first year of mourning. This is rarely possible with the many responsibilities that religious leaders have. It seems more realistic that a lay committee of the congregation contact the bereaved, stay in touch, and offer continuing support. These representatives of the religious institution, whether church or temple, would indeed prove that "religion" can be relied on to help in a crisis. The idea has to be put into action by the caring individuals of the institution. Outreach programs are gradually being developed to provide ongoing support after a crisis.

3

UNDERSTANDING THE MOURNING PROCESS

The death of a loved one is a profound experience, disorienting and disturbing to the physical and emotional balance. You may feel confused, dazed and suspended. The loss is felt as if it were an assault, a blow to the self. The onslaught is especially burdensome because you are called upon to cope with the impact of the death, attend to overwhelming feelings, and somehow continue the tasks of everyday life. Enormous energy and strength are required at a time when physical and emotional energies are diminished. Somehow you have managed to come through the funeral and perhaps the first few weeks of mourning, but the pain and confusion remain and are waiting for expression.

MOURNING: A NATURAL PROCESS

Mourning, the expression of intense emotional suffering, is a normal and natural process that must be allowed to happen. There are no prescriptions, no antidotes. It cannot be avoided and should not be rushed. The *process of mourning is a continuing development involving many steps and many changes.* Real strength is needed to endure the pain. You will also need to have faith that the pain will subside and that relief will come.

Mourning, as a natural process, requires several components to expedite its course. One component is *permission to mourn;* that is, to be allowed to feel and express your emotions. It is important to have permission from yourself as well as from others *to express your feelings.* It is also *essential to cry,* to give yourself permission to cry alone, and to be able to cry with others. It is also *essential to talk* about your feelings and to talk about the deceased. Although mourning is a process that involves you as an individual, it must be *shared with others.*

The bereaved person has another special need which is necessary to the process of mourning. This is the *need to repeat the story of the loss* and the details surrounding it, whether it begins with the diagnosis of an illness or the circumstances surrounding the death itself. This compulsion to repeat is an attempt to understand and make the event real on a mental and emotional level. The repetition serves as a catharsis and also as a method for mastering the situation. Friends and relatives may tire of hearing the same stories again and again or you may tire of repeating them, saying "I've told you this before." Perhaps it will help to know that this retelling has value. The bereaved should be encouraged to relate these stories in an attempt to expand feelings and reach new depths of feeling. The effect and intensity will change over time. The twenty-fourth telling will be different from the first. *Thus, repetition is an important aspect of the healing. Important components of the process are crying, talking, sharing, and having permission from yourself and others to engage in these releases.*

Unfortunately, a climate in which people may grieve openly is seldom provided after the initial ritualized period of mourning. After that, the bereaved may receive unspoken messages from friends and other family members that imply: "Don't cry in front of me"; "Don't tell me how it hurts." This attitude is not supportive of the mourning process. *What is supportive is for those around to give permission to share feelings and tears and to acknowledge the suffering of the bereaved. It is supportive to say simply and sincerely: "I know you hurt deeply."*

Mourning is an *adaptive process.* It is a time of transition in which the old reality which included your loved one is gradually let go, and the new reality in which the absence of your loved one is felt and realized is gradually let in. In this intermediate period you make efforts to adjust and adapt to the new social reality. A great deal of energy is used to accommodate the new reality and incorporate this change. It is a *slow process.* As you assimilate the loss, it becomes a part of you. *Mourning is the process of absorbing the reality of death, experiencing all the emotions, and then being able to let go by expressing your emotions in various ways. It is imperative to express your feelings through talking, crying, writing, physical means, and in any way that is comfortable or unique for you. You will each need to find your own creative avenue for expression.*

Death: A Crisis Event

The death of a loved one or the facing of your own imminent death after the diagnosis of a life-threatening disease is a crisis event. There is no adequate preparation for an event of this magnitude because there is no way to imagine the depth and extent of emotional pain. A crisis includes extreme feelings, fear, confusion, and a sense of being powerless. The usual coping mechanisms are not adequate, but decision and action are usually required.

The death of a significant person is a crisis when people require help. At this time individuals are usually open to receiving help from others, whether it be from family, clergy, friends, or mental health professionals. Intervention during a crisis can help prevent future emotional problems. When someone is so dreadfully burdened and assaulted, there is a willingness, in fact a need, to accept help from others.

The crisis of the death of a loved one presents both danger and opportunity. Death is a part of life and how we cope with it or try to hide from it will be a dominant factor in how we live the rest of our lives. With support, expression of feelings, and the inner resources of the aggrieved, mourning is able to run its natural course. The person who can verbalize and emotionalize about the loss will have a better chance of emerging from this crisis with a mature attitude about life's priorities.

Mourning Defined

The psychological definition of mourning as it is used in this book refers to the mental and emotional "work" following the loss of a significant person through death.[1] The normal process of mourning, with all its attendant feelings, will be experienced at the time of any loss: a death, separation, divorce, chronic or terminal illness of self or significant other, loss of a limb, or of a bodily function, birth of a handicapped child, or the loss of a hope, a country, or a home.

There are differences in various losses. In the case of illness or handicap, we lose a function but can sometimes compensate for that. We still have the presence of loved ones who care about us. With the death of a significant person, we lose the relationship, the focus of our love, and the love returned by the other. There is a dimension to the death of a loved one that causes a different kind of pain and helplessness, a special finality.

The definitions that follow, from *Webster's New World Dictionary,* Second College Edition, are for words that will be used frequently throughout the book.[2] *Grief* is defined as *"intense emotional suffering caused by loss, disaster, misfortune, etc.; acute sorrow; deep sadness."* The word derives from a Latin verb meaning "to burden." Indeed, you do feel burdened. You are carrying a heavy load of feelings. *Mourn* is defined as "to feel or express sorrow." *Mourning is the expression of grief.* The word derives from a Gothic verb meaning "to be anxious," and it comes ultimately from an Indo-European base meaning "to remember; to think of." Mourning involves remembering and thinking of the deceased and this makes you feel anxious or uncomfortable.

Bereave means "to leave in a sad or lonely state, as by loss or death." In Old English, the word meant "to deprive or rob." One mother said after her daughter's death, "I feel as if I were robbed of my most precious possession." The bereaved are survivors of a recently deceased person and are those in mourning.

Support means to endure . . . to carry or bear the weight of, to keep from falling, slipping, or sinking; hold up; to give courage, faith or confidence; help or comfort; to give active aid or to approve and to sanction; to keep intact, prevent failure. Supporting mourners reduces the loneliness of the grief experience. Support also means coaching the bereaved to express themselves and to have faith in recovery. Modeling behavior for mourning is also supportive.

Reality means pragmatic, objective fact, not taken on faith. *Mature* means full grown, fully developed as a person. It is developing at a deep level, experiencing deeply. *Process* is a continuing development involving many changes . . . a number of steps.

The mourning process is the ongoing psychological experience and the expression of grief. It is the expression of sorrow, anger, emotional suffering, and the full range of feelings experienced. The mourning process is continuous and changing.

Grief Demands Expression

The goal of the mourning process is to integrate the loss that is known to be true in outward reality in order to have it become an emotional reality. This can happen only if you are able to express the anger, pain, despair, and all the other emotions that assail you. Your feelings must be talked about; words and tears must be shared with other mourners and with family and friends. Feelings need to be released rather than blocked. If freedom of expression is denied, pushed away, or ignored, the mourning process is inhibited. As with any natural process that is inhibited, halting the mourning process can cause problems. Inhibition of grief may present a picture of strength to the world, albeit false, but stuffing sorrow away is a temporary solution. It takes a lot of energy to ignore feelings and one day, if they have been ignored, they may boomerang with full force at an inappropriate time or in a disguised fashion. Sometimes the belated reaction may seem unrelated to the earlier crisis. It is healthier to deal with the feelings when they occur and are accessible. Audrey's experience which follows illustrates this. Audrey, fifty-one years old, was widowed at twenty-one and immediately returned to her parents' home with her infant daughter.

> Although I cried a lot, alone and with others, there was little *talk* about my feelings. My parents encouraged me to start dating shortly after the death. At twenty-three I remarried and tucked away all memories of my first love and my pain at his death. Ten years later I suffered an emotional breakdown.
>
> I had never mentioned Marty's name. First my parents and then my husband colluded with me to block out what I felt and had lived through. I was restricted in mentioning Marty's name. Finally my psychologist told me I should talk about him like you would reminisce about any past event. . . . Then I began to talk. Finally I realized how I needed that. I really did. I began to feel better.

This is an example of insufficient talking and insufficient expression of feelings. The denial took the form of focusing on the future and finding a replacement for the lost person rather than on experiencing the feelings at the time of her loss. Her feelings remained and lingered on as unfinished business, only to erupt and disrupt at a later time.

When an attempt is made to block out some feelings, the whole range of feeling is affected. If you try to block out pain, sadness, and anger, you begin a *process* of blocking feelings. Therefore, all feelings are blocked and diminished. If you think of feelings as a continuum, pleasant feelings on one end and unpleasant feelings on the other, your ability to feel joy will be blocked, along with your ability to feel pain and sadness. You will end up immobilizing more than just the unpleasant feelings. You will freeze pleasant and joyful feelings as well. The process of holding back becomes ingrained and the ability to express yourself naturally and spontaneously is throttled. Turning the feelings inward may become your process. You give up your capacity to laugh and to enjoy yourself as you give up your capacity to feel pain and sorrow. Too much elapsed time and too much denial make it difficult to get back in touch with those feelings which are essential for resolving and integrating a loss. A loss needs to be fully felt and expressed in order for healing and recovery to occur.

PHASES AND FEELINGS OF GRIEF

The emotional suffering of grief encompasses many feelings that are sometimes confusing and often overwhelming. The process of mourning, that is the ongoing events and feelings, weaves a loose pattern. The feelings which weave the cloth of mourning fall loosely into phases. The feelings in each phase demand expression.

In order to help understand the process, the following categories have been used to help clarify and organize the flow of feelings. The phases are characterized by a *dominant feeling or process*. They are: shock, undoing, anger, sadness, and integration. These phases and feelings will be explained in the following pages. Some illustrations of the emotions experienced during the mourning process are given in the explanation of each phase. The phases and feelings will become clearer as they are applied to examples of different losses and various life situations.

The idea of stages of grief was introduced and popularized by Elisabeth Kübler-Ross and has been interpreted more rigidly than intended.[3] The use of the word "phase" is preferred here since it connotes the looseness of the process. The phases are used as a way of conceptualizing and understanding the emotional experience of mourning and are helpful in giving a framework to this process. These feelings are categorized to *clarify* this experience and are necessary since personal feelings are often disorganized and confusing. The phases are not time limited or sequential, nor are the feelings. Some feelings do not clearly belong in one phase or another but actually occur in several phases and are connected to other feelings. For example, feeling powerless recurs in almost every phase with some variation. Although a rough estimate of time is given for some phases, these are flexible guidelines and require interpretation and application to each individual and circumstance.

It is important to remember that the same feelings will *return* again and again and they often *overlap*. You may feel many feelings in one day and that can be overwhelming. You may believe you have dealt with a certain set of emotions and, lo and behold, they recur. As time passes, the emotions oscillating between sadness and hope change their pattern. The changes from emotional highs to emotional lows are less frequent and dramatic. The times between being weighted down becomes spread out and the sadness is of shorter duration. The feelings experienced in each stage constantly change and rearrange themselves. Be aware of feelings and phases as they change, overlap, retreat, and return until you achieve integration and balance. Allow yourself to flow with your own emotions.

During the early phases of mourning, the deceased, and your feelings about the death, are prominent. They monopolize most of your thinking and emotional life. As time goes on and feelings are attended to and expressed, thoughts of the deceased become background and other things become foreground. In working toward the integration of the loss, the balance between foreground and background changes, you can once again attend to the tasks of daily living, and other things will begin to interest you. The deceased and your grief return to the foreground when a particular reminder, special date, or holiday comes around. The foreground and background continue to change and the balance between your grief and your relief also shifts.

The First Phase: Shock

The period of shock varies considerably depending on the circumstances of the death and the individual mourner. Although *shock, disbelief,* and *denial* are dominant in this phase, it does not mean that many other emotions are not experienced. It does not eliminate sadness, anger, guilt, and other feelings that may creep into awareness. These are neither lasting nor intense, and dealing in depth with these feelings is usually postponed to a later phase.

When you first hear the news of a loss, whether it is the diagnosis of an illness or the death of a loved one, you feel stunned for a moment. It does not seem to register. It feels totally shocking. Then follows a reaction of disbelief: "No, it can't be true."

> Wilma said: "I can remember that minute or two so well; it wasn't right away. Not that I didn't believe my friend. I believed her, but I didn't want to believe what she was telling me. I remember the process of not wanting to believe he was dead, of taking and pushing it out, which is my usual process—pushing out all bad news for the first second or two before I take it in."

> When informed of her son's death in an automobile accident, Margery was in total shock. "They said 'He's DEAD' and it's like somebody took a knife and cut out the part of me that had feelings. Talk about shock! I felt absolutely, positively nothing. Like I wasn't there, numb. I knew what to do. I went through the motions of telling the children and notifying others. But it was just absolutely an unbelievable thing. I thought it really couldn't happen. It might happen to somebody else but it really couldn't be. Except I knew it was true."

The phrase "I still can't believe it" crops up again and again, usually meaning "I don't want to believe it. I wish it weren't true." Believing is also an adaptation to the reality that the death *is* true. It takes time for this to be believed emotionally. These feelings of disbelief fade in and out and intermingle with other feelings during the first year or sometimes even longer when the death is sudden or bizarre.

Some people are numb at first and there is no visible reaction, but others may begin to cry or become hysterical and talk and moan while crying. Crying is a spontaneous response to death, and tears will emerge in men and women unless an attempt is made to block them or the person is in shock.

Confusion and Bewilderment.   The initial impact may cause you to feel confused and bewildered, not really knowing what to do, whom to turn to, or how to express yourself. You may feel you need someone to guide you, to help you. When you do make contact with someone, you will find there *are* others willing to help.

The feelings of being dazed and confused may linger, especially if the death has been sudden. Many persons report an initial reaction of hysteria giving way to one or two weeks of confusion. Your sense of time becomes distorted, and it may become difficult to recall events occurring around the time of the trauma. After all, for you it is as if time had stopped.

Denial.   The experience of assault upon the self calls forth some protective mechanisms. The process of denial is an attempt to shield yourself from the impact and pain. This temporary denial serves as a protection to the self for it would be unbearable to let in all the pain at once or allow the meaning of the loss to penetrate all at once. The reality is absorbed in small doses so that the meaning of *dead* can be taken in little by little. This is a normal reaction and serves the purpose of self-protection.

If the denial continues beyond a reasonable time, it prevents you from dealing with the reality. Then it becomes harmful and is no longer a useful mechanism. If the denial stands in the way of getting treatment for illness or precipitates inappropriate behavior, it becomes a problem and not a healthy, functional defense.

Keeping busy is a way of supporting denial. Claire said, as if to her feelings: "Go away, I'm too busy." It takes time to attend to your feelings and it is necessary to take the time to feel and to allow them to emerge.

Isolation and Withdrawal.   The feelings of vulnerability and defenselessness are common in bereavement. It is not surprising that another way a mourner would seek protection is by withdrawal. During this phase you sometimes feel isolated with your grief. You may feel as if no one understands. You may withdraw, not because you do not want to be with other people, but as a way to protect yourself from further assault. It is another effort to protect the self from being hurt again. The feeling of isolation and the reaction of withdrawal seem to go together. There is a strong need to be connected to others and taken care of by others, yet ironically the emotional experience is one of being separate and alone. The shock and the assault have the effect of disconnecting you from others. This is yet another confusion to the mourner and to those in the support system as well. Ruth explained her feelings:

> I wanted to be taken care of and protected, yet I felt completely alone. I couldn't reach out to anyone else for help at this time. If someone called on the phone or asked to be helpful, I couldn't admit my need or accept help. But if someone just came to the door without asking, I was able to accept and feel comforted by their presence and concern. I didn't understand my own feelings of isolation nor my behavior of not being able to accept kind offers.

Mourners are very sensitive. It is hard to reach out and ask for help but offers are usually greatly appreciated. It is sometimes difficult for others to break the barrier, but it is extremely important to try and reach out, to be comforting to the bereaved. The withdrawal should not be mistaken for a desire or wish to be alone. This is an *emotional experience* of isolation. If others interpret this as a wish for privacy, it often does harm to the bereaved, because then the emotional experience and the social reality are the same and the bereaved will surely feel as if no one cares. If others understand that this feeling of isolation and behavior of withdrawing are emotional reactions, they can deal with them appropriately. Others should not interpret such behavior as a personal rejection but, on the contrary, should make every effort to bridge the gap, to stay in contact and in the presence of the mourner.

Sudden Death.   The period of shock will vary depending on whether the death was sudden or occurred after a long illness. It takes much longer to recover from a sudden death that has occurred from a heart attack, accident, suicide, or sudden illness. It makes you feel you cannot trust anyone or count on anything. It upsets the normal course of events. Expecting to see your loved one later on, you receive news of the death instead. It is totally contrary to the anticipation. As Wilma said: "The suddenness of his death, of course, had a special impact. There's no way to respond to something sudden. People prepare for certain things but sudden death is just plain shocking."

This first phase usually lasts for a period of two to three months. There are other feelings that slowly emerge during this time such as sadness and anger. However, the full impact and the full suffering are usually experienced after the shock wears off. Ruth described the end of the first phase of mourning:

> I remember sitting in my den on a Sunday morning when the children were in Sunday school. My husband and I used to spend those mornings together, and I missed him so much. I tried to sort some papers, but all I could really do was cry and sob. I thought I would be feeling better by this time, but I wasn't. All I could think was "How long does this go on?" I impulsively phoned a widower I knew and asked, "How long does this go on?" He had been mateless for two years, and he told me it was still going on for him, even though he had resumed a social life. Although I knew I had a lot ahead of me, I felt comforted by knowing that this is the way it really is. My feelings began to emerge in "living color" after this initial period.

It was not the end of pain but the beginning of another phase for Ruth. Different feelings emerged, and with increasing intensity.

If the circumstances are bizarre as in an accident, murder or suicide, or when someone has been mutilated, the period of shock may last longer, perhaps six or seven months. In addition to the suddenness of the death, there is the *horror* of the event to deal with as well. Catherine, whose husband was killed in an industrial accident, related:

> My friends kept coming to visit me longer than most people, I think. Most nights someone was visiting and bringing in dinner. That lasted for six months. Their visits were distracting but I didn't share my feelings with them. I think I was still in the shock stage. Then the visits became uncomfortable for me because I had all these feelings inside of me and I was about to burst. I can remember, it was almost like seven months and I think I was starting to come out of that shock stage and then the crying started. I think it was like seven months of sorrow every day.
>
> I functioned during that shock period, but after that I was lucky if I could cook meals, if I could even get out of bed.

It is after the shock wears off that the reality and the pain penetrate, and intense and varied feelings emerge in full force. Shock and denial are important processes during the first phase of mourning. They serve as a protection to the self. Friends, family, and professionals need to beware of being too confrontive and trying to rush someone through this phase.

Relief After Prolonged Illness.   When death follows a prolonged illness, a feeling of relief may be experienced at first. There is relief that the person is no longer suffering when there was no hope for a cure. There is relief for the family who had many extra obligations and tensions during the chronic or terminal illness. There is also relief from that terrible period of "waiting for death." A woman related that when her mother died, there was a phenomenal relief that it was over, for her, for her mother; it was over for everyone. "It's a terrible thing to say: 'Thank God!' But I knew she was never going to get better. All I could do was hope for a merciful end to the whole thing."

These feelings of relief experienced in the first phase shield the self from the meaning of the final separation and reality of *dead*. The stark difference between illness and death is yet to be felt. However, the family is spared the shock and surprise felt after a sudden death. There has been time to prepare emotionally for the death.

Betty's husband had been an invalid for four years, and she devoted all of her time to him. He died of an unexpected complication not related to his chronic illness. Betty said:

> When he died, I felt relieved. I felt blessed that I didn't have to go through a more serious time of life than I did. I felt I was spared. I did not feel guilty about the reaction because I had given him the best care. I thought it was okay to feel relieved because I had really done my share. I didn't know what to do with myself though. My life had revolved around his caretaking for so many years.

Betty had an awareness of guilt as people often do. It does not seem appropriate to feel relieved when someone dies. It is something you are "not supposed" to feel. Being relieved at first is natural, and many other feelings will surface as time goes on.

Betty had a large void to fill following the death. Soon afterwards, she found an outlet for her energy through church work. Although death that occurs after a long illness provides a sense of relief, it engenders another loss, a loss of role and function. During the illness considerable energy is exerted in concern, in visiting, or in caring for the sick person. You feel at loose ends for awhile, as if something is missing (and it is), until you redirect your time and emotional energy.

The Second Phase: Undoing

Undoing is a process in which the mourner attempts to undo the calamity in order to make everything as it was before. "In my daydreams I can make everything all right," a father said. "Then my daughter would be alive and healthy." Reversing the death would also mean that he would not be suffering and in such pain. Attempts at undoing the event involve thinking such as : "If only I had gone to the doctor sooner. . . .What if I had insisted that she get medical help. . . .If only I had taken her complaints seriously. . . .If the doctor had only given this other medication. . . .If only I had said, 'No, you can't go on the trip.' " All these phrases imply that if something else had been done, the deceased would be alive and healthy and everything would be normal and undisturbed. These fantasies of alternatives are attempts to undo the disaster and make everything right again. It serves the purpose of allowing temporary relief.

Guilt, Self-Blame, and Powerlessness.   The mourner may take on the responsibility for the death and feel guilty. It is as if the mourner assumes that he or she had the power to prevent the death. There is also an underlying implication that with prior knowledge it could have been prevented. Both Ruth and Rose said: "I shouldn't have let him go jogging that morning." In a way, they blamed themselves for their husbands' heart attacks and figured they could have prevented them. The implication is that the death would not have occurred if they had intervened, and that they had the *power* to intervene. "What if I had made him take a nap instead of letting him cut the lawn?" or "Maybe I should have listened to her when she complained." Stricken people want to put everything back in order again. They want to retrieve or recover the lost person, to bring the person back to life. They try to convince themselves that if they had acted differently and exercised more assertiveness, the death would have been avoided. They *want* to believe that by thinking and wishing, the situation can be reversed. It is like playing a movie backwards and creating a new ending.

Another struggle evident here is with your own limits and power. You have to confront the fact that you cannot undo the tragedy, which means that you are powerless in the face of death. It also means that you have to live with your anguish.

Power and responsibility become big issues when death has occurred through suicide: "If I had gone straight home from the party, she would not have taken the overdose of sleeping pills. I would have been there in time to save her." The survivors try to figure out how they could have prevented it and take on guilt and responsibility for the death. This is very agonizing.

Guilt feelings may come from recalling that you failed the deceased in some way or feel regret over having quarreled or disappointed the deceased. Guilt may come from actions that were omitted or opportunities missed. There are always regrets, as there are always many ways to do things, many ways to solve problems and many ways to react.

One element that becomes very misleading and can sometimes keep you hooked and going in a circular pattern is that there seems to be a small grain of truth to some of these conjectures. They may appear to be reasonable speculations. People can become very creative in inventing "if onlys" and "what ifs" and can convince themselves that this could indeed have been the case. You *can* often intervene and take different alternatives, except when death occurs. The fact is, these are *speculations* and *not* the *reality*. There is a point at which you must say, "I could not prevent it. . . . It was not in my control. It did not come out the way I wanted it to. . . . I must accept the awful truth the way it is and learn to live with it, not distract myself with fantasies. . . . I must not continue the search to recover my loved one. . . . The truth is that the person is dead."

It is natural for parents to feel responsible for their children. Parents whose child has died make great mental efforts to undo the circumstances, to make everything right again or to try to do a "retake." Then, of course, the child would still be alive. The Breen family had a terrible time after their teen-aged daughter died in a fire. Fires somehow propel us to investigate the cause, implying that prevention was possible. It is as if knowing the cause would give us back the power of prevention. This encourages the process of undoing. Mrs. Breen went over and over the circumstances of the death. "If only I had not let her sleep over. If only I had said, 'No.' I should not have let her go. If only the fire department had done its job properly," and on and on, tormenting herself with ways this horror could have been prevented. If overused the undoing process can become self-torturing rather than relieving. Although it serves the purpose of making everything right in fantasy, it stands in the way of accepting things as they are, horrible as they may be. Since the reality *is* so horrible, this serves the function of trying to reverse it as a way of cushioning the blow. This phase is a buffer between your wish and the reality, and it softens the pain so that another small portion can be absorbed when you feel ready for it. However, reflections are also torturous and counterproductive and they must eventually be abandoned. Death is permanent. This effort to undo blocks accepting the reality and stands in the way of integration. Recognize that you have done what you had the power to do and allow youself to move on.

The Third Phase: Anger

Anger is a difficult emotion for us to express in our daily lives. It becomes even more difficult to understand and to express during the mourning process, and many people do get *very* angry. When you are angry, you want to be able to express this directly to the source of your anger. You hope for some resolution to your conflict. The anger of mourning does not provide you with an opportunity for confrontation or resolution. You are left with a sense of frustration knowing that no matter how angry you are, things cannot be changed. You do not have the object of your anger to deal with directly, and you do not have any hope for resolution of the conflict.

> "I don't know what to do with the anger," Claire complained. "What should I do, where should I aim it? When you are angry you want to be able to take it up with someone, you want to pick a fight, and I have no one to fight with."

Another aspect of anger that may inhibit expression is that it does not seem logical. It does not make sense to be angry at someone for dying. After all *he* or *she* surely did not *want* to die. However, anger or other feelings do not have to be logical. They are not right or wrong. We do not make judgments about feelings. Feelings exist and need to be acknowledged and expressed.

Anger is felt at the situation, at the *happening*. "How could this happen to me?" "I am so angry that my life is disrupted." Anger may be felt at the deceased for dying, for having *abandoned* you. People have expressed the following: "How could you leave me?" "How could you do this to me? I hate you!" "You left me with all the problems." Children often verbalize: "I am angry at you for not being here for my graduation," or "I am angry at you for not watching your diet."

> An eighteen-year-old said: "I want to blame you, Dad, for dying. I am angry that you did not take care of yourself better, have that surgery, everything else that goes along with that, for leaving us because you didn't take care of yourself."

> A young widow reported: "There were two particular times that I would be acutely aware of my anger. One would be when I would sit down to pay bills. Somehow that triggered off my anger and I always felt: 'It was terrible of you to leave me with all these worries.' Another time that was terrible for me was when there were any problems with the children. I would feel these problems would never have arisen if he were alive. 'It's all because you have gone and left us and upset our family.'"

Sally Robbins also felt angry when there were problems with the children.

> "I felt that he had set up disciplinary action with the children and then was not here to carry through. I did not discipline in the same way and found it difficult to get the children to respond to my way. I would feel: 'Bob, why aren't you here to finish the job you started?'"

Displacement.   The anger is mainly felt towards the circumstances and the course of events, but often it is directed at *someone*, the family members or other persons.

When a parent dies, children often direct their anger at the surviving parent. Over and over again Ginny expressed her anger at her father for not *doing something*. She was angry at him for her mother's illness and angry because he did not give more guidance to the family during the illness. "He should have done something. Why didn't he talk to us? Why didn't he give us a chance to say how we felt? Why didn't he *help* me?" Children feel it is up to the parent to take care of them and make everything right and are angry at the parent when he or she is unable to live up to this expectation. There are times when no one can make things right. Cari was also angry at her family, "You guys [her mother and brothers] are around to support each other and I'm going to be all alone, not knowing what's going on. I have to be by myself. I have to go back to college. Who is going to help *me*?"

Anger is often directed toward the medical professionals for not knowing enough or not doing enough to keep the loved one healthy and alive. They will be blamed for mistakes they have made or alternatives that could have been taken. It still comes back to being angry about the death, no matter who becomes the target. The anger exists because the circumstances cannot be changed, the death cannot be reversed.

People often feel angry at God and express the feeling that "God should not have let this happen to me." Some feel that God has been unfair when they have led a good and religious life and thus expected God would spare them any tragedy or pain. Some people put their anger at God into action and leave their religion or their place of worship. Jenny stood on the church steps immediately following the religious memorial service for her husband who had been killed in the crash of a commercial airliner. Her anger was fierce and she directed it to the church. A cascade of words expressed her wrath. "All they cared about was his soul," she exclaimed bitterly. "They didn't care about Fred, the man. Father George knew him and was his friend but you'd think he had never met him. All he wanted to do was save Fred's soul." Jenny alienated herself from the church. Even after years of widowhood, remarriage and a divorce, Jenny is still exploring other religions, looking for something she can really believe in. It appears that Jenny's anger colored the rest of her life. She has not understood the source of her anger, nor has she adequately expressed it. It seems that she is still expecting God or a religion to make everything "right" for her.

Expression of Anger.   The expression of anger is a difficult task and will be dealt with later in more detail. You need to be aware, to acknowledge angry feelings, to talk them out and express them in many ways. There must be physical and verbal expressions of anger. Each of you must find your own method of expression, your own unique way of venting your anger, but the *expression of anger is essential.*

Powerlessness. During the anger phase you may struggle with your powerlessness again. This may be expressed in feeling angry about your own limited powers and inability to stop the course of death. For some people powerlessness is dealt with in each phase of mourning, especially people who had a strong sense that their lives would be happy and good if they worked hard and were honorable. A young widow said: "I could not believe there was nothing I could do about it all. I had always tried so hard to do the right thing and we both had always worked so hard. Somehow I thought that those efforts would make everything turn out okay. I felt so powerless."

It is hard to accept that we are not promised a life without pain and loss, no matter how upstanding we have been.

Feelings Overlap.   Many emotions become intertwined and become more difficult to understand and deal with. Guilt often becomes involved with anger. People feel angry at the deceased and then guilty about having angry feelings. Then anger may follow the guilt as it is such an unpleasant emotion to experience. It becomes very confusing.

Anger is sometimes a cover-up for sadness. Beware of this as it is necessary to acknowledge and experience sadness as a separate feeling. Feelings are layered. Excessive anger is a signal that other feelings are being converted to anger.

Other feelings which are experienced in the anger phase are feelings of being cheated and that you have been dealt with unfairly. You may feel cheated out of your continuing relationship with the deceased. You are cheated out of the future you had imagined together. You are cheated out of happiness and expectations. In their place you have pain. You may feel that what has happened to you or to the deceased is unfair, that you did not deserve such a fate, that it is unfair for you to be so distressed when others can still enjoy their lives. It is true you have been cheated, and it is essential to accept and acknowledge these feelings.

Resentment and Revenge.   Other feelings which are experienced in this phase of anger are feeling cheated out of "what is rightfully mine," and feeling resentful toward others who seemingly have everything "just right." Revenge is a strong emotion when the death has occurred through accident or murder. The direction of anger for the survivors will be the wish for revenge on the murderer. This is often put into action by following the court proceedings and imprisonment to make sure the individual gets just punishment. When there has been an industrial accident or automobile accident, people struggle with these feelings because there usually is no retribution except perhaps insurance, always inadequate compared to a life.

Paradoxically, there may be an attempt to exhibit understanding toward a person who has caused an accident. Lanny's death was caused by a nineteen-year-old driver of a van who ran a red light. Her mother said: "I feel sorry for him. Sorry that he has to live with that. I don't think about him except every time I'm in church and say the words asking God to 'forgive us our trespasses as we forgive those who trespass against us.' *I can never say that line without seeing that guy trespassing against us.* He certainly did not mean to kill her but he was doing wrong."

> Fifteen-year-old Sandy feels differently about the driver. "All I could think of was how bad it would be to have that hanging over your head for the rest of your life. Hank, Jr. wanted to kill him, but how many times has *he* run a red light? Or you, Mom, run a red light? Everybody does it."
> Returning to her feelings about the driver of the van that killed her sister, Sandy said, "I read all the papers, his reactions. He put his head down on the steering wheel and cried. He's only four years older than me. Can you imagine me dealing with that? It's bad for him and it's bad for us, too."

This attitude neutralizes the anger and resentment and may, in fact, serve as a denial.

A young college woman related the story of the violent death of her uncle. She described her own process and her awareness of it. Most prominent is the rage and revenge experienced by the surviving brother, her father.

> I turned hesitantly to face my mother's bloody red eyes, to face the news. "Somebody killed John on his way home from work," she managed to say, hopelessly staring at me. Some people, as I did, repress, blunt, or deaden their feelings because it is not tolerable to feel anything, but my father in an uncontrollable surge of rage smashed his hand against the wall. "Dammit!" he said, his teeth clenched. "If only I could have been there!"
> My father and I talked as he drove me to school. He heatedly expressed his feelings of anger as he wiped the hot tears from his eyes. "They say it's good to cry," he said. He explained that he felt like a cold-blooded killer and that if it were not for us he would be out in the dark streets hunting for them. "Oh, God," I said angrily, "I bet you're gonna end up in jail before I even get back."

Now two months later, my father has gained back all of his weight and more, but hardly any of his humanity. "I'm mean!" he proclaims.

When asked what should be done about the killers, he reacted explosively. He replied that the killers should be turned over to the family. He would tie them to a tree. "They won't walk. They won't talk. They won't kill again!" he said.

Then he faced us quietly. "When will I ever get over it?"

As Ruth and Mr. Barnes asked, you may ask, "When will I be over it?" The mourning process is painful and long, but as you continue to be aware of your emotions and express them you will find relief.

The Fourth Phase: Sadness

Sadness is the predominant feeling when the reality of the death is really sinking in and being absorbed. In this phase you will feel the hurt and agony very deeply. A longing is felt for the deceased as well as a realization of the absence and the permanence of this absence. You feel very disappointed that things have not turned out the way you had hoped they would and feel helpless because you cannot do anything to change it. A hopelessness about the future may follow this. "How can the future have any meaning without my loved one? How can I survive this anguish and this pain?"

You will get in touch with your limitations, the things that you cannot do. We all confront our limitations when it comes to a matter of death. This is one place indeed where we do not have any control. On the other hand, in facing our limitations we can also realize where we do have the power and control to direct our lives.

The sadness is an emotional recognition of this terrible thing that has happened to you. It is a very painful phase, but essential before integration can occur. You may again feel alone and isolated, as if no one could possibly understand or feel as you do. As a bridge from this isolation, find someone with whom to share your feelings. You need to feel connected to another person.

It is difficult to describe sadness. There are so few words that fit the feeling. It is profound; felt down to the core of you. It comes from and stays in the very center of you. Sadness is darkness and aloneness. Sadness is associated with acknowledging that your loved one is gone, not available to you, not retrievable, and really dead. The loved one is missed and you know that you will go on missing this person who was special in your life. A ten-year-old girl wailed pathetically about her older sister: "I want her. . . . I am so sad." A bereaved mother said:

"*Sad* is an understatement. It is so deep." A twenty-five-year-old woman expressed her sadness about the death of her younger sister:

My sister is dead. I feel desperation. How can I ever adequately verbalize these feelings of devastation?

I have had to work through feelings of shock, disbelief, helplessness, frustration, anger, righteous indignation, and sadness. Yet, sadness remains forefront, a constant, perpetual reminder that as I live she no longer lives. With each step taken, she is one more step behind.

Lydia's sadness is different. She wept: "I don't feel sad for myself. I feel sad when I think about my sisters. They died too young. Their lives were unfulfilled."

Six weeks after her father's death Cari shared: "Sometimes I just want to cry for you Daddy. Other times I just don't know what to do. It's very hard to live with death. I wish you had life as do I . . . more than anything I wish you had life."

Cari's sadness lingered for years after her father's death. "I miss him not being around. I can remember his face . . . can remember as if he were standing here. I miss him not being in on a lot of things that happened to me, like growing. I really feel sad that my husband will never know him and that my children won't and they will never have a grandfather anywhere."

Another young woman began:

I miss my mother so much and, as if talking to her, said: "I just don't understand why you had to die. I feel like I would give everything I have just to talk to you for five minutes."

When I went to the cemetery I was talking to her about our decision to have a baby. I began crying so hard because I wouldn't be able to give her the baby to hold. That is one of the nicest ways to say you love your parents—that they gave you enough of the joy of life that you want to pass it on to someone else—and she wouldn't be there to participate. It is so unfair for all of us not to have her around to share these kinds of moments. It diminishes all the moments because she's not here. Nothing is ever quite as nice again.

Ruth tried to put her sadness into words:

There are times when no one else will do. *You can tell something to only one person and that person is gone.* He's the only person I could share a certain thing with, the only person to help, the only person that would understand the words and the feelings. And I know it will always be that way. My sadness is that I know it will last, just as his space will always be empty.

This significant person had a role in your life and the loss will forever leave an empty space. Norma talked about the loss of her friend:

> Missing has to do with how much space a person has taken up inside and outside. It feels like a lot of gaps, a lot of different gaps, and I don't know about it until a new experience arises and then the gap is there.

Aaron's grandfather died. Their relationship had been as a father and son because Aaron had not known his own father. As a youngster he had lived with his grandparents.

> I still grieve his loss. It seems that it will not go away—this pain I feel at the loss of his love, or perhaps, from my inability to give him mine. I'll always miss him; I'll always love him. Only now I will have to carry it with me, no longer can our love intertwine.

There is sadness for the loss of the relationship as well as for the loss of the individual. The hopes and dreams for the relationship must be given up. As long as persons are alive and together they have hopes for resolving conflicts and having happy times together. With the death you must give up all the expectations for the relationship and for the future together. There are many changes in the picture of your life. In addition to the loss of the individual and the relationship, there is a loss in the family as a unit, in the configuration of the family. At first it appears that you are no longer a family, but that is not true. The family changes and rearranges itself and eventually reaches a new configuration.

Avoidance of Feeling Sad.   Feelings of sadness are difficult to bear. They are often avoided or converted to other feelings. A flurry of activity and busyness may serve as a distraction from feelings. As Claire said, "Go away. I'm too busy now."

Another avoidance or denial is inhibiting the expression of sadness, whether through words or tears. Through avoidance of feeling or expression, the sadness produces an edge that may be experienced as anxiety. This is a signal that feelings have been submerged. You need awareness of your feelings and need a release for the pain of sadness.

Sadness is often converted to anger. Rather than staying with sad feelings because they are so deep and devastating, the sadness is changed and expressed as anger. Anger is easier than sadness to deal with for some persons.

Sadness and anger often become intertwined and the anger becomes doubled in intensity. Sometimes expressing your anger and working with it, will get you in touch with your sadness. The anger is often a layer above the sadness. Very often children will anesthetize their sad feelings with anger. If there is excessive anger and a notable lack of sadness, be on the lookout for this conversion.

When you get rid of your anger and sadness, you will have room for other feelings.

Self-Pity.   Another dominant feeling of this phase is self-pity. It is all right to feel sorry for yourself when something terrible has happened. It is certainly appropriate. People often try to talk themselves out of self-pity by thinking that it is not acceptable to pity yourself. Worrying about what others might think of you or making self-judgments will serve to inhibit your feelings. You need to believe in your own process. What you feel is natural and necessary. It is part of mourning. Give yourself permission for self-pity just as you would for all other feelings. *You need to allow yourself the pity and the expression of it so you can move beyond it.* Self-pity may leave its scar as "poor me," just as the remainder of anger leaves its scar as bitterness. Danny felt sorry for himself many times when with his friends.

"All the other boys have fathers and I don't. I miss him when I'm doing the same things he did and when I meet people that knew him. I feel sorry for myself because he's not here to help."

Sharon cried on her twelfth birthday. "Today is my birthday and I miss my Dad. My friends have daddies to be at their birthdays but I don't." Missing, longing and sadness are interwoven with self-pity. This is often expressed by children and adults. Widows will often say, "I have to do everything myself. I look around and see others who have someone to share responsibility with." There is an undercurrent here of anger, resentment, self-pity, and sadness that things are the way they are, all mixed up.

Depression.   During this phase of sadness many persons will say that they feel depressed. This is a feeling of heaviness, of feeling burdened, similar to the definition of grief. There may also be a period during which it is difficult to become mobilized, to get up and do things. Mourning requires a lot of energy because energy is used to feel and to express so many emotions. Therefore, there is limited energy available and little interest in other things, except the essential tasks.

Many persons use the term *depression* to refer to a combination of feelings or as a shorthand for an emotional experience. It often includes intermittent spontaneous crying or a feeling that tears may well up at any time, being preoccupied with painful thoughts, no interest or motivation, feeling burdened by the loss. These feelings are related to sadness, and the emotional exhaustion experienced in the process of mourning. "Depressed" may aptly describe this combination of feelings related to the loss, but it is different from the use of the term to mean a clinical or chronic depression.

A depressed feeling in the sadness phase of mourning should not be confused with the term depression used so freely and widely in our society today, or the depression used as a diagnosis for an emotional problem. Depression is overused in our society to describe even a short term feeling of sadness, lack of energy, or feeling "down." The word "depression" is sometimes used as a catchall term. Underlying the exterior signs of depression are unexpressed feelings that may range from sadness to anger. The goal is to uncover the feelings beneath this depression and express those feelings. During the mourning process you are encouraged to keep track of your feelings, be aware of them, recognize them, and acknowledge and express them fully with words and tears. If you keep up with your feelings and identify your sadness, you will probably avoid a clinical depression.

There are many symptoms of grief similar to the symptoms of a clinical depression. These will be discussed later under Acute Symptoms. These symptoms are normal for grieving but would be cause for concern and psychiatric attention if they occurred at another time of life. When these symptoms occur during the normal phases of grieving, they can be understood as part of the mourning process, unless they are exaggerated or prolonged. If there is any doubt, professional help should be sought.

Living With It. When someone dies, a part of you also goes and sadness takes its place. You do not forget your loved one. You do not forget your sadness; it will still hurt at times. Sadness becomes part of you. You will become a changed person with an added dimension to yourself. You will be able to go on and address yourself to new aspects of your life.

A young woman expressed the process of her mourning with the following poem.

Deep grief:
Deep down in the heart

Wish things were different, grief.
Deep wish I could
Let go of the load.
Grief:
Feeling of disappointment,
Not able to give.
Little girl grief,
Not able to grow up.
Grief:
Focused on self
Unable to be
any other way.
Grief:
Pain we all suffer.
The hurt
Of final separation.
The bond is still there.
Afraid to let go
And be free and separate.
I am not just Emily.
I am Emily
After 35 summers.
35 winters, and
Grief:
Different than Emily
At another time.

Starting to believe
In my own journey
Toward wholeness.
Grief:
Life as we understand it
Has a beginning and an end.
Separation that must be.
No choice.
Living from the heart
Is not possible
In a state of
Grief,
But is in a state of
relief

Where grief
Plays its role
But does not live
As the honored guest.

Emily Williams

You need to allow yourself to experience your sadness fully. It is terribly painful. Real strength is required to endure sadness. If you experience it, express it, and share it. eventually it will take its place within you and be integrated. This integration will also make room for other feelings. From what seems to be a meaningless void, meaning will emerge again as you move toward integration of the loss.

The Fifth Phase: Integration

Integration takes place slowly during the mourning process. The working out of feelings in each phase makes integration possible. The sense of finishing up that is felt with integration is part of settling into the new reality. It means becoming more comfortable with the way things *are* rather than continuing to struggle to make things as they *were*. Verbs and pronouns change from "is" to "was," from "we" to "I," from "ours" to "mine."

Integration is the phase in which the reality becomes part of you, absorbed by you. The emotional reality finally becomes fused with the intellectual reality. The death has been "taken in" and digested. You begin to "know" emotionally what you have known rationally; your loved one is dead. The struggle ceases and you put this knowledge in its place. The pain changes from being sharp and stabbing to a dull ache, to a sensitive spot within you. When a reminder or memory touches that spot, the pain may return for a moment, an hour, or a few days. The sadness does not disappear, but it does become background. The current facets of your life become the foreground upon which you focus. *The sadness coexists* with other feelings awakened within you: the ability to laugh and enjoy things again, the ability to experience pleasure and beauty. Your appetites are reawakened. You are no longer a mourner, but you do not forget the deceased. The many parts of you have said goodbye to the many parts of the other—the goodbyes that began with the memorial service and that have been repeated over and over during several years. The goodbye that takes place during integration is a deep and final goodbye, one with full realization of its meaning. Your loved one will not return. You feel freedom from past emotional ties.

Acceptance does not mean, "Well, it is all done and over with and I won't be bothered with that anymore." It is more a matter of, "This is how things are now and I need to face it even though I don't like it. I need to make my life meaningful." You take up the strands of your past life but many things are different. The changes in your life can be accepted as challenges. The loss is absorbed and integrated and you finally emerge as a changed person, having developed new facets of yourself.

This is a time when you accept your limitations. You have had to confront your powerlessness and helplessness as well as the opposite, your power and control. You need to exert control in all areas of your life where it is possible. Psychological energy used for mourning is freed up as you move toward the goal of integration. You will have more energy available to reorganize your life and reinvest in new interests and new relationships. As energy is freed up, you are able to work on establishing a new identity and redirect the part of you that related to the deceased. You become adjusted to the role change that has taken place with the loss of the relationship.

The following quotations capture the gradual process of integration and the meaning it holds for some individuals:

> I rarely cry now. Though it is still painful at times, I don't feel that awful feeling in my gut anymore.

> The sadness still comes but without the peccant thoughts of before; memories sting with loneliness, but not as overwhelming as before.

> I always know that the world lost too much laughter and goodness when my sister left. My hurt and loss have changed me.

> My conception and value of time has changed. I live very much for deriving pleasure in the present and recognizing joy in life's simplest gifts.

> Death has awakened my taste buds, whetted my appetite for life. Knowing the blackness of death, I want more of the lightness of life.

> I've heard it takes getting through each holiday and birthday once and that the first year is so difficult because of this. I can say it took more than one holiday, birthday, and anniversary to feel better about them. It took me several years before I could face one without dread. I'm still aware of somone missing, but I can enjoy them at last.

Although most persons take up the threads of their lives gradually with some meaning, it takes a long time to feel good and unburdened. Many persons have said that somewhere along two to three years after the death, they have a "lighter" feeling. Claire said, "I can do some of the old things without clawing at others. I can put my heel down, not just slough along." Ruth finally experienced a difference:

> One day I realized that I was starting to feel good again. I had short periods of relief all along but the periods lasted longer and felt like more than relief. It felt good. I felt some happiness and hope. I had come a long way.

Remembering. Remembering and recalling are important parts of integration. One of the ways of keeping a person's memory alive is to continue to talk about him or her, to tell anecdotes, to share reminders, and talk spontaneously and naturally, as well as sharing feelings about the person and the death. It is important to talk about the whole person and relationships with that person. Too often the deceased is talked about in glowing terms as if perfect, forgetting or ignoring the negatives and conflicts. You want to reminisce about experiences together, especially the pleasant times. Too often people forget that the deceased was human and had some qualities that were not endearing. Sometimes a fiction develops that the deceased was an angel, especially when the death has been untimely. There is a "growing goodness" about a person after death. It is important to remember and talk about the weaknesses and faults of the deceased, the imperfections, the qualities you did not like, and the hard times together. It is essential to acknowledge the disappointments in the relationship and the loss of fulfillment. Mourning takes place not only for the death of an individual but also for the loss of the relationship and the loss of the future together which includes the changes and losses in the picture of your everyday life and your future. Integration does not take place unless the whole person and the whole relationship are acknowledged rather than idealized.

Painful memories need not be shunned and pushed aside. Unpleasant memories of the relationship or the last look of death fade as mourning and time go on. Pleasant and happy times will be remembered along with the deceased's appearance when alive and vital. Jean related:

> When I think of Mattie I remember mostly the good times. The pleasant memories are more dominant in my thinking than those months of horror when she was so sick.

Norma said:

> You can't replace anything, really. If I take the word apart, replace/ment, I must talk about filling those gaps, all the little times when I

think about the help he would have given me in a particular situation, the things he would have said, the way he would have behaved. No one can duplicate that. I know it is true that after many years those gaps don't appear in the same way; they begin to fade. I would then have a different sense of who to turn to for those responses or as a resource. Other things would develop but it would not be a replacement.

Aaron shared this experience:

My grandfather passed on his secret for living with his last words to me, "I fought as hard as I could." And so I must. Fight hard. I cherish this last living memory. Life does go on despite the absence of a loved one. This I find sad, yet there is hope in it as well. Death has brought fond, treasured memories along with its bitter sting.

Remembering comforts us and keeps the loved one with us in a healthy way. We each wish to be remembered after our own death. It is a way of keeping meaning in our life and our beloved's.

This is healthy remembering, remembering that sustains us and makes us all feel that we will not be forgotten after our own death. It is a way to keep the person with us and is the immortality of our loved one.

One of the ways of keeping the person alive is to continue to talk about this significant person, to share reminders, and to continue to share feelings. The sadness and lonesomeness for your loved one will continue, but the memories will have a comforting quality.

ACUTE SYMPTOMS

The acute symptoms of grief take many forms and occur early in mourning. These are experienced as physical distress. Among them are sleep disturbances, loss of appetite and weight, extreme fatigue, palpitations, shortness of breath and headaches. Some people suffer from chronic indigestion, difficulty in swallowing, and generally have many aches and pains. Confusion and disorientation are common in the early phase of mourning. Many will experience dramatic mood swings and extreme sensitivity. Some people report visual and auditory hallucinations. Most bereaved people are free of acute symptoms after a year.[4,5,6]

Sleep Disturbances

Disturbances of sleep are common and sometimes outlast other symptoms. The quality of sleep is poor, manifested in the inability to fall asleep or to stay asleep, early awakening, or interrupted sleep. The feeling of vulnerability and the fear of another disaster interfere with restful sleep.

> Ruth had no trouble falling asleep but only slept four to five hours a night and would awaken at 4:00 or 5:00 A.M. It was too early to rise but she was too restless to fall back to sleep. "As much as I wanted to sleep, to have some relief from this agony, it was difficult. I would awaken during the night and feel so alone and frightened. I felt so vulnerable and exposed and so helpless."

Very often you get more sleep than you realize. Surprisingly, you can get along on four or five hours of sleep or intermittent sleep for a period of time. When you cannot fall asleep or awaken after a short sleep, thoughts roil in your mind. Even if you sleep in short spates, you have a feeling of not having slept at all. Being awake at night is difficult at any time. Midnight wakefulness brings on negative thoughts and it is hard to work through a nagging idea. It becomes frustrating and heightens the feeling of restlessness and agitation. If lack of sleep continues for an extended period to the point of exhaustion, then some mild sedative might be indicated. Before turning to your physician for medication, try the old-fashioned remedies of daily exercise, warm milk, reading or writing down your thoughts. Many persons begin the use of sedatives and sleeping pills as an attempt to conquer the sleeplessness, but often they are ineffective, or lead to dependency.

> Chuck's worst night came about a month after Jane's death. A sleeping pill at bedtime was no help. After restless hours he took another one. Still unable to sleep, he paced about the house for awhile, stretched out on the couch in the den and finally fell asleep as daylight began to show on the horizon. "That was the worst night I had. Sleep was not easy."

It is a struggle for many to get out of bed in the morning. You may wake up with an oppressive thought and prefer to sink back into the forgetfulness of sleep. Every awakening brings another realization that the person is absent; it forces the awareness of the reality. "Every time I woke up was another realization that my husband was absent, not next to me, not in life," Ruth said. "Every awakening was like getting the news again that Jeff was dead."

Some persons may also seek escape through an excessive amount of sleep. Debby found she was sleeping an inordinate amount and had trouble getting out of bed in the morning.

> I did not want to wake up to the reality of it. Mornings were especially bad because Art died in the morning. It was such a nightmare. I would

wake up and think, "Did I dream it all?" hoping it was a dream. It was really hard to wake up.

Most people manage to drag out of bed and get through the day even though it is difficult. There *does* come a time when it becomes less difficult. The awareness of the death is lessened and the focus on the day ahead increases.

Loss of Appetite

Loss of appetite is another common symptom that appears soon after death. It seems to confirm that death is an assault on the whole being. Your system is not functioning normally, and you may not have a desire for food. Many people say they just cannot eat. It will not go down. Many people report they cannot swallow. This seems to be symbolic. Emotionally, they do not want to swallow what has happened.

> Sarah had suffered two miscarriages. A few days after the second miscarriage she took an aspirin, and it seemed to stick in her throat. The sensation of the stuck pill stayed with her for weeks. An aspirin dissolves easily so how could this small pill stay in her throat? She realized she still had not "swallowed" the idea of the loss. That is what was really stuck in her throat.
>
> The saying, "That's a tough pill to swallow" is familiar to us all.

Fatigue and Confusion

Tremendous fatigue is another reflection of the assault on your total being. It is related to the inability to sleep and eat properly, in addition to the emotional stress of death. It takes a lot of energy and strength to bear the burden of your feelings. The psychological work of mourning is exhausting. Being aware and dealing with your feelings uses up so much energy, that there is little energy left for other things. Trying to ignore or push feelings aside is a struggle which also uses up enormous amounts of energy and does not lead anywhere. *The energy used in the work of mourning leads to the eventual freeing up of energy as you approach integration of the loss.*

The mourning process is all-consuming, overwhelming, and draining. It is like being hit on the head. It knocks the sensibilities out of you. Disorientation, confusion, and difficulty in remembering may result. This is usually a temporary phenomenon. You may not remember where you put things, if someone has told you something, or how to do things which were previously automatic. You are so overburdened with emotions that there is no room in your mind for mundane things. You are distracted and unable to focus your attention on anything but your grief.

For the mourner time becomes blurred. People actually say, "Time stopped for me." Time becomes meaningless just as everything else becomes meaningless, except the struggle with life and death. Looking back and trying to orient yourself in time is difficult. Often people cannot remember events that happened around the time of the trauma.

Emotional Instability or Dramatic Mood Changes

There may be brief periods of relief from the despairing feelings of grief, but it does not take much to lose the temporary sense of well-being. Mourners are extremely sensitive and a fleeting thought, a small incident, or a word from someone else can cause a sudden mood change. It is surprising how quickly you can go from up to down. You can be feeling better and some irregularity, reminder, or small demand can push you into an unhappy or agitated mood again.

There will be times the bereaved feels extremely sad and blue, then feels better again. When you feel better, you may think, "Everything is going to be all right from now on. I am going to be able to go on with my life." However, before long there is another mood swing into sadness again. Many people are discouraged by this and think they are through with feeling bad and should continue to feel better. There are periods of hopefulness and periods of hopelessness. Over a period of time the mood changes lessen and the periods of sadness shorten. This is the pattern of recovery.

Illusions and Hallucinations

It can be frightening if the bereaved person is not aware that illusions and hallucinations are quite common following the loss of a loved one. You may fear a "breakdown" or loss of emotional stability. You may hesitate to tell anyone for fear of criticism or disdain. These experiences have been referred to as "searching behavior," trying to find the one who is lost. The visions are also evidence of the loneliness inherent in the situation. Many people feel a "presence of the dead" and are helped by their illusions.[4]

People have reported hearing the voice or seeing an apparition of the deceased; they have heard the doorbell ring at the time the deceased would normally arrive home, or the phone ring when he or she would usually call. These fantasies are tied to the strong wish that the person were still a part of their lives. They also are a sign of the struggle with the reality of the death. Case studies show that the "seeing" or "hearing" are often precipitated by a familiar sight or sound that would in the past precede the arrival of the loved one. There are many manifestations of these kinds of experiences. Hearing the stairs creak might remind one of the mate coming up to bed; hearing someone whistling in the street might give rise to the illusion the son is returning from school. A young woman imagined she smelled the smoke from her father's cigarette. One is convinced the dead husband was sitting alive in his chair across the room, or the child who used to come for comfort in the dark of the night stood by the bedside. It is a way of feeling the person is still alive. Hypnagogic (half-awake) hallucinations are hard to shake even when one returns to full awareness. The bereaved person may be comforted by the knowledge that there is nothing abnormal about these phenomena during the mourning process and can be reassured that they will fade as the loss is integrated.[4,5]

Shaking and Trembling

Involuntary and uncontrollable shaking occurs with many persons. It feels as if something powerful is happening inside you that you cannot control and do not understand. Sometimes it lasts for a short period of time and passes. Occasionally it may last for a longer period of time and is accompanied by shivering. The feelings may be similar to the reaction of a high fever. People may feel weak in the knees or lightheaded.

Emotions have a strong effect on your whole body and demand expression in some form. You may have had the experience of being very angry at the boss or a person in authority when expression of the anger would have been inappropriate or cost you your job or a fine. You may have walked away trembling with anger and stuck with it inside of you. Trembling with fear is a better known reaction and is also the result of overwhelming emotion. The physical reaction is similar, although the source of the feelings may differ.

This shaking and trembling are usually reactions to an emotion strongly felt but not expressed in any way. Sometimes it has been expressed partially in words, but the greater part of the emotion, the power of it, is still seething within you. Not understanding it and not being able to control it adds to your worry. Identifying your emotions, acknowledging them, and verbalizing and expressing them in various ways equal to their intensity will prevent this reaction or help to calm you when it does happen.

DREAMS

Dreams are important psychological events that represent efforts to work through conflicts and to resolve and integrate the loss. They are a normal and healthy part of mourning. Dreams have interesting and important symbolic meaning, and in the dreams of mourners the meaning and feelings are often easy to understand and interpret.

Dreams of the bereaved person usually illustrate the struggle within the mourner between the wish to have the significant person alive, against the knowledge that the person is dead. Sometimes the dreams are pleasant, involving the deceased in a lively, vivid, or affectionate manner. Sometimes they contribute to the mourner's agitation, illustrating the conflict with the death and the adjustment to the new reality.[4] Often the image of the deceased will be clear, but the contact is minimal or evasive. There is seldom direct communication, illustrating the awareness that this is no longer possible.

Some examples of dreams are given to demonstrate the apparent and symbolic representation of the struggle with feelings about the death and the deceased within the bereaved person. Claire's dream is typical.

> It was a wonderful dream. It was in a big room with lots of people—a horseshoe type of room like the pictures you see of the United Nations. People were there in flowing robes. They were standing. There was something at the top, hovering above, and I thought it was Gerald. When I came into the room they clapped for me. They were happy. Then they turned against me and Gerald was gone. I couldn't reach him.

Happy, then sad and evasive, these aspects of Claire's dream are common. At first she was happy because she was in a churchlike setting for what seemed to her to be a wedding. Sight of her beloved made her feel that he had not died. When the people turned away from her and Gerald left, she felt abandoned, just as the bereaved feel abandoned. She could see Gerald but could not touch him. "I would just like to touch him," she said after relating the dream. "I would like to have a chance to touch him once more." The desire to touch again is common; it is the desire for another chance, another contact. Claire said, "I wish I could have another chance; I wish I could do it over. I wish there could be a different ending." This illustrates the undoing phase of the process of mourning, the attempt to make the situation turn out right and recover the loved one.

Many people see the deceased very clearly in their dreams. They are able to describe the appearance in detail, what they were wearing, and the facial features. "She seemed so alive," is a common remark. Despite the visual image, there is seldom lasting contact.

> Ruth had many dreams about her deceased husband. She said she loved dreaming about him. "It is a way of having him with me for awhile." Her dreams illustrated the dominant feelings of her ongoing personal experience. A dream she described was one in which she started to run to greet Jeff but he passed her without a glance. In another dream she was again in a public place; this time she felt fully exposed with no one to protect her. Jeff passed her by again with no recognition.
>
> Despite being able to see his image vividly, she was not able to touch him or talk with him.
>
> During the months following Jeff's death, Ruth dreamt often about being at a favorite vacation cottage and in trouble. "He brought us orange life jackets to save me and the children and directed us to put them on." She often had the feeling of being in trouble and needing to be saved.

The dreams came early in her bereavement when her emotions were very raw. She felt abandoned, vulnerable, and in need of help. Obviously, she wished for him to be alive again, but alas there was no contact. It is interesting that years later she had the following dream:

> I dreamt that I was with my dearest friends and they were talking about Dr. Brownlee. They said they had made an appointment with him and had heard he was very competent. I was dumbfounded and hurt and couldn't talk without crying. They didn't seem to remember that it was Dr. Brownlee who treated my husband. I felt his medical error caused my husband's death. I felt betrayed not only by the physician toward whom I was still so angry, but also betrayed by my friends. I felt I couldn't count on anyone. They all abandoned me. I felt alone.

The feelings of abandonment and aloneness were aroused by an important event, her daughter's wedding. The dream occurred shortly after the wedding which was a difficult event to carry out as a widowed mother. At this special event the absence of husband and father was deeply felt and hurt feelings rose once again to the surface.

An occasion such as a celebration or an anniversary, when the deceased is especially missed, may trigger a dream many years later. Dreams will occur at a special time when the absence of the loved one is underscored, as when there are family gatherings and the family constellation is focal.

It takes many years for children and adolescents to work through their mourning. It was not unusual that Daniel had the following dreams six to seven years after his father's death.

Before Thanksgiving he dreamt that his brother was home, someone he also missed who lived out of town. "I came into the kitchen and Dad was standing there. I hugged him and kissed him and then went out to work. It is the first time I ever dreamt about him."

Shortly afterwards he had another dream that dealt with his father's death, although it was clothed in symbolism.

I got a call that an adult friend of mine died of a heart attack. His secretary called me to tell me, and I could not believe it was true. Then I hung up the phone, I went into the kitchen. My brother and a business man in a grey suit were there, and I tried to tell them what happened. At first they ignored me, and then all they did was look over at me. The businessman was standing by the stove. He had just taken a chicken out of the oven. He had stuck a fork into the breast of the chicken and was ripping it off. The chicken was undercooked and bloody and he just took it and put it on the cutting board near my brother. Neither spoke to me.

Dreams can be understood on different levels but usually require the help of a therapist to examine the many meanings. One level of the significance of a dream is the apparent meaning. Another level has symbolic meaning. The process or what is going on in the dream and the feelings are important. Exploration of the significance of his dream added to Danny's understanding of himself and aided his mourning. Danny's dream actually tells the story of what happened the day his father died. The scenario is similar; even the persons represented in the dream are similar to reality. The friend that died of a heart attack represented Danny's father and was even in the same profession. The secretary that called represented his mother who worked together with his father and did his secretarial work. The afternoon of the death they had both been working on some papers, and she had cooked a chicken for supper. The businessman represents many people who were present but were formal and seemed unemotional, people who were at the house when Danny arrived after school: the undertaker, an uncle, and others. They seemed concerned with the business or the task at hand and did not convey feelings. They represented all the people who were physically there but who really did not give emotional support.

The chicken has symbolic meaning. It may have represented his father who was still a "young chicken" when he died. It was undercooked, meaning "not ready to die" or that the death was untimely; he was struck dead before his time. Ripping the breast off the chicken was also symbolic of Danny's feelings. It was as if his own heart were ripped out of him in the agony that he experienced after the death of his father.

His prominent feelings were shock, disbelief, isolation, and a sense of lack of support. He felt ignored and as if no one could do anything or change anything. Danny said, "I felt hurt. . . . I *was* hurt, and no one understood. I wanted to tell somebody, to be comforted."

There was little that could comfort a twelve-year-old at that traumatic time. In a healthy way, he continued to make use of his dream material to facilitate mourning and integrate the loss.

A middle-aged woman suffered the death of her young daughter. In her dream, a bus pulled up in front of the hotel where she was staying, and she and her daughter boarded it excited at the prospect of riding to unknown places. They were surprised to find the bus filled with slot machines but no people. In this dream, mother and daughter were again united. Death is symbolized by riding to unknown places. The slot machines are symbolic of the chances we all take or the risks we experience living from day to day.

Once struck by a tragedy, a person's awareness of death is heightened. It is common to be fearful that some other terrible thing will happen. You do not go on believing that these things happen only to others. You know it can happen to you. Before this it is possible to believe "It won't happen to me."

After his daughter's sudden death a father dreamed he lost his son. He said it was ghastly. The dream illustrates his fear of another disaster. Another father's dream had the same meaning. "I dreamt Peggy came back but only to take my younger daughter with her."

After his father died, Steve, fifteen years old, had dreams that something happened to his mother. Fortunately, he related these dreams to her and they could discuss them and his feelings. She could help allay his fears. It illustrates the same vulnerability and fear that permeates mourners. Feelings about the deceased linger on at some level and do not disappear completely for many people. Margaret still dreams about her father seven years after his death.

> I frequently have dreams about him when I am under a lot of pressure. I guess that's because a lot of times he was a good sounding board for me. Sometimes I see him fleetingly, other times he is very clear. A recent dream was extremely vivid. I'd come home for the weekend and I'd opened the door and he greeted me with a big hug. All this I could see in my dream and I could hear him say: "Skipper, what happened today?" I actually felt him embrace me in the dream and I woke laughing.

Margaret is one of the few persons interviewed who, in her dreams, has actually felt physical contact with her deceased loved one. She repeated several times that in many of her dreams she could feel his arms around her.

Usually, as the person works through the mourning process toward resolution, the dreams occur with less frequency, but dreams will recur years after the death. If the grief has been unresolved, the dreams may reappear, often with a recurring theme.

> Cathy's father committed suicide 17 years ago when she was eighteen years old. She still dreams about him. She senses he is somewhere on the "outskirts" of her life. "It is as if he was away some place, and I've discovered he is still alive. Most of the dreams take place in his office but he is not glad to see me."

Cathy's sister and brother, twins, who were twelve at the time of their father's death, reported similar dreams throughout the years. Even the setting was similar. The wish to have their father alive as opposed to the vague recognition of the death is clear. The fact that the two sisters and brother, now adults, still dream of their father is evidence that they still miss him and struggle with his death. There was minimal talking and sharing of feelings after the event.

Dreams help in understanding your own process and feelings. They help to bring your feelings into awareness with marked clarity. Many people report receiving great comfort and good feelings after dreaming of a deceased loved one. It is almost like being in the person's presence for a brief visit. Many look forward to the experience. Dreams offer an opportunity for insight into feelings and help in the process toward integration. It is necessary to record dreams, talk about them, and share feelings in order to get the most out of them.

EXPRESSION OF GRIEF

Mourning is all-encompassing and all-consuming. The intensity of grief wracks the whole body. It is a physiological event. There are many means of expression that help you carry out the task of mourning, such as crying, talking, writing, ritualized activity, physical movement, and other action. We experience an emotion or locate it in our body and attach a mental label or words to it such as happy, sad, angry, afraid. We search for a vocabulary of grief. Words for describing feelings are very limited, even though they are the major mode for expression of emotions. We need language to attach to our feelings. It is often difficult to find the words because they seem inadequate compared with the intensity of the experience. When you talk, the feelings and images become more real. Therefore, there is often resistance to talking about feelings. At first, talking stimulates the feelings. It may seem better for the moment to push the feelings aside because of the pain. Talking may not give you *immediate* relief since it stirs up feelings and makes them real. *Talking* is one of the steps along the road which will lead to *eventual relief*. Talking and sharing may be difficult at first, but they are the path to relief and closeness with others. Silent grief is still more painful, and does not help you move through the phases of mourning. Without words, crying, and other expressions, the pain stays within and ferments. Then there can be no relief, no end, no integration.

Some people feel vulnerable if they reveal and expose their feelings. Actually, it is utterly human and gives us the opportunity to be close to one another. There is a commonality of feelings among us all as human beings, and it is reassuring to share and have our emotional experience validated by others.

Allowing The Process To Flow

Do not hide from your grief—face it, express it. Sorrow needs words. Ruth followed her own healthy instincts to guide her in mourning. She shared the following:

> Instinctively I knew that I had to pay attention to my feelings and not hide by keeping busy or whatever. I was going to indulge my feelings and express them fully. I also knew instinctively that this would take time, and I did take the time. My work schedule was light, and I put other obligations aside. *I FELT DEEPLY AND I CRIED.* I believe to this day that it was the healthiest way to mourn and recommend this for all mourners. Don't hide from your feelings! Express them! One thing for sure, though, it takes an awful lot of strength to bear all that pain—a lot of strength. But most people have more strength than they give themselves credit for.

Crying

Crying is a physical expression of emotions. *Although many harbor the myth that not crying is strong, crying has nothing to do with strength or weakness. Crying has to do only with the expression of feelings.* Men and women both need to cry. The belief that crying should be controlled is detrimental to the mourning process. Mourning by its very definition is the expression of grief. People find ways to stop themselves from crying such as laughing, swallowing, denying, tightening up, constricting breathing, and biting the lip. Some people say, "What good will it do? It won't change anything. It won't bring the person back." That is true. It will not bring the person back or make everything right. The purpose of crying is to express feelings and not to change anything in the environment. It is obviously not possible to change death. Inhibiting the spontaneous reaction begins a process of turning feelings inward and interferes with the *natural process* of mourning. It becomes more and more difficult to bring forth the healing tears.

Sometimes tears come at unexpected moments and for unexplainable reasons. It is an involuntary reaction. You find yourself crying or wanting or needing to cry. This is true for men and women and is normal. Allowing this will support your mourning process. Experiencing tears near the surface lasts, in varying degrees, about a year. That does not mean the bereaved stop crying. On the contrary, memories, sadness, and tears may be triggered over a very long period of time by anniversaries, the sound of a special piece of music, picking up a particular book, or many other little things.

Ruth said *"I cried every day for a year.* I cried the next year also, but skipped some days. I was speaking with a principal one day and began to cry in her office when she asked me about Thanksgiving." Margery started out everyday by crying for hours.

> Debby told her four-and-a-half-year-old daughter: "Don't be afraid to cry. That's what you're supposed to do. I do it, and it's not anything to be ashamed of. We'll cry together."
>
> "And we cried a lot," Debby said. "She would cry and I would cry with her. Or I would start and she would join me. When she remembers her father she cries and is sad and we talk about it."

> Chuck never cried when anyone was around, but there were times when he was alone that he was overwhelmed: "It's the most peculiar feeling. I live on the coast and I use imagery. The only way I can describe it is that out of the blue there's a great big tidal wave that washes over me and engulfs me and I break up."

Chuck's description of being engulfed by a "wave" of feeling is not unique. Many people use the same metaphor. They describe a "wave of sadness, a wave of emotions, a wave of tears."

> Howard related: "I wept so much those first few months that I thought there had to be something wrong with me.... I never knew just what would trigger a crying spell...a song, a letter from a friend, a kind remark. I used to tell my friends just not to be kind...be mean. I could handle that better. Of course, that didn't work either."

The men of Engine 69 of the New York City Fire Department gathered in the firehouse drawn together by the bond of sorrow. Two of their colleagues had fallen to their deaths the day before attempting to rescue residents of a burning tenement. A fireman described the scene in the second floor room of the firehouse: "There must have been 30 or 40 guys up there. You'd be talking, talking about why it happened, then a silence would come like somebody just turned the radio off. A minute of silence, then you'd hear the coughing, the sobbing, and the crying."

"All of these big burly guys with hair on their chest. They'd walk over to the corner or put their head on the pool table and just cry like babies. In the beginning, they didn't want to see each other cry. But by about 7:00 A.M., there was just a big circle of guys hugging each other and sobbing. There must be 10 gallons of tears up there."[7]

Crying is the main expression of sadness and hurt. As Ginny said, "I feel this core of pain inside of me. When I cry a little piece of it goes away." An elderly woman whose husband died described something similar. "I felt this great ache inside me. I lay down on my bed and cried for hours. After that, I still had great sadness, but I didn't have that great ache." If words precede or follow the tears, the words and tears support one another in a more complete expression of anguish and sadness.

Catherine said, "I was so sad. All I did was cry for a while. It came out and it wouldn't stop. Everytime I turned around I was crying. Some days I cried all day, it seemed like."

Aaron shared "I am positively flooded with emotion, fearing that unless constrained this flow will overwhelm me. It feels good to cry; like bleeding aids the healing of a physical wound, my tears work to repair my damaged spirit. The tears do not bring back my grandfather, nothing will ever do that, but they do restore me, bring *me* back to life."

Some persons say they do not feel better after crying. "My head hurts" is a common complaint. *Crying must be done with abandon, without any holding back. You must keep your mouth open and allow crying with your whole body.* You must not stop yourself prematurely and say: "That is enough." You must cry until you are all cried out for those minutes in time. Some people cry for a half hour or for hours. That is not unusual. Cry until you feel exhausted of tears, until the next time. *Give yourself permission* to cry it out and you will feel better. You may still have a headache, or an aching throat or whatever, and you may feel very tired; but after a while, you will feel great relief. Usually if you cry and sob with your *mouth open* and your throat open, allow sounds to come forth, you will not have localized pain.

Dealing With Angry Feelings

Many people (especially women) will cry when they are angry, but anger needs to be yelled about, screamed about, pounded out. Pounding on one's pillow or pounding the bed with a tennis racket and attaching words and feelings to that physical expression help many people. Ruth said:

> One day I was raring to go, I just had to get it out of my system. I grabbed a yardstick but that quickly broke. The pillow was too soft so I took a tennis racket. It was a release to hit it on the bed and yell at the same time. It tired me out and I accidentally damaged the headboard, but that was minor to the damage it would have done to me to keep that rage inside.

Some people use physical exercise to release their tension. Anger needs to be expressed with abandon and not be bound by rules, form, and concern about winning a game. A woman whose son had died said that when she felt the anger and tensions building up inside her, she would put on her jogging clothes and go out and run and run.

Anger needs to be drawn out, to be expressed gradually by each person until it has run its course. If anger is not expressed, it permeates the personality and you run the risk of becoming a bitter person. We have all known people whose faces and tone tell us immediately they are seething with anger inside. This anger not only interferes with relationships but causes suffering within you. Alfreda said:

> My father died when I was ten. Everything in my life was colored by my unexpressed anger. I didn't even know I was angry. I didn't bury him until I was forty, when I finally worked out my feelings.

A mother whose daughter had died would not let herself be openly angry at her daughter, "How can I be angry at her when I loved her so much. She was such a wonderful child. I just can't be angry at her." However, her words belied her actions because it was apparent in the mother's face and reactions to other people that she was extremely angry. Even though she was aware that she was angry at the circumstances, she continued to displace her anger onto other family members. Carrying anger around is damaging for everyone, the bearer and the receivers.

Some people look for a target for their anger. Having no one to confront and no possibility of resolution or change they find their anger too frustrating to tolerate. It is difficult to talk about anger without direct confrontation or any resistance to the anger. Various targets will be chosen for the anger in the absence of the deceased. Children are often angry at the surviving parent; family members may direct their anger at each other or blame others for not preventing the disaster; anger may be directed at the medical profession or toward God as in the previous example of Jenny.

Sometimes it helps to express anger with the help of an understanding person, a friend, or a therapist. Some persons are worried about their children or someone else hearing them scream so they have tried screaming in the shower, with the vacuum cleaner on, or in their car. You need to find your own way, but find it. Do not sit on it. Develop your own repertoire of effective ways to express angry feelings.

Some people get in touch with their anger early in the mourning process. For other people it is delayed. Following are two examples of this.

> It was a year after her father's death that Margaret realized and admitted her anger. "You know why it took me so long? I think it was because I was single and mother looked to me more than to the other children. She was being very calm and I felt I had to be 'strong' for her. When I got together with my siblings, they didn't show any anger. Each of them had a mate with whom they shared their anger. I was angry and it was a year before I admitted it to myself. I was angry that my father died and I thought that feeling was abnormal because nobody else seemed angry. I finally said to my sister-in-law: '*I'm angry! I'm angry!*' And she said: 'But don't you think everybody was?' No! I felt absolutely like a freak because everybody *seemed* calm."

Emotions are not always what they *seem* to be to others. Trust yourself and your own process.

> Ruth related: "I didn't feel angry for a long time, maybe a year and a half. I kept saying, 'I don't know why, but I don't feel anger. I don't even feel angry at the kids or like yelling at them.' Then anger slowly came to the surface, and actually, I felt more normal, more alive."

The expression of anger frees up a lot of energy. It is a true unburdening.

Some people have tantrums that never end. They are so angry that things are not the way they want them to be that they do not try to work through their anger in order to get to the other side of it. The behavior is like a child's temper tantrum. The child continues to kick and scream until things are just right. This tantrum in mourning will not bring relief because it is not possible to get what you want. A young woman related: "Like a child I want what I cannot have. I want my sister to have her life. I want my sister to be 'in life' with me. As an adult I live with the bitter realization that she cannot."

It is true that you cannot change the reality in any way. You cannot reverse the death. If you maintain an angry posture, it stands in the way of accepting the situation, as unpleasant and unwanted as it is.

Symbolic Expression

Metaphors often help to capture or describe an emotion and relate it to the physical sensation. Fear is often described as a tightness in the chest or the throat, or an awareness that the heart is beating very fast. When we are excited, we may say "my heart is pounding" or "I have butterflies in my stomach." "A lump in my throat" is a metaphor for sadness and unexpressed tears. Happiness may be represented in the words, "I am flying." These word pictures help to tie the physical sensations to words thereby bringing emotions into awareness.

Using such symbolic imagery is very helpful. This broadens the ways in which the bereaved can creatively experience their grief. It serves to chip away at the task of mourning. Do what is comfortable and familiar for you. You will find yourself reacting in new ways that require different avenues of expression. If you do not have a repertoire of expression from your past, you will have to be creative and find new ways for yourself.

Inhibiting the Expression of Feelings

The *expression* of feelings is not only essential for movement through the mourning process, but the *inhibition* of feelings may be harmful to you. Verbal and bodily expressions are needed to express the full range of emotions. Energy is required to inhibit the expression of a feeling whether it be by crying, talking, or other physical means. To inhibit means actively holding back, thus immobilizing parts of the body that would be involved in that expression. You may stop or deaden the sensation so the expression does not develop. Darwin concluded many years ago through observing muscle reaction that screaming is a spontaneous response to loss.[8] Most people do not allow themselves to scream. As a result, there is muscle tension that is locked up because the spontaneous expression has not been allowed.

Energy expended in blocking the expression of feelings does not lead to the goal of integration of the loss. Your movement and growth are stopped. It locks up your grief and deprives you of considerable energy. Mourning takes energy; however, not mourning or ignoring feelings takes more energy. You lose energy; you lose sensation; you lose the ability to feel. You thereby diminish yourself as the feeling parts of you become less available.

At first it is painful to get in touch with feelings and express them. However, you will feel better in the long run by doing those things which are painful at first. It will reduce tension and give you relief. Blocking feelings increases the tension even though it pushes the pain aside temporarily.

Methods of denying feelings as the mourning process continues are different from the denial in the first phase of mourning, which is part of being in shock. This denial is more pervasive. It is an avoidance of mourning, that is, of the expression of feelings, rather than a protection of the self. It is denying the existence of your agony, sadness, and anger. It is like pretending that these feelings do not exist. The self-protective aspect of denial becomes counter-productive to the process of mourning because it prohibits the *gradual* expression of emotions.

Some people stop themselves from expressing any feelings by saying they are afraid they will lose control or fall apart. Once they begin to express their feelings, they are afraid there will be no end. They will be completely distraught. They are frightened by the intensity or strength of the emotions. Ironically, the feelings become more intense, painful, and frightening by keeping tight control. The tension escalates and some people may be overcome by the sensation that they are going to burst. This inhibition causes anxiety and sometimes the shaking, trembling and shivering described earlier. The slow and gradual release of emotions through crying, talking, and other physical means will provide ongoing relief and avoid the buildup of pressure.

People find many reasons for inhibiting the expression of their feelings. They often say they want to be strong for their family. Actually, *real strength is needed to feel and experience emotions.* It is not strength but fear that motivates persons to push feelings aside and not pay attention to them.

Many persons say they are embarrassed about crying, although it is perfectly natural and appropriate. Some people feel inhibited about crying in anyone's presence. They may say they worry their tears may inflict others with pain or that they will embarrass others by their show of emotion. They bite their lips or swallow hard and try to keep the tears from bursting forth. Tears must be shared with others. It is an important part of the mourning process.

Parents may say they want to demonstrate to their children that life must go on. It is important for adults to provide a model for mourning and the appropriate expression of feelings. It is possible to have a balance between maintaining daily tasks for living and expressing the pain of loss.

Another reason people inhibit the expression of their feelings is because they experience conflict regarding permission and messages from other people. They may get a message which is either spoken or unspoken from others that they do not have permission to talk and to cry with them. They may have the need to talk and cry, but they feel a prohibition against expression of their feelings so they drive their feelings back inside. It is important to share with someone who will be sensitive, responsive, and accepting. It is also important not to let others who are not bereaved set a standard for you. Sometimes this conflict is the result of what an individual imagines others think. This may also be another excuse for denying or holding back the expression of feelings.

There are ways of avoiding feelings by engaging in certain behaviors. Bereaved people sometimes throw themselves into activity, busyness, work or travel as a way to avoid dealing with the loss. Some people look for a substitute for the lost person very soon after the death as a diversion or attempt at replacement. Of course it is not possible to replace anyone. Significant new relationships will be more wholesome if they are developed some distance from the time of the death and integration of the loss.   All these ways of inhibiting feelings and inhibiting the expression of feelings just push them inward, only to return later. It keeps the loss within you, unresolved and unworked. You need to whittle away at this painful experience that is being carried around. You have to come back to the sadness, stay with your feelings, and allow expression. *The process has value.* You have to believe this and allow the process to unfold. You will ultimately be relieved and find your way to integration of the death, calmness, and renewed energy.

The Physical Counterpart of Emotions

Physical sensation and tension are counterparts of emotion and demand release. Tension, tightness or aches may develop in certain spots in the body where action has been inhibited. If spontaneous expression of any kind is held back for a period of time, the focus of the sensation may become a persistent pain. This spot may become a stress point and weaken, and may become a place where illness is more likely to develop. A healthy goal would be to develop awareness of feelings and sufficient verbal and physical expression, so that the physical experience will not become distressing and chronic. If there is inadequate verbal expression, a physical sensation may become separated from the emotion and become exaggerated. It is then more difficult to recognize the origin of the symptom. It is of utmost importance not to send feelings underground where they may possibly be expressed in physical illness or contribute to a chronic condition. The following case is an example of unexpressed feelings which have taken the form of physical symptoms.

A seventy-two-year-old woman became widowed after 58 years of marriage. It was a relationship which spanned her lifetime and on which she had been totally dependent.

After the death of her husband, she went to live with one of her children. When she expressed her emotional pain in various ways, they would admonish her to stop and pull herself together. She was hospitalized twice for the symptoms of inability to sleep and eat, hallucinations, and her inability to walk. During the second hospitalization, she said she did not have any feelings in her legs and that she could not stand on her feet. She had poor control over her hands, refusing to feed herself or hold a glass.

The therapist came to the hospital at the family's request. She was encouraged to talk about her deceased husband, given support and sympathy, pressed to express her feelings. "Can I cry in front of you?" she asked. "You need to talk," her grandson reassured her, and stroked her hand and talked about Grandpa with her. Gradually she began to move her legs and took her arms out from underneath the covers. She moved her body and lowered her legs, and dangled them over the side. Her grandson was amazed at the way her energy was freed up after the short conversation.

The metaphor of being able to stand on her own two feet was used as a way of awakening her control, independence, and drawing a relationship between her physical symptoms and emotional experience. It was an exhilarating experience for all to see her energy released before their very eyes after her expression of sadness.

In her immobility this woman was expressing her feeling that she could not go on without her husband, how she wanted to die and be as he was. Her feeling of dependence on him was expressed in not being able to stand on her own two feet. It was a clear example of the relationship between unexpressed feelings and the conversion to a physical symptom. The symptom was dramatically relieved through the support of the expression of grief.

Serious conditions sometimes develop or an existing weakness or illness may become more severe as with headaches, backaches, colitis, spastic colon, asthma, rheumatoid arthritis, sinus problems, or other somatic disturbances.[9] When the symptoms are distressing, it is advisable to undergo a complete physical examination to determine whether there is treatment available. You may need your doctor's sympathetic ear more than his or her prescription for medicine, but it is wise to have yourself checked.

The relationship between emotional stress, especially the stress of the death of a significant person, and physical disease has been researched for many years. There are strong indications that a relationship exists between emotional stress and the onset of physical and emotional disease, including heart disease and cancer, resulting from a breakdown in the immune system of the body.[10,11,12,13,14,15]

Thomas Holmes and Richard H. Rahe have developed a scale that measures the magnitude of stressful life events based on the relationship between biological, social, and psychological phenomena.[16,17,18] The Social Readjustment Rating Scale assigns a numerical value to various life events. The numerical score indicates the chance of illness following a major life event. Research into the process of health and disease produced powerful evidence that stressful life events, by evoking psychophysiological reactions, play an important role in the natural history of many diseases. There is no clear cause and effect relationship, but evidence suggests that loss of a loved one does contribute to physical reactions within the body.[4,19,20,21,22]

Social readjustment includes the amount and duration of change in one's accustomed pattern of life resulting from various life events. As defined for this scale, social readjustment measures intensity and length of time necessary to accommodate to a life event regardless of the desirability of this event. Studies have been done on the Social Readjustment Rating Scale and illness onset or major health changes, particularly within the two-year period following the occurrence of the change. Health changes following a life crisis were greater than chance. The greater the magnitude of life change or life crisis, the greater the probability the change will be associated with disease onset. There was a strong correlation between the magnitude of the crisis and the seriousness of the chronic illness. The health changes observed were psychiatric, medical, and surgical. It was postulated that life-change events lower bodily resistance and thereby increase the probability of disease occurrence. Adaptive efforts are made by the individual which are faulty in kind and duration. Thousands of patients were studied to lead to this conclusion.[23] Death of a spouse is assigned the highest stress value on the Holmes and Rahe scale. Death of a close family member is fifth in the stress it produces, according to this extensive research which spans various cultures and social classes.[16,17] The following are examples of the onset of illness after the loss of a loved one, believed by the individuals to be related.

> Two women reported their belief that their cancer disease was related to their loss of a loved one. One middle-aged woman had cancer several years after the death of her first husband. After her second husband died she came and said, "*I want help*. I do not want to get sick again."

Another woman believed her disease was related to the death of her father whom she never adequately mourned.

Frank, age 79, developed cancer one year following the sudden death of his wife.

Stress produces changes in the body that result in tissue and cell changes and imbalance in various secretions, hormones, etc.[10] For example, we know that when frightened, the body produces an excess of adrenalin. The body is always striving to reach a balance or homeostasis. In order to do this the products of excessive secretions need to be eliminated. The ways the body secretes unwanted material are through sweating, urinating and so forth. It has been postulated that crying may also be a way of eliminating secretions in an effort to restore the body's balance. The research has demonstrated a difference in the chemical makeup of irritant tears, that is, tears shed from peeling an onion, as different from tears of sadness shed while watching a sad movie.[24,25]

> ...tears are nature's way of excreting bodily chemicals that build up in response to stress. From a biochemical viewpoint people who are sad or depressed could be suffering from a chemical imbalance...that is restored, at least partially, by the excretion of certain substances in tears. "I submit that the secretion of tears is central, not incidental, to the relief mechanism. So when people say they want to 'cry something out,' this may be literally what occurs."[24,25]

It seems logical that tears from profound personal sadness would have a greater concentration of chemicals than tears shed from watching a sad movie. In addition to the emotional release of crying which has value in itself, it may also be true the whole body is helped in being restored to its natural balance after crying.

Other experts on stress and stress management have also drawn a relationship between emotions and physical disorders. They suggest some disorders are caused by the restrained way stress is handled.[26] Attention has been called to crying as a release for stress. The inhibition of crying, particularly in men, as a way of expressing feelings and relieving stress may lead to the greater incidence of disease and early death.[27] This could be related to the theory that crying releases toxins from the body.[25]

These references to the chemical relationship of tears and emotions lend support to the psychological imperative that a bereaved person express grief through crying as well as talking and other physical outlets.

Sedatives and Other Medications

Many persons in our society rely excessively on medication to take away pain, emotional as well as physical. There are some physicians who succumb to the same philosophy when a mourner or members of the family appeal for sedatives to "get a little relief." The attempt to expunge the emotional pain removes the opportunity to deal with it. You cannot mourn if your feelings are not available to you. Many professionals working with the bereaved believe it is better to encourage and support the expression of grief than to mask the agony with sedatives and tranquilizers.[28,29]

Mourning is to *feel* and *express*. If you take a palliative to dull the awareness of feelings, you will cut off the natural process of mourning. People need encouragement to live with and to suffer the feelings. It requires real strength to endure this pain. Bereaved people will benefit by staying with the process through integration. Relief will come through *expression* of painful feelings. Sedatives can be destructive to the mourning process except in extreme cases where they are indicated. Much of the healing potential in tradition and ritual is often prevented by doctors who give bereaved people sedatives that sweep away grief.[30]

When their son died, the Jones' physician gave them both medication. They took tranquilizers to help them through the wake. Afterwards, Mrs. Jones reported, "It was very unreal. I was greeting people as if it were a reception. I just went through it. I didn't feel anything. It seemed like my behavior didn't fit the situation."

It is fortunate that medications for psychological emergencies have been developed and are available for proper use. There certainly are circumstances that indicate medication would be the appropriate form of treatment and temporary use would be advisable. It is recommended that you consult with a psychiatrist to determine whether medication is indicated or desirable, indicating your own wishes and abilities to maintain good contact with the reality of your feelings throughout the ordeal. Following is an example in which a prescription for diazepam (Valium) resulted in inhibiting and postponing a grief reaction.

Mrs. McCormick put her energy into "going on with her life" after the murder of her husband. Her mourning did not run its full course and there were many unsettling feelings still inside of her. Many social situations or public places caused her to be anxious. Early in her bereavement she was given a tranquilizer by her physician. She got into the habit of taking a tranquilizer in the morning for fear she would have an anxiety attack and she would take one whenever she felt any discomfort. The mourning process had been aborted for her as she struggled to keep her fears at bay. The shock, the horror, the sadness, the anger, all of her complicated feelings had been unidentified. In order to do the work of mourning she needed to be totally in touch with her feelings, not have them minimized or dulled by a tranquilizer. She was afraid she would not be able to get through these periods of anxiety.

She developed awareness of the source of her feelings and what precipitated them, and was finally able to identify her feelings, rather than experience a blur of anxiety. She was able to give up the Valium with great relief and a sense of pride.

Tranquilizers are often an impediment to the mourning process as the person becomes more dependent on them. The individual may also develop a sense of weakness rather than confidence. It is always better to have support from another human being for the awareness and acknowledgment of emotions rather than becoming dependent on a drug.

CARRYING ON IS DIFFICULT

Mourners have conflicting feelings about doing certain things that were previously part of everyday routines. It is also difficult to face new situations. When at home you want to be out; when you are out you want to be home. The garden needs work but you cannot bear to walk out there. You think about watching television to pass the time, but the programming is too sentimental or too violent. It is lonely to be alone but hard to be with others in a social setting. During bereavement nothing feels right. Your everyday reality is upside down. The awareness of your loss has this effect on you.

Some of the difficult things to do are disposing of the belongings of your loved one, using or rearranging the bedroom, deciding whether or not to display pictures, going out in public or even to the grocery store, working, socializing, entertaining, vacationing, and celebrating holidays and other special occasions. Getting through a particular day of the week or time of day when the death occurred is stressful. A certain place may stir up unpleasant memories. Activities that were once enjoyable or taken for granted become major projects.

Approach each thing you do with caution. Pay attention to your feelings. *In the beginning* if a situation is not tolerable, do not force yourself. Do what is best for you. Gradually you can venture back into things as you feel less vulnerable and more confident.

Giving Away Belongings of the Deceased

One very difficult task following a death is disposing of the possessions of the deceased. It is not advisable to give things away quickly or all at one time. It is best to do this slowly and gradually. It is not natural to reject the person's memory all at once. It is important to keep the person with you for awhile and let go gradually. Letting go of possessions is a parallel process to letting go emotionally; it needs to be done slowly and with attention to feelings.

The disposal should be done in stages. The first step might be to give some precious things like a piece of jewelry or clothing, a favorite pen and pencil set, a special book or record, to relatives or friends who were close to the deceased and would be happy to have a tangible reminder of the person. Then, as if doing spring cleaning, give some old or out of style clothing to a thrift shop or rummage sale; things the person would have given away in the natural course of events. At a later time you can give away other things to a favorite charity.

Some persons have the idea that belongings should be given away soon after the death. They think that removing the reminders of the person will also remove the pain of the person's absence. Possessions of the deceased should not be cleared out with one impulsive action. Their removal does not remove the hurt and sadness, and it may be a counterpart of the process of blocking out feelings rather than dealing *with* feelings. Giving away belongings is symbolic of the whole process of giving up the deceased and is an adjunct to mourning.

There are those who want to erase every vestige of the deceased from their lives. Removing external reminders does not remove the internal pain, and sometime later you will find you cherish some special items. Following are two examples.

> A widow had her son immediately remove all of her husband's possessions from their apartment after he died. Several months later when she spent the night at her son's home, she discovered one of her husband's shirts hanging in the closet of the guest room. "Now I always wear that shirt instead of my nightgown when I stay overnight at George's. It is comforting," she said.

> Mark was twelve when his father died. His mother kept a few things: sweaters, blue jeans, a jacket. Mark has grown into the clothes now and says he likes to wear them because they make him feel closer to his father. One Father's Day he put on an old shirt of his father's even though it was torn. It was his way of having his father with him on a day when he missed him painfully.

Seeing and touching things that belonged to your loved one may help you get in touch with your sorrow and support expression of it. The memories attached to certain things become comforting. They will become precious to you. Many persons like to hold onto some special things forever or wear a watch or ring that belonged to their loved one.

> Ruth saved the cassette tape from her husband's telephone answering machine. Occasionally she will play the tape to listen to his voice. She also saved a note pad and several letters and cards with his handwriting.

Henry helped his mother and aunt clear out his grandfather's house and dry goods store after the old man's death. His grandpa sold shoes and Henry remembers as a small child watching him measure people's feet with a special ruler with a movable part that was pressed against the toe. The ruler now has its little place on a shelf in his home. He also treasures a small footstool upon which his grandmother had rested her feet after a day of working in the store even though the upholstery is tattered and the springs sag.

Nancy Hickok described the way she gave away her daughter's things:

> Once I got into cleaning out her room, it was really good therapy. I sorted into different piles items to be passed to the Center, others to keep, etc. I do have one drawer where I put some things, clothes I just didn't want to part with, and I do look at them once in awhile. It made me feel good to know Lanny's clothes were going to someone who could make use of them. I took sacks full of toys, too, but first asked the other children if they wanted something. They each took a stuffed toy for themselves.

Instinctively, Nancy had done the right thing. She had sorted through her child's possessions, allowed the other children and relatives to choose a memento, and kept a few things that had meaning for her. The procedure allowed her memories to surface and tears to flow. Sometimes it is helpful to share this task with another member of the family or a close friend.

There are others who refuse to remove daily reminders of the deceased from their lives. They keep clothes hanging in the closet, dresser drawers as they were left, toys on the shelf. It appears that the person is expected to return and still make use of these personal items. This is a denial of the change that has taken place, a denial of the reality and the permanence of the death.

Each person has his or her own time schedule for confronting this task. As with other aspects of grieving, there will be differences depending on the suddenness of the death or whether a period of illness preceded it. The more sudden the death, the longer the material things need to be around to aid in the gradual absorbing of the reality. Margery shared her experience of dealing with the removal of her son's personal items.

> I didn't move anything for a long, long time, like a year or more. I knew his clothes hung in that closet; I knew he wouldn't come home. Maybe at first I thought he would. I washed all his underwear and put it back in his drawer. I had to have it all clean. But I cried when I did it. I really knew he was never going to come back. I think you have to live with the presence of something that belongs to your loved one to get you through the period.

All of his things came one day from the Navy. We still have his uniform. My husband and I went through them and put them in a trunk. It's still downstairs in the storage closet. I have his school books. I just can't give them away.

There needs to be some attempt to distribute special possessions or give away some things after a year or so. How soon this can be approached also depends on the relationship to the deceased. For most persons it does not take so long to part with the possessions of an elderly parent who has died. Widows and widowers vary considerably. This task is most difficult for parents when a child has died. They tend to keep possessions and to leave a room intact for a longer time. This is understandable. Each piece of clothing and possession carries with it tender feelings and pain at separating and is part of the process of saying goodbye.

The Use or Change of A Special Room

The bedroom, den, or the workroom of the deceased is a reminder of the absence of your significant person. You may find yourself in conflict about whether to keep the door opened or closed; whether to use the room or avoid it, whether to change the room and redecorate it or keep it intact. When the deceased has been the sole occupant of the room, it may seem as if it is out of bounds. The bedroom of a deceased child is painful to look at, but closing the door may close out your feelings as well. If the room has been shared with another sibling, it usually continues to be used, but the bed and personal belongings remain to be dealt with. Widows and widowers may find the bedroom or bed previously shared an unwelcome place. However, continuing use of the room and the bed is a direct confrontation with the changed reality.

You need to do some things at home that recognize your loved one is no longer part of your everyday routine. After one or two years, or sooner if it feels right to you, the room should be used or changed. Otherwise, the room may become a shrine or a "no man's land." This hinders you in unbinding the past.

A mother felt she wanted to use her daughter's room and make it into a sitting room. "I've taken the ironing board up there and my sewing machine. I think we ought to be in that room and I feel comfortable in there."

Harriet brought her mother who suffered from emphysema to live with her. The large airy bedroom was given to her mother and she herself moved into the small guest room. Two years after her mother's death Harriet was still sleeping in the tiny bedroom, leaving the other room unoccupied and unused. She finally decided to redecorate the bedroom and turn the guest room into a study for herself.

Some men and women who have died in wars become idols in their households. Sometimes a corner of a room has been dedicated to the deceased. A shrine has been built around pictures and memorabilia of the fallen hero. The life and death of the loved one are ever present, not allowed to become background in a natural way. If a bedroom or special chair is left unused, it may become a shrine to the deceased. It also feeds the fantasy that the person may return. Eventually, the empty places and spaces left by the deceased need to be filled in by those who are living.

Displaying Pictures of the Deceased

People often ask: "Should I leave her picture out or put it away?" The answer lies within each individual and depends on how you feel when you look at it. Some people find it helpful and comforting to display pictures of the deceased or a family picture including the loved one. Others find the pain unbearable. Some people say: "I do feel pain when I look at the picure, but I still want to see it." Seeing pictures and other memorabilia of the deceased may make you sad, but it can be another key to open the latch to your feelings. If seeing a picture causes too much pain, put it away for awhile. You are in enough pain already; do not add another abrasion at this time. When you are ready, you will take it out. It is a process of trial and error. You can always put it away again and try another time. After a year or so your reaction to displaying pictures may change.

After the death some persons have reported a strong desire, almost a compulsion, to duplicate pictures of the deceased, hang them up or distribute them to family members. Sometimes snapshots are enlarged again and again, from 5 × 7 inches to 8 × 10 inches to 11 × 14 inches. It is a symbolic attempt to recapture the person's presence. If this is comforting, do it. It is a way to keep the deceased with you and helps to keep good memories alive.

Often the same stimulus does not have a uniform effect on everyone. It is important to take into consideration the feelings of all the members of the family. In one family the mother liked having a picture of her late daughter displayed on the piano, but this was found to be terribly painful when viewed by the sister. The family should talk it over and try to reach a decision that is mutually comfortable. If only one person desires the picture displayed, it can stay in that person's room. Sally had large pictures of their father made for each of the children. They cherished them and asked for one of the parents together. Pictures and photograph albums are helpful in observing the anniversary of the death and reminiscing about your loved one.

Many Hurdles to Jump

It seems that the world goes on as if nothing had happened but to the bereaved simple things can be loathsome. Taking over the everyday chores that used to be done by the deceased, picking up the daily newspaper, going to the post office, opening and sorting the mail, or paying bills remind you of his or her absence. You may find things you once enjoyed doing with your loved one are now aversive, like taking a walk, gardening, playing golf, Christmas shopping, going to church, playing games or cards, or sharing newspaper stories.

Chance meetings are stressful. That is the reason it is so hard to go to a supermarket or department store or a large gathering of people. This is especially difficult for many persons. You dread the possibility that you may meet someone who will want to talk. These feelings are often shared. "I was afraid I'd cry if anyone spoke to me or if they asked me how I was. I felt I had to say all right but I really felt miserable." It is unsettling to see someone for the first time in a public place. Someone may express their sympathy and stir up your feelings when you have steeled yourself to be out in public.

Everyone has his or her special things that had been done or shared by the deceased that are hard to continue. Some persons find it impossible to set foot in certain places for a long time—maybe your child's school, the store, church, a theater or going to a baseball game.

> Attending concerts had been Ruth and Jeff's principle recreation. It was such a special thing for them she could not face sitting next to anyone who might occupy Jeff's seat. She gave away the tickets for that season. "When I finally decided to attend again I didn't enjoy the music. I was so restless. It took me a couple of years before I could enjoy a concert. Often the music evoked tears. It also was a special place for me to mourn, but difficult because it was public."

You feel like a wounded bird. Sometimes a kindness will move you into tears. Small disappointments may push you to your tolerance point. Little unexpected things can set off feelings of sadness or anger.

> Edna sat down to pay some bills, a very ordinary thing to do, and wrote the date on the first check. Unexpectedly tears welled in her eyes as she

realized it was the date of her father's birthday. He had been dead nearly two years, and she had not thought about him for weeks; but the physical act of writing the date evoked memories and sadness.

A particular place, day of the week, or time of day when the death occurred may fill you with a sense of foreboding. For a long time, every Tuesday at 8:00 P.M., a mother was filled with sadness. It was the time of her daughter's death. At a particular time for you, you may feel restless or have a sense that time has stopped. A young woman dreads riding by the hospital where her mother was pronounced dead.

Nancy related that she drives by the site of the accident where her nine-year-old daughter was killed. "I drive by that corner so many times. I try not to, but there is no other way to go. Sometimes I can drive by without even thinking about it, but other times it is very painful.

The lunch hour is an excruciating time. I really pray and ask God to help me not remember the exact moment she was killed."

Experiences like these are painful to endure. Eventually they fade into the background and do not command the attention. You become less aware of the day, the hour, the place.

Returning To Work

There seems to be an unstated message from somewhere that you are supposed to go back to work after a week if you are employed, but psychologically you may not feel ready. What you think is expected of you is often so different from the way you feel. You are overcome with emotion, have difficulty being efficient and concentrating, and it is hard to converse with others about business matters and everyday things. Following are some personal examples.

A week after the funeral Sarah was sitting in her office with a friend and co-worker. They talked for a short time and then Sarah said: "I don't know what I am doing here. I really don't think I can stay here. I don't think I can work. I have to go home."

John related: "I went back to work the week after my wife died. By the end of the day I could barely contain my anguish. I felt as if I was going to fall apart. I would go to the parking lot, get into my car, close the doors, and just let out a few screams."

Shortly before Jane's death in June, Chuck, a writer, signed a contract for two children's books. Expectations were that he would complete them before the end of the year. From July to mid-September he was obsessed with writing about the circumstances surrounding her death. "That was the only thing I could put my mind on at the time."

A middle-aged man whose wife died suddenly followed his own inclination. He took a month off and returned to work gradually. At first he worked for several hours, then half days, then full days, according to his own endurance. This approach is self-accepting and realistic. It is unfortunate that many jobs demand an early return and do not allow for an initial recovery period. This indicates a lack of permission to mourn from society. You need to give yourself permission to do what is best for you.

Mealtime and Cooking

Many men *and* women find it difficult to cook. Many widowed men take over the function of cooking for themselves and/or their family; some men resist it and eat out. Although it is the traditional role for women, many find it distasteful and the family has "pick-up" dinners or eats in restaurants frequently. At mealtime the focus is on the family as a whole, and it becomes so apparent the family has changed. Often each person has an appointed seat at the table. When everyone sits down, it is upsetting to see the empty chair, or traumatic to see someone else in it.

> More than two years have passed since Mr. Borden died but the family has not sat down to a meal together at the table. Mrs. Borden continues to eat standing up; the children are served their meals on plates which they carry into the den and watch TV.
> Although Ruth never abandoned the preparation of meals, she has lost interest in cooking. There are many special dishes she has not prepared since her husband's death. However, she has always maintained the precedent of the family gathering for meals. Dinnertime has retained the significance of exemplifying the family unit, even though the configuration has changed.

This demonstrates to the bereaved, both adults and children, the continuation of life and importance of family members to each other.

Socializing

It takes time before you feel like going to a party or meeting or even a small gathering of friends. The bereaved person is afraid of being poor company or of being restless. Small talk seems inane. Your thoughts are filled with your own pain and matters of life and death and it is hard to engage in conversation about movies or books or politics. It is hard to realize the world goes on when your own world is shattered. Being out with others may be a strain, but staying home and isolated is not comfortable either. It is hard to find the right place to be. It is that same feeling so aptly put, "When I am home I want to be out, but when I am out I want to be home." It is kind of family or friends to offer you a ride, but it is better for you to be able to leave when you have reached your tolerance level. It is easier to leave a movie, a museum, library, supermarket, or church if you have independent mobility without concern for someone else's time schedule.

Often others do not know how to approach you. It is awkward seeing someone in public for the first time after a death. A party or other public place is not where most people welcome a verbal expression of sympathy, yet some acknowledgment of the event is appropriate. Usually saying, "It's good to see you," or "I'm glad you are here," is sufficient.

Invitations come when you may not want to socialize or be with large groups. They are important many months after the death but often people have ceased extending themselves and do not include you. Hopefully friends will try to understand the bereaved person and continue to offer the opportunity for distraction and companionship. The invitations are appreciated, and one day the bereaved will be receptive. Some people take the refusals as a personal rebuff and the invitations are discontinued after two or three turndowns. Sometimes they mistakenly believe the bereaved person is not interested in being with them. Instead of feeling rejected, friends and relatives need to understand that the bereaved person is not ready to cross the bridge to sociability. Continue to keep the lines of communication open. Family and friends can encourage the person to do what is best for him or her. The time will come when he or she will be able to socialize again. Until that time, the mourner needs acceptance of his or her own time schedule.

Friends and family bring us through our sorrow. It is difficult for the bereaved person to initiate contact, but it is greatly appreciated when others phone, visit, or extend invitations. Just knowing someone cares is a most important part of surviving. Ruth said, "People reached out to me. I couldn't reach back at the time, but I cherished their offers and will never forget their friendship."

Margery told about the support she received from her friends. "My friends reached out to all of us for such a long time. They made a point of including us and kept in contact. Maybe I didn't want to be there when they invited me, but at least I could show up if I wanted to. I appreciated the fact they made the effort to include me. I couldn't make any advance plans, but often I would go if someone would call again the last minute.''

Lydia tried to get her mother reinvolved after the deaths of her two sisters had left her mother listless and indifferent. She enlisted the help of a friend whose turn it was to entertain the church study group at home. The friend called and asked Mrs. Baker to serve as hostess instead. Doing a favor for her friend helped Mrs. Baker return to other church activities, too.

Ruth did not have that encouragement. She and Jeff had been part of an adult education group. They had attended a meeting the night before Jeff's death. It was their last social activity together. After his death it was very painful to continue. She told the leader of the group it might help to rekindle her interest if they came to her home. There was no follow-up and Ruth felt abandoned by the group. "Whenever I'd meet one of them, they would invite me to come and I appreciated it, but I needed more. I needed someone to phone and say, 'I'll pick you up tonight,' or 'Can you have the next meeting?' "

The mourner needs patience and understanding from others and support for reentry into activities. The time comes when you do things even though you may not enjoy them at first. You cannot stay by yourself indefinitely. You have to start going out or you will become socially and emotionally isolated.

A Special Place to Mourn

There may be places or activities that have special significance. It may be a room in the house, a garden tended by the deceased, or an activity shared by the family. These places or activities stimulate memories and provide an opportunity to express feelings about the absence of your loved one.

Many parents find that sitting in their child's room and handling his or her clothes or toys assists them in mourning. A mother whose son died suddenly as a result of an accident related, "Every morning after everyone had gone to work and school, I would crawl into his bed and cry. After a while I would get up and make the bed and go about my business for the day. His room and bed served as the focus of my mourning.''

Children miss an activity they shared with a parent or sibling. It is helpful to engage in this with another person whether it is eating breakfast together or going bicycle riding. This gives the child an opportunity to talk about the deceased, how they formerly engaged in this together, and how he or she misses the loved one.

Some people like to return to special vacation spots where the family has enjoyed time together. On holidays and birthdays Claire likes to drive to a spot near the lake where she and her husband had many happy times. Well-meaning friends may tell you to find other places to go so you will not be reminded of your grief and your loved one. It is often constructive for those feelings to be revived. You can get in touch with them, express them, and do another part of the work of mourning.

> Ruth continued to return to the family's favorite beach. Only two weeks before Jeff's death the family had spent a glorious vacation there. A picture of Ruth and Jeff in smiling embrace hangs on the wall of the study. The joy expressed in that photo is almost palpable. When Ruth planned the first vacation for herself and the children 11 months after Jeff's death, a friend tried to discourage her from returning to a place that would elicit so many emotions. "I was scared," she said. "But somehow I knew I could do it; be in complete charge of three kids, the trip, the driving. We stayed in the same cottage. At first the kids were angry and said, 'We're on vacation but look at you, you are so unhappy.' They didn't understand that it was very important for me to be able to cry there and miss Jeff's being there. By the end of the vacation, I felt I had done some important mourning I couldn't have done any place else. For the children too, it was a place to remember their father and many happy times together. It provided a setting to do some grief work. That beach still beckons."

Reminders jog the memory and are an aid to mourning. Sufficient attention and expression of the thoughts and emotions generated by memories will have a healing effect.

GRIEF RETURNS: HOLIDAYS AND ANNIVERSARIES

It is normal to have an intense reaction on the anniversary of the death or other special occasions like birthdays, wedding anniversaries, holidays, celebrations, or other special dates. The significant date brings the loss into focus again, and it is normal to go through a mini-mourning period. Anticipating these dates and allowing your emotions to emerge will help you to cope with these times. It is common to experience a psychological awareness of an important date even where there has been no conscious recognition of it.

Even years after the date of the death, it is natural for feelings of sorrow to be aroused by a special occasion or particular date. The intensity diminishes but the sadness recurs even in people who have revamped their lives and are content. Often people may not be consciously aware of the anniversary and cannot understand why they feel uncomfortable, unhappy or even unwell. Some who do remember try to push aside thoughts about the deceased. They plan a busy day filled with many things to do. The sadness will often hit them in the middle of the activity or one or two days afterwards. It is better to acknowledge special days and prepare for them psychologically. Allow yourself to do some mourning. After the days have come and gone, and you have acknowledged the reality of your feelings about the loss, you will have finished up another little piece of mourning.

Holidays

Holidays and the gathering of family emphasize the absence of your loved one. It is helpful and supportive to be open in acknowledging the difficulty in getting through holidays. As trying as it is, it is important to maintain family tradition. It is a healthy way to demonstrate that life does go on and the family remains connected.

Sally finds Christmas most difficult. She and her husband had always spent the day cooking together. "I wish I didn't have to do it at all. I'd like to do something entirely different, like go out west to be with my parents. But the children wanted everything exactly the same and on the same schedule. The tree, the trains, the breakfast, the dinner all needed to be done at exactly the same time and with the same menu. I found I couldn't do it all. My son wanted it so much he cooked the meal."

In the same family, the thirteen-year-old, Sharon, made out her Christmas list. "I made out my list," she announced to her mother. "There are two people missing that I want on there, Daddy and Aunt Rose."

Dee talked about how every Christmas carol she heard made her cry. "The anticipation and preparation is harder for me than the day itself. I cried so when we took out the ornaments. They had been so perfectly put away by my husband last Christmas, each one wrapped so carefully."

Margery shared the pain of her first Christmas. "The Christmas following my son's death was agonizing. I was getting out the Christmas things and his stocking was there. I cried and cried. Finally, I put it aside."

Ruth finds the holidays difficult. There were times when she and Jeff invited all the family—the brothers, sisters, parents, nieces, and nephews to gather at their home for dinner. At these times Jeff's absence is underscored. Ruth continues the traditional holiday assemblage, but it is always preceded for her by a period of physical and emotional ill-feeling. "Nothing serious," she says, "but I feel like I have the flu. The extended family is important to me. Somehow I manage; I get through the time. As time goes on, it becomes more natural, less painful, and even happy again."

The Breen family had to confront the first holiday in their home after the death of their teen-aged daughter. Although it was terribly difficult and painful, they made all the preparations for the gathering of the 20 people in the extended family. As they sat down to dinner, the young sister began to cry, as did the mother. Mother said, "Come sit on my lap and we will cry together. Everyone knows why we are crying, that we miss Peggy, and it's all right." It was a difficult evening and an important hurdle. They got through it.

This family provides an excellent example of courage and sharing. Acknowledging their loss within the group, and sharing their tears made it possible for them to carry on their tradition.

Anniversary of The Death

It is natural for grief to return on the anniversary of your loved one's death. If you expect yourself to react and deal with your feelings, you will have accomplished more of the work of mourning. You may find yourself reviewing the circumstances of the illness and death.

Natalie related the way in which she experiences the anniversary of the death of her loved one. "Every year on the anniversary I do not feel good. I don't always realize what it is, then it dawns on me why I am ill. You absorb it in your very bones and it remains. What is left is not a bad thing. I relive the events in my mind. It is worth a couple of days of discomfort for me to periodically be reminded. It makes me think about her and Bob's father, and my own parents who are still living. I don't want it to be all blotted out and sanitized. It should be part of our living experience, the knowledge that life is finite."

Anniversary Rituals

Some religions have ceremonies which provide a structured expression for grief aroused at this time. This offers something "to do" and opportunities for remembering. Many people find this a solace.

A special mass can be offered for the deceased. Families will often visit the grave to bring flowers and to pray. A vigil light or candle can be lit in the church.

The Jewish religion acknowledges the need for remembering. Each year on the anniversary of the death, a 24-hour candle is lit at home. Remembrance prayers are recited at a synagogue service and the deceased's name is read.

Some people initiate their own rituals for remembering or add personal meaning to existing tradition. Looking at old photographs stimulates memories and feelings.

Ruth and her children visit the cemetery at the traditional time preceding the religious holidays and Father's Day. In addition to the traditional prayers, they take turns reading poetry that is meaningful to each of them. On anniversaries they take out the slide projector and look at pictures of past vacations and celebrations. It stimulates feelings they can talk about with each other. It is an opportunity for family sharing and closeness. Although painful it is therapeutic. Most importantly, it keeps their father's memory alive and the meaning of his life. It keeps the experiences and happiness that were part of their growing up in the forefront of their memory. It has helped the children with their mourning.

On the first anniversary of her husband's death, Catherine Blackman bought five roses. She and the girls took one to the cemetery, and the other four, symbolizing their family when it was complete, they brought home.

Referring to the second anniversary she said: "It's just important to be able to say it to someone: 'This is the second anniversary of my husband's death.' I don't feel the need for a special Mass because every Mass seems especially for him. We're also going to the cemetery. Then we'll go out to dinner or just do something special so that we take the time, the three of us, to remember him."

When your religion does not offer guidelines for anniversaries, you can create your own ritual.

Janet and her six-year-old son Mark made a special day of the second anniversary of the husband/father's death. They had shopped for a model car, a white Datsun similar to the one Daddy used to drive. They selected three lovely flowers at the florist, not to be placed on the grave because the father is buried in a distant state, but for a vase in their home to symbolize how the three of them had once made a family unit.

With the flowers in full view in the kitchen, mother and child sat down to put together the model car, a pleasant activity and attached to the memories of Daddy. Mark suggested getting out the photograph album. They cuddled together while looking at the pictures and talked about the places they had been together, about their relationship, about the fun they had had, and about how much Daddy loved Mark. They also talked about their sadness and how much they missed him.

The next day Janet experienced a spontaneous outpouring of tears as she was getting ready for the day. It was the final catharsis of the intense emotional experience of the weekend.

All of the two-day remembrance activities had been planned carefully. Ways of handling questions Mark might ask were anticipated. Janet wanted to be sensitive to just how much of his sadness he could deal with at this time. It is important not to press a child any further than he or she is ready to go, but it is also of utmost importance not to ignore his or her feelings and the fact that the child needs help to express them. Planning and sharing this sadness was supportive for both mother and son.

DURATION OF MOURNING

You must follow your own feelings and allow your own process to flow. Mourning outlives the social and religious guidelines that provide structure for grief after the death of a loved one. You may get the mistaken idea that grief should end when the rituals and guidelines end. One thing you need to do is get rid of these "shoulds" and expectations. You need to follow your own timetable for mourning and not let others write the script for you.

Misleading expectations have developed regarding grief. As a result of cultural messages, you may get the idea that there are proper times to end your mourning and that to continue to feel sad or complain is abnormal. Not being directly affected, friends and extended family are able to put the matter aside, but your unrelenting pain continues. Margery shared, "Everyone expects you to be all right, but you know inside you are not. I didn't dare tell anybody that hadn't experienced the same thing that it *does* take such a long time."

Sometimes there are expectations that the mourner will be "feeling better" after two or three months. Actually, this is ordinarily the end of the initial phase of mourning. The impact and meaning of the death become more real and feelings may become more intense at this time. It is confusing to expect to be feeling better when in actuality you may be feeling worse. A transition to another phase may bring difficult times. This is the normal course of mourning. It is important to be patient and accepting of yourself and of others, and important for family and friends to accept the normalcy of your feelings and behavior.

It takes a long time to assimilate and integrate the death of a significant person. Sometimes people are frightened to think they will suffer for a year or so. It is better to be prepared for this than to worry that you are abnormal when your emotional pain persists. Remember, there are periods of relief, and you will feel better as you express yourself throughout time.

Individuals have varying psychological time schedules and unique ways of coping with stress and loss according to their personalities. Some feelings are more difficult for certain persons to deal with, even though the process of mourning is similar. The relationship to the bereaved and with the bereaved, the manner of the death, the degree of change in your everyday life, as well as individual differences, will chart the course of grief. The degree of dependency, the age of the deceased, the age of the survivors, how much of your life was wrapped up in the relationship, the amount of unresolved conflict, and the length of illness or suddenness of the death will all influence the duration of grief.

For most persons the first year after the death of a loved one is extremely agonizing and many acute feelings and symptoms emerge. The symptoms and longings gradually abate as the attachment loosens and increased periods of calm and hopefulness are experienced.

The first anniversary of the death is an important psychological time. You are beginning to know emotionally what you have known intellectually. The emotions and the intellect have slowly fused in accepting the reality of the death. The end of the first year underscores the permanence of the loss. Missing the person and longing are strong. The reality that the loved one is no longer an active part of your life sinks in. Anguish lessens, but missing increases.

Most of the acute symptoms are gone by the end of the first year and gradual improvement and change are noticeable. The periods of sadness are less frequent and last a shorter time. The periods of hopefulness increase. However, the same feelings will crop up again from time to time as mourning continues into the second year. There will be individual differences regarding the continuation of mourning into the second year. This is usual in the loss of a child or spouse. To an adult, the death of an elderly parent is usually integrated and accepted by the first anniversary of the death, providing the relationship was not ridden with excessive conflict or the circumstances bizarre. The death of a child's parent will require *many years* of intermittent mourning until integration can occur.

There is an overlap in mourning and in the resumption of activities and friendships. More energy becomes available to take up old and new interests and to cultivate new relationships. Although you do not forget your loved one, you sometimes forget you are a mourner. Soon you will no longer be a mourner. It often takes from two to three years for adults to *feel good again* after a sudden death or the loss of a relationship that was an integral part of your life. Many have said, "I just feel lighter or like a whole person again." It is important to know this so that you can be accepting of your own process, avoid unrealistic expectations, and be supportive of other family and friends. Periods of intense emotion will still arise, but usually the worst is over if mourning has progressed naturally. Movement through the phases is needed. Reminders will stir up old and familiar feelings but emotions are not so near the surface. Mourning ends but memories remain.

Sudden Death

There is nothing to compare with the impact and profound shock of a sudden unexpected death. The assault is a jolt to the system. After a sudden death the period of shock and disbelief is long lasting. Those who have suffered the sudden death of a loved one will experience a longer period of numbness and denial. They will need to go over the circumstances of the death repeatedly in order to make it "real." They make more attempts to undo the circumstances of the death. The survivors are deprived of the opportunity to take care of the relative and a chance to show they care. They do not have the *opportunity to say goodbye* to their loved one. This is of great importance in facilitating the mourning process and in emotional separation from the deceased. The family may be left with a feeling of suspension or unfinished business until they can work it through another way.

If there has been a short period of expectation of death, due to the sudden onset of an illness or an accident, it may still be experienced as a sudden death since there is little time to anticipate the death and begin mourning. The family usually focuses on hopes of recovery. The possibility of no recovery barely begins to sink in. Mourning is of longer duration after a sudden death than after an anticipated death. More time is required to integrate the reality.

Death Following An Extended Illness

Death after a prolonged illness will ease the beginning of the mourning period for the family since it softens the impact of the death. A prolonged illness in itself has many problems for the patient and the family. Often the patient is worn out physically and emotionally by the bout with illness and pain. Family and friends also become tired from meeting the demands of the patient, the trips to the hospital, and the emotional strain of witnessing the significant person suffer and become debilitated. It is hard to stand by feeling helpless and powerless to change the situation. A sense of relief from these stresses is often experienced which replaces the shock.

Those experiencing a prolonged or terminal illness of a loved one will have both opportunities and tasks that are burdensome. There is an opportunity to do preparatory mourning and a chance to say goodbye gradually to your loved one. You can share your feelings about the anticipation of the death. These tasks are challenging because it is hard to confront the *thought* of death before the *fact* of death. Mourning at the time of the diagnosis and during the illness does not eliminate the bereavement period after the death, but it will facilitate it. Unfortunately, many people do not use this opportunity but maintain denial and avoid talking openly and with sensitive honesty to other members of the family or the person who is ill.

Some of the tasks are paradoxical. You deal with the threat of the loss of your loved one while maintaining a meaningful and close relationship. You have to cope with the impact of the disease on an everyday basis and mourn the loss of function and also what is yet to come. Accepting your own feelings and expressing them and also responding to the feelings of the dying person are difficult because you may be in different phases of grieving at a particular time. It also involves giving support and being able to receive support. You are constantly adjusting to new patterns of interaction as roles change during the illness. The patient fears being abandoned and wants love, acceptance and assurance that the relationship will be sustained until the end. It is difficult for the family to maintain closeness and share intimate feelings while anticipating separation from the significant person. Although these are demanding tasks, they are immeasurably valuable to perform.

It is indeed a time "to get affairs in order." There is more to getting affairs in order than making out a will, planning one's funeral, or other tasks of this kind. *The most important affairs are one's relationships.* The time of anticipated death can be used to enhance a relationship, exchange deep feelings with each other, reminisce about past events, and repair old rifts. The very minimum and also the most important is a declaration of your love. Many people find this period to be very moving and meaningful for the patient and for the family.

It is best to avoid judgements about which is a "better" way to die. The dying and death of a loved one are terrible and difficult for all concerned. There is no way that one is better than another; it is just different. Different opportunities are possible or not possible. Opportunities should be used to their fullest to aid and support the dying and the family.

Bizarre Circumstances of Death

Sudden death means a longer bereavement period since more time is needed to assimilate the event. When it has occurred under bizarre circumstances, there is greater intensification of all emotions and it takes even longer to recover. The shock and disbelief are more penetrating. When death was caused by murder, suicide, accident, drug overdose or other unusual situations, the death is contrary even to the expectations of the causes of death. It is incomprehensible.

It is natural for the bereaved person to mull over the circumstance of any death, but when the loss has been sudden because of heart attack, stroke, accident, or the result of horrifying events, it is too much to comprehend. There is a stronger need to go over and over what has happened, the repetition is an attempt to experience and grasp the reality. Attempts at undoing, guilt, and blaming, whether self, others, God, the deceased, or the circumstances, are heightened beyond the level usually felt when death occurs after a prolonged illness or at the end of a normal life span.

Murder

In cases of unprovoked murder the surviving family is vehement in its desire for revenge. The family has a strong need to get even, to make the person who inflicted the death suffer as much as they are suffering. It is almost unbearable if the murderer is granted an early parole or evades a long jail sentence by pleading insanity. That verdict often leads to release after a stay in a mental institution. The fear and anger of the victim's family can be formidable barriers to the integration of the grief. It is natural for them to want the murderer punished by at least a lifetime in jail. It is natural, too, for fear to stalk the survivors. If the murderer has a distinctive characteristic the fear of persons with similar characteristics may persist. The sight of someone vaguely similar to the murderer can dredge up the anxiety, fear, anger, and rancor even many years after the event. There may be a fear of going near the place where the event occurred, whether it is a city street or a room in the house. One traumatic event can have a powerful effect in creating a phobia. The horror of the event complicates the mourning process. This requires special attention and special help in working toward integration.

Suicide and Addiction

When a loved one has committed suicide, there is often a perseveration of "ifs": "If I'd only paid attention; if I'd only been with him; if I'd only listened." One keeps trying to undo what happened, trying to make things right by bargaining and reiterating all the "might-have-beens." Survivors are wracked by guilt and anger and it takes extra time to work them through. Complicating the problem is the feeling that others are critical or blameful. There is embarrassment and fear of being accused of having been a poor parent or poor spouse. *It is not the fault of the family or friends.* Suicide is the result of the *individual's* emotional state at the particular time of the death. Sometimes it is a temporary mental illness.

Although the family suffers greatly, indulging in self-blame and excessive guilt is harmful. The support of an outside person is often needed to
help survivors deal with their torturous feelings.

When someone has died of a drug overdose, the idea that it was an
accidental death may assuage the painful feeling of the survivors. Drug
addiction and alcoholism are self-destructive behaviors. The death may
not be clearly suicidal, but the behavior is on a continuum toward death,
although often denied by the participant. Guilt and blame are prominent
along with anger. Often feelings of frustration and helplessness may have
pervaded the family while the significant person was alive.

Whether death was the result of an accident, suicide, murder, or other
unexpected or grotesque cause, the bereavement is complicated. The survivors must deal not only with the loss but also with the manner of death
or horror attached to the occurrence. Therefore, it is necessary that they
be given an extraordinary amount of support from family, friends, and
the community. It takes a long time to integrate the loss and, even then,
remnants of many feelings may remain. Professional intervention is
recommended to support and facilitate the mourning process.

Delayed Mourning

It is expected and appropriate that mourning with all its various phases
and feelings takes place within the context of the death. The expression
of emotions needs to begin at the time of the event and proceed through
time. Time alone does not heal, as the cliché says, but it is the use of time
for active mourning that contributes to healing.

When there is little or no expression of grief and the individual pushes
away and blocks feelings, the mourning is delayed. These feelings usually
emerge at some point in the future and press for expression. Although
there is variation in each person's capacity to resist feeling, repression
does not usually last forever. The defensive mechanism will eventually
fail to work at some time in the future, and the work of mourning will
still need to be done. When suppressed and delayed, the emerging sensations may not be clearly defined as related to grief, but are experienced as
anxiety or depression, especially if considerable time has elapsed. It takes
some exploration to determine the cause and relate it to the loss. The
resistance to feelings must be penetrated even though the difficulty
increases as time passes because the feelings become less available.

The absence of grief should not be mistaken as a good adjustment to
the loss but rather as a signal that appropriate mourning is not taking
place. Grief that is not expressed may be disguised and come out in other

ways. It may take the form of a physical symptom or illness, or be manifested as an emotional problem. The individual may harbor a fear of another loss which becomes a problem in itself, and which may also interfere with forming relationships. Furthermore, it takes considerable energy to ignore feelings, so sufficient energy may not be available for everyday tasks and relationships.

Prolonged Mourning

No timetable can be set for a person to reach integration of a death. Although generalities have been discussed, each person moves through the mourning process at his or her own pace. Children need more time than adults. Sudden death and unusual circumstances require more time. *It is crucial to see changes and movement through the phases and feelings.* When there is little or no movement or when someone gets stuck in a particular phase, there is cause for concern. Another indication of prolonged grief is the persistence of the acute symptoms and the inability gradually to resume the ordinary functions of daily living.

When feelings remain very near the surface after a year and a half or two, or when there is an overcontrol of feelings, the grief may be prolonged. If the deceased continues to occupy and dominate the thoughts and emotional life of the bereaved into the third year after the death, and when there is *little change or movement* in these feelings or thoughts, it becomes apparent that the mourning has been prolonged. Grief therapy is often necessary to help the individual in the expression of feelings and to facilitate movement through the mourning process.

The duration of the dominant feelings in each phase will vary according to the individual's dynamics. Some feelings are more prominent and last longer than others. Note the *change of emotions and the movement through the process of mourning.* Being stuck in a phase or with particular emotions indicates a blockage in the process and a signal that help is needed. Therefore, it is not so much the duration of grief as it is the movement through the phases and the change over time that are signs of healing and recovery.

Grief therapy is indicated for persons with the problem of delayed or prolonged grief. Eventually the individual must go back to the very beginning of the process and mourn as if the death has just occurred. It is hard to retrieve the feelings because they have been blocked for this period of time. This is difficult but necessary psychological work so that the individual can be freed from past emotional ties and release energy for confronting each day.

After awhile an individual may sense something serious is wrong and develop insight that it is the lack of integration of the death. Although it is so painful, many express relief in being able to *feel* once again, even to be able to feel pain.

Avoiding visiting the cemetery at appropriate times such as holidays or anniversaries of the death may indicate an unwillingness to deal with the death. Visiting the cemetery is an acknowledgment that the loved one is indeed dead. A visit to the cemetery often helps to retrieve feelings that have been pushed away.

> Ginny avoided visiting her mother's grave for 10 years after her death. She said, "I thought that visiting the cemetery was a way to let you know that your loved one is dead. But it also reminds me of when Mother lived and how much I miss her. I also can remember things more, but remembering things makes me miss her more and that's more painful."

The result of blocking painful feelings is the loss of positive feelings and memories. The pain is not felt, but you also lose the memories and the significance of your loved one's life and its meaning to you. You may temporarily protect yourself from pain but you lose the comforting memories as well.

BEREAVEMENT THERAPY

Bereavement therapy is primarily guidance by a trained professional through the process of mourning. This specialist offers support and understanding, encourages the expression of all feelings, and facilitates movement through the phases of grief toward integration of the loss. Non-judgmental and accepting, the therapist lends the bereaved strength and faith in living.

Therapy is a safe place for the expression of all kinds of feelings. It is an opportunity to examine the relationship with the deceased with all its happiness and disappointments. The loss and the pain permeate every part of the mourner's life, and he or she is helped to understand how it affects the individual's perceptions, reactions and other relationships. Extra psychological work is done when the mourner is stuck in a certain phase.

A professional therapist can help a family give support and comfort to each other and minimize silence and separation. There may develop an unspoken agreement in which no one talks about feelings. The parents discourage children from talking because they are overwhelmed by their own emotions. They may misinterpret the children's silence to mean they are coping with the loss and making a good adjustment.

A mother referred to her fifteen-year-old daughter as "self-contained" and "coping very well" with the unexpected accidental death of her nine-year-old sister. The mother has not encouraged her daughter to exchange expressions of grief with her because she is still working out her own feelings. The self-control displayed by the daughter is not really coping but actually an inhibition of mourning. The daughter and other two surviving children all need adult guidance to help them express their grief. Often the only way to overcome the resistance and denial is through professional help.

Many believe it is weak to ask others for help or to seek professional help. This is a myth which prevents many from getting the support they need. It is a sign of strength to know when you need outside help and to do what is necessary to initiate it. It is difficult for each family member to be supportive of others when each is needy and struggling with a different set of feelings at a given time. Sometimes it feels as if there is no one to lean on and as if no one knows what to do. You see the others as upset as you are. The strength of someone outside the family who is not in mourning is needed. Having someone available who does not need anything in return is reassuring.

Those who are bereaved are needy themselves and have little to offer others in the family. It is also difficult to see those you love crying continuously and in pain. When we see others cry and sad, it reminds us of our own sadness. An individual from the outside who is not suffering and has the ego strength as well as the knowledge of the mourning process may be needed to guide mourners through their grief.

The bereaved need family, friends, clergypersons, and others to give continuing support and comfort. If others are not available or if there is no support system for an individual or family, then a professional person is imperative. *Grief needs to be shared.* Even when there is available help from others, a professional person can be important. Others may tire of hearing the repetition of stories and feelings which is so necessary in mourning. Often, others feel helpless and at a loss to make the person feel better. It is also difficult for others to hear because it evokes personal feelings of fear and sadness and a constant reminder of their own vulnerability.

The loss of a loved one is a profound emotional experience. It demands a major psychological readjustment. Energy and strength are required to do the work of mourning. The support and comfort of others are essential. It is never a mistake, nor is it an indication of emotional imbalance, to get professional help at any point in bereavement. It is possible you are progressing in the mourning process in a satisfactory manner and need only to understand that your symptoms are normal. Grandma Lasher was reassured her reaction was normal after consulting a therapist.

It was a sad day when the Lasher family received the diagnosis of their infant's disability. Despite the prognosis, Nell and George are finding joy in their baby's existence. They are sad and mourn the circumstances and are supportive of each other. They are fortunate that their friends have been kind, understanding, and helpful.

Nell's parents live in a distant city, and all they knew was that their grandson had a birth defect that would result in mental and physical retardation. They did not see him for months at a time. Nell's father refused to discuss the situation and the disappointment with Nell's mother and chided her for crying. Grandma mourned and cried about the circumstances. Nell's brother said there must be something wrong and suggested she needed to see a psychiatrist.

When the parents visited their children, they consulted a therapist. They were reassured to learn that the only thing "wrong" with Grandma was that no one had allowed her to express her sorrow.

Now Nell's mother reports: "Ever since Dr. Weizman gave me permission to cry, I haven't felt the need to. I feel understood." When a person cries because of a death or other loss, the family should not be critical. The person may or may not need professional help, but the conclusion that something "is wrong" should not be drawn simply because the person cries. That surely is a proper expression for sadness and disappointments.

There are many circumstances when professional help might be imperative: when there is an absence of appropriate mourning; if there is an inadequate support system; when there is little or no movement and change in the phases of mourning; when there is insufficient expression of emotions or a breakdown in communication within the family; to help children mourn; when the death has occurred under bizarre circumstances or when there is the threat of suicide by the survivors. In cases of complicated, prolonged, or delayed grief, professional guidance is needed. Therapy is indicated if the relationship with the deceased involved considerable conflict and ambivalent feelings and if the survivors have experienced multiple losses.

Life has changed for you, and the transition will be painful. You will take up some of the strands of your past life but many things will be different. First you *must be allowed and allow yourself and others to go through the mourning process.* Usually bereavement runs its course with support and an individual's resources. For most people healing takes place without complications. If the process is stifled, emotional problems can arise that will require psychotherapy. That does not imply that you have to wait for a serious problem before seeking professional help; it does not preclude professional consultation at any time during bereavement if you feel worried, alone, or unsupported. In fact, early consultation can facilitate the mourning process and avert an emotional disruption years later.

Finding Professional Help

There are agencies and private practitioners where you can find help. You must be careful to select a person who is *empathetic and qualified,* who knows how to be helpful and who has resolved his or her own feelings about loss and death. Although most professionals—psychiatrists, psychologists, social workers, doctors, nurses, and clergypersons—do encounter loss and death in their practices, they are not necessarily prepared to work with bereaved persons. They may not have an understanding of the process of mourning and could aggravate the problem by mishandling. There are people who are specially trained and have a special dimension and sensitivity that allow them to help the grief-stricken. Some clergypersons are possessed of that quality and, generally, are comforting and reassuring. However, religious support is usually time-limited due to other demands on the clergy's time. Use your judgement in choosing a professional. Many persons today have established reputations in bereavement therapy, and a few inquiries will lead you to the right person.

A young woman related how she felt about the beginning of her bereavement therapy.

> I have never talked to a therapist before. I respect your professional expertise but also thought you would be an automatic plug in, that you would know what I am talking about because you have been through it, too.

Her therapist had been recommended by several reliable people. She began therapy with confidence in the professional relationship.

The bereavement therapist must have special qualifications. This person needs to be educated in the psychological aspects of mourning from the vantage of many theorists; well read and studied in the literature available by and for professionals and the layperson. An important dimension is to have experienced a personal loss, mourned in a healthy and normal way, and to have attained integration of that loss. This adds a human dimension to the work of the therapist. The studies of death and dying and grief therapy are more than academic. They are heavily laden emotional topics. The therapist, teacher, nurse, physician, or anyone dealing with those who are ill or bereaved must preserve their own human and sensitive reactions. The therapist must be perceived as a feeling person, and also have a balanced perspective and be able to appreciate the importance of life that the loss of a loved one underscores.

Support Groups

The best support is often found in talking with others who have had a similar experience. Many support groups have been established during recent years with professional leadership or self-help. Comfort comes through mutual sharing and the commonality of experience. Sharing on a meaningful level helps people move on through the mourning process. Following is an example of the benefits gained from participating in a support group.

> Betty O'Neil was widowed after nursing her husband through a long illness. She considered herself totally self-sufficient, leaning on no one for solace, "handling" her grief in a stalwart and independent manner. Several months after her husband's death, she began to feel the pressures of her unexpressed grief and decided, despite an antipathy toward psychiatrists and the idea of therapy, to enroll in an eight-week support group for widows conducted by Dr. Weizman.
>
> "I felt strange but I really kind of enjoyed it. I thought I must be gaining something. I always felt good and stronger each time I left. It was a strengthening of the soul or an inner feeling. Something made me feel stronger."
>
> Betty admitted later she had not been "tuned into it" before the first session. Despite her wariness, she did a lot of sharing with the other widows and a lot of crying. It was the first time in all the years of her husband's illness and since his death that she had articulated her feelings and had cried with others. "I really don't share with people and I don't like to put my problems on other people. I think my own intelligence and my own common sense ought to get me through life."

Despite that attitude she attended all the group sessions and found they helped her cope with her loss. In fact, she said, "If the group had continued, I would still be attending because I seemed to get a new strength so that I could get through each day and do what I had to do. It was a relief of tension and I looked forward to coming back."

You may find help through your local church, hospital, university, social service agency or private therapist.

4

THE FAMILY

A Natural Support Group
For Mourning*

The family can be a haven of mutual support as it is a ready-made support group for mourners. Feelings can be safely shared and you can gather together for comfort. Each member experiences the loss of the same individual. There is a special level of understanding and communication possible among persons when they have shared an attachment and share the loss.

It is difficult to get good support for mourning. It is difficult to find someone you *can talk to as much as you need to talk, to be able to cry without being embarrassed, and to be able to be real.* Home is a place where you do not have to worry about being accepted or rejected. Grief can be most naturally and fully expressed within the family.

The *process of mourning* and many of the emotions experienced are similar for all bereaved persons. There are differences in the experience depending on the person's *relationship* to the deceased, whether spouse, parent, child, or sibling. No matter which loved one dies, no one mourns in a vacuum. In most instances there is a *family* who is bereaved. If a family mourns openly and together, if they share their feelings and tears, they can help each other through the process of mourning. Closeness bridges the isolation felt by each family member. If each person gets wrapped in misery, ignoring the feelings of other family members and not sharing personal feelings, distance rather than closeness is created.

The family is the center of all the separate relationships within the group. The losses addressed in the subsequent chapters occur within the

*From a paper entitled: *The Family: A Natural Support Group for Mourning*, presented at the 3rd International Congress of Family Therapy, Tel Aviv, Israel, July 3, 1979, by Savine Gross Weizman, Ph.D.

family context as described in this chapter. Exploring mourning within the context of the family can help each person understand his or her own personal loss of the relationship, the loss experienced in the family as a group and also how the family system is affected.

THE FAMILY AS A SYSTEM

The members of a family make up a system. The family is an arrangement of persons related and connected to each other, and contributing toward a whole unit. It is an arena for many relationships, and a general feeling exists when all are together. The family has characteristic ways of operating, solving problems, caring for each other emotionally, performing tasks, providing food and clothing, dividing chores, having fun, and handling crises. There are family traditions, beliefs, and values. Ways of communicating have been developed.

The family strives to reach a sense of equilibrium. Every part is important and crucial so that if there is one change in the system or a change in an individual it affects all participants. If an injury or loss occurs in one member, the equilibrium is disturbed. When a member dies, it creates a major change, and all parts of the system are affected. Everyone in the group readjusts his or her position when someone is removed. Not only is one individual relationship severed for each person, but the image or picture of the family as a whole is completely different. Characteristic ways of operating no longer work, and the family members flail around in an attempt to reestablish a new balance. Roles need to be readjusted and redefined. Many attempts are made to adjust to the changes in the system even while it is in a state of flux.

Each person loses an individual relationship and experiences a personal loss whether it is the loss of a spouse, a child, a parent, or a sibling. In addition, each of these persons also loses within the context of the family. A group loss is experienced. The loss is a double one. "I have lost a sister but I have also lost a member of my family group; I have a personal loss; I have a group loss because this whole family now looks different to me; 'We' as a family group are different." Each person has a unique perception and experience of the personal loss and of the loss and change in the family system.

Some will say, "We are still a family." That is true, but it is also true that it is not the same family "picture." Some will say, "We are not a family anymore" because the familiar picture has been disrupted. The ways in which the deceased has complemented and added to the family are underscored. A loss disrupts the structure of the family and the roles within the family. When a member of the family has died, the fabric of the family has a hole in it, and it needs to be repaired, actually rewoven by the remaining members of the family. When this has been done the members accept the "new look" of the family.

DOUBLE TASKS: MOURNING AND THE REORGANIZATION OF THE FAMILY

Mourners are confronted with two challenges, each one requiring immense emotional energy. The two tasks are *mourning,* tremendous in itself, and *adjusting to the changes* in the family system. The family has a new form, but the reorganization of the family cannot take place until the old form is abandoned. This means it is imperative for mourning to be supported and continued until integration so the new form of the family created by the death can be accommodated. If the mourning is abridged or aborted, the reorganization of the family cannot take place. The two processes are interdependent because accepting the new family form means acknowledging the absence of a member. The immediate tasks for survival, working, household tasks, and attending school often take precedence by necessity. Mourning may be neglected or set aside because of the overwhelming tasks facing the family. There is barely enough energy for both mourning and daily tasks in addition to the family tasks.

Everyone in the family is very absorbed in individual grieving. There is not much energy for parents to take care of children's emotional needs and also to take care of themselves. What often happens is that parents make a choice. They may either submerge their own grief and attend to the children, or they may attend to themselves and neglect the children emotionally. *Children need help in staying with their feelings and talking about the deceased.* Rather than make a choice some people *attempt* to do both. It is difficult and necessary to mourn and support mourning in others, or the family unit weakens.

When children are quiet or tearless, adults may believe they are not grieving, that they are adjusting well. They may not realize that children have difficulty in articulating their sadness and need the adults to help them find words for feelings. The absence of mourning indicates a problem rather than a sign of adjustment because mourning is the natural reaction to a death or other loss. Years after her mother died, Harriet, now an adult said:

I never had the words before to say how sad I was. I never had a chance to say the words. It's like something tied down at the bottom of the ocean, like an old shipwreck. A feeling comes to the surface. You have to dive down to the bottom and see what it was attached to.

A child may try to talk but is squelched or ignored because the adult is not prepared to talk openly. There are times when the parent is so wrapped up in his or her own pain that there is no recognition the child is suffering, too.

Sometimes the effect on the family is not apparent at the time.

> Recently, a thirty-six-year-old woman said, "I came across an old snapshot of mother, my brothers and sister, and me taken at an amusement park a couple of weeks after our father's death. It's funny. I always remembered that as a happy, fun-filled day. Now that I look at that old picture I see four terribly sad little waifs. Our mother looks out of the picture with a grim visage. I guess the camera caught something we were never able to say."

Lack of communication breaks down relationships and causes each person to feel isolated. Regardless of personal pain or the child's resistance, it is the responsibility of the adult to open the way. The first steps toward communication may be difficult, especially when there is little or no model of past dialogue. Tragedy sometimes can help overcome this pattern because the need to talk is so great, feelings are so strong, and the need to maintain contact with each other is so keenly felt.

Changes in Family Members

The family must also adjust to the others around them who have been changed by the loss. In addition to the loss through the death, a loss is experienced through the changed behavior and demeanor of parents, children, and siblings. A boy who was 15 when his father died related years after the death: "I realized that not only had I lost a father to a heart attack but also lost a mother to emotionalism [mourning]." Two young girls said to their mother, "You're always talking about sister." Although the children grieved deeply for their sister themselves, they had reactions to their mother's mourning. They missed her lightness and energy. They felt less important than the deceased. They needed to feel that they, alive and well, were important. Only talking and clarifying can reinforce mutual caring and contribute to understanding.

Adults Provide Guidance

The family as a whole and in combinations of two or more persons needs to cry and talk together. It may feel awkward or strange at first to speak of fears and sadness, but it will help each one to realize the feelings and reactions are happening to parents and children alike. This will create a feeling of being connected.

It is the adult's responsibility to initiate, encourage, and model the open expression of feelings about the loss in the family, whether the loss has been a child, a sibling, or a parent. Children need a model for grieving. They need permission to express their feelings, and they need an adult to take charge. It is helpful if there has been a history in the family of talking things over and talking about feelings. If no precedent has existed, this crisis can be used as an opportunity to develop new kinds of behavior. *The integration of the loss and adapting to the new family group depend on mutual sharing and mutual support.* The parent or parents need to provide an atmosphere for the free flow of feelings from one person to another.

The Inhibition of Family Sharing

At first the family huddles together in shock and misery. Its members cling to each other for comfort. As time and pain continue, there is a tendency to pull apart. It is difficult to sustain the mutual sharing of feelings and support for each other during the prolonged process of mourning. If the family is the natural setting for the sharing of true feelings, a place where you can be real, why is it so difficult to continue to depend on each other for comfort and so difficult to maintain support for mourning? Some of the things that inhibit us are the same as with others outside the family. We are still afraid of death; we do not understand the process of mourning; we do not know how we are "supposed" to feel and we do not have permission from ourselves or from other family members to talk and continue talking. The family may not have an established pattern of sitting down and talking together or talking about feelings. *By giving permission to share, the mourning process will be facilitated for all.*

Adults often have the idea that they protect the others by not talking, by keeping a "stiff upper lip" and not showing emotion. "I have to be strong for the others, I want to show them that life goes on," is often said. It is important for children that the adults be able to maintain some regularity and routine. Having the laundry clean and regular mealtimes help children feel that they will be cared for and that structure continues in their lives. However, that does not eliminate the need for talking and sharing feelings. By being honest and open with feelings, you are better able to carry on daily obligations. Some parents and children have the fantasy that they just have to go on doing what they have to do. They cannot stop to talk or cry. A lot of energy is then arrested in stopping the process. This affects your own individual process and the family process as well because there is no free passage of feelings. Without mourning, the realignment of roles and adjusting to the new family unit cannot take place. If a significant portion of energy is bottled up in suppressing feelings and communication stops, mourning will not proceed naturally and the reorganization of the family does not take place. When the needs of mourning are not met within the family, the bonds are loosened and the system deteriorates.

Another dynamic that stops persons from sharing within the family is that each person is acutely aware of his or her own suffering, which is typical for grieving. Each person is very self absorbed and may withdraw, reducing contact with others and eliminating opportunity for support. Even within your own family, you may feel "No one understands me; no one hurts the way I do."

An additional problem is that each member of the family feels very needy. They do not know if they will get their needs met because others are needy also. Each one has little to give and it seems as if there is no one to lean on. Persons are afraid to share their feelings because they fear they may be asked to give support also. The giving and receiving are mutually supportive and sustaining rather than depleting.

Certain phrases are used to inhibit talking about feelings like: "I will hurt you if I talk about it or if I cry in front of you." The fantasy is that "I am the only one who hurts." This is a denial that the others hurt, too. There is a mistaken idea that talking makes the hurt. It brings it to the surface, but the hurt abides in everyone. You and the other family members already hurt, talking about it is not going to make the others hurt. The death itself created the hurt. If you talk about something, it makes it more real and brings feelings to the surface. Although expression is painful at the time, it has the long-term effect of relieving the pain for everyone. It will give family members an opportunity for closeness and comfort. The family can be experienced as a safe place to talk and to be natural. Rather than duplication of the social atmosphere outside the home, there is confirmation of the safety of home and family and a sense of security which comes from acceptance.

Another reason people are reluctant to talk within their family is because their feelings are mirrored in the faces and words of the others. "I look at you and you are crying and you are hurt and that's how I feel too. You really reflect my own feelings." A mother said: "It hurts me to see them hurt." There is an awareness of a double dose of hurt, yours and the hurt you see. So adults may keep their hurt private, and pretend the others are not hurting. Each is off alone, deprived of support and caring. A young woman described this experience after her sister's death.

> The pain I feel is not limited. A feeling of perpetual drowning occurs as I search the eyes of my parents and brother. I hope to catch a glimpse of tranquility on their faces, but instead see their pain. I cannot help them. It is not enough to sustain the tragedy of her death and to live on the edge, but as a family we must constantly confront each other's grief. Grief demands closeness, but I feel alone.

Phases and feelings may differ at a given time for each person in the family. An exchange of feelings is healing, regardless of the phase the individual is undergoing. Everyone does not have to be experiencing the same feeling in order to be helpful to each other. Start sharing your emotions as you feel them. Provide the necessary model for your family.

It is not really possible to hide and disguise feelings with those who care about you. Husbands and wives are often in tune with each other and children can sense their parents' vulnerability. Sometimes it is acted out behaviorally if not put into words. It is surprising how perceptive children are of their parents' emotions. "Jerry is always hugging me," Nancy Hickock said. "He's quick with his eyes. When someone mentions Lanny, he looks at me to see my reaction. He's always very observant of how it will affect me."

It is an unnecessary effort to put on a facade and act as if everything is all right when it is not. All family members are in emotional pain, and the family is the place to share, and get relief and acceptance.

Displacement of Feelings

Everyone feels sensitive and irritable. There is an underlying layer of sadness and a pervasive feeling of disruption. These feelings are often expressed in impatient reactions to others, being irritable about behavior usually accepted, or children teasing each other. Verbalizing feelings with other members of the family will help to minimize displacement of feelings onto others and overreacting to everyday problems. Otherwise, children and adults are confused by others' reactions. It is confusing to be the recipient or object of displaced feelings and unwarranted reactions. Such behavior leaves the person bewildered, thinking, "What did I do to deserve this?" and feeling righteously indignant over such treatment. This leads to resentment and anger and creates distance in relationships.

An excessive amount of arguing among children is a sign that they have emotions which are not being put into words. The following family interactions demonstrate this.

> There had been a minimum of overt mourning by Mr. Blackman's daughters, Edie, 16, and Lauren, 14, during the two years following his death. "I kept waiting for the explosion," Mrs. Blackman reported.
>
> Mrs. Blackman observed months later: "It seems like I'm remembering more now and noticing more now about the girls than I was initially. It does seem like they say things a lot more in conversation. It was very awkward at first when I mentioned their Dad. It was really a difficult situation to try to bring him up in conversation."

Each of them was embroiled in her own feelings, pretending to be adjusting, but tensions were unwittingly exposed by outbursts of anger. This happens often among siblings. They over-reacted with anger to many situations and converted their sadness to anger as well. Each was surprised to realize how hard it had been from the beginning for the others. Talking about this promoted mutual understanding and reduced the arguments.

TALKING ABOUT THE DECEASED

It is important to remember the deceased and let go of the attachment very gradually. One way to do this is to talk together about what the deceased was like: good points, favorite sayings, sense of humor, and *things you did not like.* You need to explore the roles performed and the contributions to the family. It clarifies what was special about the person and also what will be missed.

Redistribution of Roles

You will have to discuss together all the empty spaces left by your loved one and the ways you can help each other to fill in those spaces. Ways must be found to redistribute the role so that each member of the family can take up some of the slack.

Children may be frightened about who will take care of their emotional and physical needs when a parent has died. The concern may focus on the financial situation or daily maintenance tasks. Children need reassurance that they will be taken care of and the family will stay together. They need to know that you will all manage together. When changes are unavoidable, prepare them adequately with explanations and emotional support.

The adult survivor may also worry about how he or she will fulfill the roles of the two parents. "How will I cook dinner, pay the bills, mow the lawn, be comforting when there is illness, be firm when discipline is necessary?" It is overwhelming for adults and children alike.

When a child dies, the parents may miss the joy or problems that particular child brought. A sibling may wonder, "Who will go bike riding with me or who will bake cookies with me?"

As time goes on, various members of the family will voluntarily take over some of the tasks of the deceased. Edie said: "I'll do Dad's job. I'll take the tree down this year." Tom automatically took over the yard maintenance and set up the trains at Christmas time, exactly the way his Dad had done it, even though he missed sharing the task with his Dad. Danny, Steve, and Cari always planted the vegetable garden to carry on the tradition. The surviving parent will fill in for the other, whether that is seeking employment, cooking, paying the bills, or nursing a bruise. Each task that is taken over will be a reminder of the loss in addition to underscoring that another responsibility has to be assumed. This is hard work, emotionally, and perhaps physically. It helps when your efforts are acknowledged and appreciated.

Adults are responsible for the emotional and physical maintenance of the family and the household. You need to be cautious that a child is not saddled with the idea that he is now "the man in the family" or that she is "the little Mother." Sometimes unknowing friends will say this to a child. Children may want to help with certain responsibilities if they are physically and emotionally able, but it is unfair and inappropriate for them to be treated like adults. Dealing with feelings about the death is more than enough for a child or adolescent to handle.

SUPPORT THROUGH PROFESSIONAL INTERVENTION

Mourning, the reorganization of the family, and taking care of the emotional and physical needs of the family are overlapping and burdensome tasks. The mourning itself is an energy drain and often the adults do not have the energy for doing all this work. At the time the children most need structure, support, caring, and open communication, the parents or parent are least able to provide them because of the strain on their own resources. The energy of someone who is not engrossed in mourning is needed. You need an individual who will give permission for the expression of emotions, reaffirm the normalcy and necessity of mourning, recognize when needs are not being satisfied.

Sometimes the extended family provide the degree of support needed by those directly affected by the loss. In South Africa an old custom remains. A relative will move into the home when a parent has died. This person serves as an emotional support to all the family, is a surrogate parent and helps with household tasks. The length of stay depends on the needs of the family but is generally about a year. This custom gives recognition to the emotional needs of the family and is a lovely example of caring.

Often the individual needs of each family member are so overwhelming that a family bereavement therapist is advisable to help the family learn to share their feelings, support one another, and take care of each other in a new way.

The Breen family came together to talk about their grief; each one shared feelings and stories about the deceased daughter and sister. It was difficult for them to do so when they were alone. They needed the facilitation and encouragement of someone outside the family. The children talked about their relationship with their sister and they cried. The nine-year-old sister said, "I miss her. I want her." The family was able to speak freely about feelings in therapy.

It is characteristic of children to show resistance to coming for therapy sessions. They don't understand the importance of keeping their feelings available and putting those feelings into words. It is the responsibility of the adults in the family to see that the children keep talking and that they do not yield to the children's resistance and allow their feelings and memories to go underground as a temporary relief of pain. The emotions will ferment from within or erupt at a later time. When feelings are suppressed, you run the risk of displacement of feelings, and interference in existing relationships.

Following are some illustrations of how family therapy can facilitate the mourning process. The cases are examples of the problems that afflict families and of the facilitation of readjustment when there is open expression of grief.

Each family illustrates progression through the phases of grief, fixation at a particular stage, verbal expression of feelings within the family, acting out by children and adults, effect of the loss on relationships within the family, and the effect of professional intervention. Examination of the four histories offers a picture of the effect of a sudden death on families and illustrates many of the normal reactions during the mourning process.

The Arnolds: Successful Family Mourning

The sixteen-year-old son, Dwayne, died from a malignant tumor, leaving his parents, two brothers (aged twenty and nine), and a sister (eighteen). Four months after the boy's death they requested therapy.

The nine-year-old, Joel, had a very special relationship with his brother. They shared the same room and many activities. After the death he was restless, had difficulty sleeping, was having a hard time concentrating and doing school work. Repetitive hand motions were another symptom of his distress. Although the mother and father shared *their* anguish, they had not shared feelings within the family group.

The Arnolds met regularly with the therapist for four months and returned again for several meetings eight months later. They were always encouraged to share their feelings, their sadness, and their tears. It was especially helpful for the youngest son. His father's expressions of emotion and unashamed weeping set a good example for the boy. The twenty-year-old assured the nine-year-old that he, too, cried often. The father and older brother were a model for the nine-year-old who then cried openly and was able to talk about his feelings.

The follow-up revealed they all were continuing normally through the mourning process. Joel regained his capacity to study and excel in school, and his sleep problems and other symptoms abated. Each of the family members learned it was acceptable to talk about their grief with each other and not be ashamed of crying.

The Johnsons: Regriefing (Delayed Grief)

The regriefing process is always more difficult than normal progression through grief at the time of the death, because it is out of context with the event itself. Suppression buries the feelings almost to inaccessibility. The longer the suppression, the more formidable the task of raising the feelings to the surface. That point was so well articulated by Harriet in the quote mentioned earlier in this chapter: "It's like something tied down at the bottom of the ocean...you have to dive down to the bottom to see what it (the feeling) was attached to." If grief is not brought into the open when a spouse/parent dies, the repressed and suppressed feelings can interfere with normal growth for the children and the physical and emotional well-being of the parent.

Don Johnson died of a drug overdose leaving Janet, his twenty-eight-year-old widow, and son Mark, four and a half years old. Both mother and child were in a state of delayed grief when they sought out a therapist one year and eight months after the death.

There was little verbal expression of grief between them; both were stuck in the denial stage. Janet drowned herself in work, reasoning that she had to earn a living for them. She had little emotional energy for her son.

Janet's suppressed grief evidenced itself in an inability to eat, in being unable to breathe, and recurrent migraine headaches. Mark developed a fear of falling. The genesis of this fear was the fabrication of a story about his father's death by his paternal grandparents. They told the boy his father died after a fall from the porch roof. This distortion had to be corrected to help Mark overcome this fear. He was identifying with the *manner* of his father's death.

Mark was fearful and would cry inappropriately at insignificant things but resisted talking about his feelings and the death. It took about six months of therapy and help from his mother before he was able to volunteer some of his feelings. The mother guided him in expressing his feelings and in correcting his misconceptions about the death.

Anger was a strong unexpressed emotion for both mother and son. In addition, time was spent helping create remembrances of the relationship that existed when the three of them were a family, and minimizing the identification with the manner of the death.

Two years after Don's death, Mark was still having sleep problems. He finally found the words to tell his mother he was afraid to go to sleep. "I'm so scared. I'm afraid I'll die." She stayed with him many nights and comforted him with explanations of the difference between sleep and death. Eventually he said, "I feel all right now. You can leave. Good night, Mother."

Recently Mark attended a wake with his mother. Special circumstances will often jog the memory. Mark suddenly remembered seeing his mother put his picture into his father's hand as he lay in the casket. Later at home, Janet and Mark talked about the wake and the memories it brought of the picture in Dad's hand. Then he startled Janet: "He took drugs, didn't he? He died because he took drugs," the boy stated. Janet later told the therapist: "It shocked me. As many times as I tried to tell him the truth over the past five years, it seemed as if he didn't hear me. But, obviously, he did hear me." Despite the pain evoked, Janet had the courage to respond to Mark's need to discuss the facts.

Often people are afraid when unusual circumstances surround a death and tend to lie or omit the truth, thus undermining the trust in the existing relationship. A child needs the truth but only in amounts he or she can deal with appropriate to the level of understanding and emotional maturity. Talking in a sensitive and tactful way helps the child face the truth and make use of it in a constructive way. The important task is to avoid identification with the manner of the death. It is important to recall the total relationship with the deceased, talk about his or her qualities, and support identification with the positive aspects of the person.

At the end of one lengthy conversation between mother and son, Mark said: "Thanks for talking to me. You've really helped me a lot. Since my Dad died you've kept me happy all these years so I don't feel so bad."

It has taken five years for Janet and Mark to reach the intimacy and understanding revealed by Mark's words.

The Richards: Early Professional Intervention

The Richards family is another instance of a parent's unexpected death. Mr. Richards died of a heart attack while out of town, leaving his wife Rhoda and two young boys under the age of five. Six months later Rhoda sought consultation for the family.

> The younger boy had developed a learning problem and both boys were acting out by fighting with each other. The mother grew dependent on and possessive of them. Both boys were overwhelmed by the contradictory feeling of intense fear of losing their mother and their discomfort from her smothering demands upon them. The children were too young to understand death and were confused.
>
> Guidance enabled mother and children to talk about their feelings. Tony and Bobby also worked out their feelings in play. The younger boy often played games pretending his father would come back. His brother said he knew this would not happen but he still wished it would. The boys eventually had an understanding of the meaning of death. Eventually a better parent/child relationship developed. Bobby's learning problem was remedied and the fighting between the boys decreased.

The Robbins Family: An Overload of Feelings

Occasionally even the good example of a parent's open expression of grief cannot guarantee progression through the mourning process for the children. If a child becomes focused on one part of the grief or flails out aggressively instead of verbalizing, it will take special help to dislodge the fixation and displacement and permit movement toward resolution of grief.

> Thirty-five-year-old Sally Robbins began therapy three months after her husband's death. She was having trouble controlling thirteen-year-old Tom's aggressive behavior toward Sharon, eleven, and Rene, eight. The mother described his attitude: "He anesthetizes his feelings with anger." During a family session weeks later, Sharon described her brother's inability to show any emotion but anger: "His nerve endings are severed." In addition to Tom's constant picking on his sisters, the three children were venting their anger on their mother.
>
> Sally had found help for herself through a support group she attended for eight weeks. She was a good model for the children and she urged them to join her in open expression of their grief. They did not respond. At first

they were intent on blaming their father and then displacing these feelings. They finally began to understand that many people are angry at the deceased for dying, but since that person is not around, the tendency is to turn the anger against the nearest target, their mother and each other. They became more verbal and the acting out and in-fighting began to decrease.

Once, when they were discussing plans for Christmas, Tom participated in the conversation until someone used the word "sad." Tom jumped from his chair and became provocative and disruptive. He was trying to evade his sadness. "Sad is unsafe," commented Sharon succinctly. Apparently, despite his behavior, Tom absorbed what was being said and benefited from the sessions. Sally reported he was always less aggressive at home following therapy.

Following her father's death, Rene, the eight-year-old, regressed to immature behavior. She finally disclosed her fear of touching the bed where her father had slept, thinking that dying was "catching." Therapy has helped her reach a developmental stage commensurate with her age. However, when she is upset she still reverts to immature behavior.

Twelve-year-old Sharon has developed a very close relationship with her mother and can talk about her worries and sadness. About a year after the father's death, Sally started dating and now has a special friend. This has been the subject of discussion at several family therapy sessions. The children have been antagonistic about their mother's friend. One day Sharon broached the subject of remarriage with her mother. "Oh no, you won't do that. You can't sleep with anybody except my father." It was not yet possible for her to accept her mother paired with another man. Sally assured her that a relationship with another man would not negate their father's importance in any of their lives.

The children's behavior toward their mother's dating is not unique. Children often resent the thought of the surviving parent finding enjoyment with someone who might appear to be taking the place of the deceased parent. On the other hand, very young children are often anxious to replace the missing parent. All they know is that someone is missing and they want someone in that empty place. One might often see a small child approach any adult with the question: "Won't you be my daddy?"

Another facet of the mourning process is the tendency to remember only the "good" side of the deceased. It takes a long time before survivors, especially children, can acknowledge that the parent who died was not a saint.

The Robbins children, especially Tom, talk about their father as though he were perfect. In reality their father was authoritarian and demanding toward the children, but they cannot face these truths yet. Tom is much like his father. His parents' relationship was a dominant/submissive one, and young Tom seems to be trying to emulate his father in his own behavior toward his mother. Sally said "They don't remember when they had run-in's with him. Tom can't see yet that his Dad had shortcomings. I could just see him if his Dad were alive today. How the two of them would really lock horns!"

Other things that came out during family sessions were the children's fear that their mother would not be able to take care of them. She kept reassuring them that being sad did not mean she could not manage the household matters. They were concerned about the hereditary aspects of heart disease. The doctor explained the medical and genetic possibilities so they could understand them and take care of themselves with proper diet and exercise.

The cases described here, plus other family histories included throughout the book, are evidence that family therapy can be an important way to facilitate movement through the mourning process. It is recommended that help be sought within the critical time soon after the death or within six months. If there is a long delay, the emotions that are a normal part of grief may be suppressed, and it becomes a formidable task to retrieve these emotions. It is during this time that a pattern of sharing and mutual support can be established. A trauma can fracture or synthesize the family structure. Professional intervention can aid in repairing the injury to the family system after the death of a significant person.

Each person is unique, reacting to grief according to age, experience, personality, and the relationship to the deceased. Although the feelings of grief are similar, individuals express them differently and experience them at different times during the mourning process. The following chapters address the mourning process with the similarities and differences in mind. It is hoped that each chapter enables you to gain strength for confronting a traumatic period in your life and to understand how the other bereaved among you are reacting to the same loss.

5

DEATH OF A MATE

My heart is still coiled in your love,
My love in your heart.
Flowing like a mountain spring,
Coiled like a bedspring, firm, and supportive.

Awareness comes in painful sorrow:
It is ended. Not flowing, uncoiled. You are dead.
Is that the fate of all love upon one of the two?

Michael Alick

When you married, you knew somewhere deep within you that one of you would die first and the other would be left behind. Those thoughts were pushed into the background as you continued to hope and believe that you would grow old together; that it would not happen until far into the future, too far away to worry about. One day you confront the end of your relationship through the death of your mate. The loss is a source of unbelievable hurt. Every marriage relationship has conflicts and problems, but even when the problems are acute or death comes after a long illness, the separation is painful. In addition, your role of mate, which has been part of your identity, is severed. The feeling of being the only adult in the household who is responsible for everything is burdensome. You feel weakened by the assault, but you must continue to carry out tasks for yourself and by yourself, for your children and the household.

The Social Readjustment Rating Scale, by Holmes and Rahe, lists the death of a spouse as the major life stress an individual may experience.[1] This is an indication of the degree of change and readjustment necessary after this life event. The age of the survivor and the stage in life pose different problems to be mastered. A husband or wife as a single parent has many emotional and maintenance tasks to perform. An older widow or widower has fewer resources to meet the demands of readjustment and the loneliness of living as a single person.

CARRYING ON ALONE

During the time you are struggling through the perplexities of grief, attending to maintenance tasks, working, taking care of the children, and adjusting to being widowed, it is hard to carry on. In the beginning you may be absorbed with yourself and indifferent to what goes on around you. You may ignore even the most fundamental requirements for good health such as cooking and eating, taking medication, and continuing activities that were part of your regimen before the death. The ordinary becomes arduous. Everyday occurrences underscore the absence of your mate. Sitting down to breakfast, or dinner, opening mail, hearing a special song, going to bed, all become sources of pain when they were formerly sources of pleasure. Each day is full of challenges and heartbreaks.

Sleeping Alone

The sudden emptiness on the other side of the bed, or the other bed, is one of the hardest things with which to deal. The bed is an intimate place and yearning for the spouse may disrupt established sleep patterns. It is hard to get into bed at night and some people delay bedtime. It is hard to fall alseep; it is hard to stay asleep.

Sidney could not bear to return to the bed or even the room he had shared with his wife. For more than a year he slept on the living room sofa every night.

Ruth related her struggle in adjusting to the empty bed. Ruth and Jeff had a king-size bed so they could be close but have plenty of room. For two years after the death, Ruth continued to sleep in the same bed, but her sleep was rarely restful. She said: "I miss sleeping with love." Finally she rearranged the room. As a way of acknowledging her widowhood, she said: "Look, I'm only one person now, I don't need such a large bed. Ultimately however, I found my sleep more restful when I moved a standard-size double bed into my room."

Sally Robbins spent months of sleepless nights huddled in her bed, conscious of the empty space beside her. "I was so lonely; I missed the sound of Bob's snore that used to be annoying. One night, at the end of a difficult week with the children, I closed myself in the bedroom overcome by a crying spell. In my bed, missing Bob and wanting to be close to him, I crawled from my side to what had been his side. Clutching the pillow on which his head had once rested, my tears subsided and I fell asleep. I sleep on his side of the bed occasionally and find I rest well."

Sally's gesture of clutching the pillow is a variation of what others do with pillows. Some put pillows or a rolled-up bedspread in the empty place to give the illusion that someone is there. Others quickly redecorate the bedroom and shift the furniture or move to another room. Widows and widowers often wake up in the morning with an uneasy sensation or a heavy feeling and have difficulty getting out of bed. It is a struggle that represents the awareness and adjustment to being alone.

Sometimes the widowed person shares the bed with a child as a comfort for each of them. This practice is not advisable and should be avoided. It may produce a situation that will not be easy to correct and could lead to problems and dependency. It is better to comfort the child and let him or her fall asleep on his or her own bed. Like Ruth, Sidney, Sally, and countless others, you will have to confront your sleeplessness in a way that is best for you. It may take a long time to work out, but eventually restful sleep will return.

Mealtime

Sitting down at the table underscores the fact that a person is missing. You may not have much appetite for food and the empty chair destroys what little desire there may be. Some families find food preparation difficult and others avoid sitting around the table.

Catherine Blackman and her daughters lived for months on the meals brought to them by friends. When that stopped, she found meal preparation irksome and none of them remember much about what they ate. Fast-food restaurants were frequented.

Much of Claire's caring for her husband was expressed through cooking and baking his favorite dishes. After his death she lost all interest in her culinary talents. She just put together quick meals for herself and her sons.

If you have no children, there is no impelling reason to prepare an appealing meal because there is no one with whom to share it.

Frank said:

> Living alone is rough to adjust to after 42 years of marriage. I eat at irregular hours and very often go without eating. When I do finally eat, I am just going through the motions because I know I should.

Cooking and eating are basic to living. They are symbolic of carrying on at a time when you do not feel like carrying on. Many widows and widowers become run down and are more vulnerable to illness because of their inability to prepare meals for themselves.

Regular meals are important to your overall health as well as anchoring you to a routine. Widows and widowers who do not have children living with them often use the television for company or arrange to dine with someone in similar circumstances. When there are children at home, dinner time is an opportunity for contact and promoting a family feeling, and contributes to constructing a new family picture.

ALONE, LONELY, AND LONESOME

You cannot avoid being lonesome and missing the person with whom you have had an intimate attachment. A middle-aged man said: "I miss the physical and emotional closeness." Ruth said: "I miss his arms around me and his wide smile as he came through the door." Widows and widowers describe their loneliness as having no one with whom to talk over the day; no one who knows whether or not you arrived home safely from work in a snowstorm; no one with whom to share pride in the children's achievements; no one to share frustrations or celebrations. The following lines were spontaneously written by a forty-one year old widow while attending a musical program at church.

> Just suppose your loving spouse were to suddenly die,
> Who would you share a loving glance with,
> Who would you reach out and touch,
> Who would you hold close to you,
> Whose hand would you hold,
> Who would listen to your dreams and feelings?

She and her daughter sat behind a family that was similar to hers when her husband died several years earlier. Many persons find that their loneliness is aroused when at church, listening to music or seeing other families intact.

You may even be lonely for someone who had been an occasional irritant.

Gwen said she used to be annoyed every morning when her husband disturbed her sleep to kiss her goodbye. Now she misses that disturbance. She longs for that goodbye kiss.

Eileen explained about their sometimes rocky marriage. "He had irritating habits like leaving cigarettes burning and his socks on the floor. Now that he's gone that irritant is no longer there. I miss it and him."

Even if you disagreed on a matter you were still not alone. Discussing or arguing about an issue usually helps clarify things and hopefully contributes to a resolution. When raising children there is often a difference of opinion, but it is still helpful to have a partner to bounce around ideas. Widows and widowers miss having a partner with whom to do this.

Aloneness is being by yourself, a state that is sometimes welcome. When your aloneness is involuntary and open-ended, you feel abandoned and empty.

Ruth reported:

I used to love the quiet times alone in the house but now I can't stand being alone. It's not like having time alone that is a premium. It's knowing my husband will never be here; being alone will not end. It's not the same as private time before you expect your mate to return. It is forever.

Eileen said:

I was used to being alone. Jim traveled a lot and I'm a loner anyway. I like my solitude. But now there is the terrible aloneness. There is no end to it, like his return from a trip.

Lonely widows and widowers sometimes become restless and express this by walking or driving around without motive or destination. Sidney bowled every Sunday morning, visited the cemetery, and then drove around for hours.

It is lonely to do things without your spouse which you know he or she would especially have enjoyed. Attending sports events for the children, open houses or concerts where they perform, is gut-wrenching. Even though there are other people around, your spouse is not at your side enjoying it with you.

At home you face the absence of the person with whom you once shared your life in love and in conflict. When you begin to go out a little, seeking companionship and change of scene, you still have to come home alone when the evening is over. This is a sad fact of widowhood.

Common Irritations

There are countless situations which are unavoidable and often unpredictable that pierce your heart. It may never occur to anyone else that these everyday things can awaken your hurt. A certain day of the week or the hour of the day when the death occurred may evoke your grief. For many persons, the hardest hours are from dusk to dawn when the mate had been there to share a meal, talk, do chores, socialize with friends, help the children, sleep together. Opening and reading mail addressed to "Mr. and Mrs." rips at your feelings. A telephone solicitor asking brusquely to speak to "Mr. Jones, please!" would abrade the feelings of a recent widow. So many things left undone: trips that were planned; milestone birthdays to be celebrated; projects not completed. All these reminders make the days and nights hard to get through, and add up to the challenge of carrying on.

Physical Reactions

One development following the loss of a mate is a greater incidence of health problems among survivors. The deleterious effect of grief may be felt soon after the death but is often delayed. Doctors recognize loss as a contributory factor in illness and death.[1,2,3,4,5,6,7]

A phenomenon of bereavement which is common among the widowed is hallucinating the presence of the deceased. It is not unusual for the spouse to experience "a sense of the presence of the dead person."[2] This is described in a study where nearly half of the widows and widowers interviewed felt the presence or thought they saw or heard the deceased. Many persons found the experience helpful for their grief. Most of them told the interviewers that they kept the episodes secret from family and friends for fear of being thought unbalanced. This study concluded that hallucinations are a normal experience of conjugal bereavement irrespective of sex, race, creed, or domicile and that they are psychologically helpful.[5] This is similar to dreaming as a way of expressing the struggle with the fact of the death.

Conflict in Marriage

No matter whether your marriage was of long or short duration, or riddled with problems and conflict, a pattern of couple behavior and attachment developed, and it will take time to adjust to the differences. There having been excessive conflict and unhappiness in the marriage does not lessen the grief. Old hurts, angers, and disappointment are aroused, and dealing with these feelings becomes part of the mourning process. Hope for resolution of conflicts comes to an end. Relief from the stress is also a normal reaction, but sadness will surface eventually over the losses in the relationship and the loss through death. The working through of conflictual feelings from the past is important in integrating the loss and if not dealt with may become a barrier to future relationships.

DECISIONS AND ADJUSTMENTS

It is best that important decisions be postponed. Readjusting to your changed circumstances is a harrowing experience that distorts judgment. Decisions made under stress may not be in your own nor your family's best interests and in the long run may be difficult to undo. You may think you want to move or change your job. Be cautious! You are very vulnerable and it is best to eliminate additional changes. If you have children, a move would pile other losses on top of the traumatic loss of their parent. Children would lose familiar surroundings, both in the house and the neighborhood; they would have to change schools and would lose the proximity to their friends. It is best to stay in the same home for at least a year, if economically feasible. *The best decision you can make during the first few months following the death of your loved one is to make no decision for a while.* Give yourself time. Your judgment is clouded because of the overwhelming assault and your unusual needs.

It is not uncommon to behave in a way which is not characteristic of you. Many widows and widowers have been known to go through large sums of money in the first year. Financial irresponsibility, untimely vacations, neglect of children, sexual encounters or hasty marriages, and moving in with adult children are some of the ways the newly widowed act because of their loneliness and confusion. There are things you might do which worry you. You may start to phone your mate to say you are on your way home. A widower may think, "Wait till I tell that to Ellen; she'll get a big laugh out of that." A widow may say to herself, "I should remind Steve the game is on." You may find yourself hurrying along the street to catch up with someone you *know* is your loved one. These are signs of not yet adjusting to the new reality, of still living in the past.

Most people get through the first year without too much permanent damage to their finances, psyches, or families. Wait until the first year has passed before you think about making any major changes. By then you will have worked through the most devastating emotions and your good judgment will gradually return. You will begin to feel more organized and will be able to restore structure and meaning to your life.

Loss of Role and Identity

The role of mate is an important part of your identity. It is a way of perceiving yourself and defining yourself. In addition it involves many functions acted out in daily behaviors. The loss of the role is another loss added to the primary loss of the death of your mate. For awhile you don't know what to do with this part of yourself. You feel in limbo.

If a person is not employed and children are grown, the role and function of spouse occupy a greater portion of the identity. In these instances, the loss of the role of mate is more traumatic. This was true for Mrs. Douglas whose identity was totally tied in with being a wife. When her husband died she said, "I was always Mrs. Douglas, and now I am nobody." She was dependent on her role as mate for her complete identity and experienced a loss of self in addition to the loss of her husband. You will need to redefine yourself as a person, that is, from spouse, to widowed, to single, and reconstitute your roles and goals.

Among the elderly there often develops an increased emotional dependency on the mate. Physical limitations brought on by aging and the lack of mobility may restrict activities and social contacts. The resources necessary for accommodating to the changes caused by the death of the mate are limited. The circle of friends diminishes as the years take their toll. This is an added burden for senior citizens and those who have retired. Although there is some comfort and good fortune acknowledged in the length of the marriage, this does not ease the lonesomeness or isolation. The adjustment is difficult. Seventy-nine-year-old Frank's first year of bereavement was difficult.

> I haven't had a day go by without thinking about my wife. She died suddenly and I felt disoriented. I didn't go out of the house or visit friends. I was lonely but I couldn't bring myself to be with people.
> I finally took a smaller apartment with a community meeting place. It was hard at first but now I can navigate alone and still be an asset rather than a liability to my family. Occasionally a few friends will stop by and see me. I volunteer at the hospital and do my own chores.

It took Frank more than a year to routinize his life and adjust to his changed status, but he rallied his resources and strength to make his life meaningful again.

Support for Widows and Widowers

The ongoing necessity of taking care of everyday matters continues during the mourning process. Therefore it may seem to others that the bereaved mate is managing well, making it easier for others to disregard the need for support. Men and women who are working and have regularity and structure to their lives appear adjusted, but actually have less time and energy for the expression of feelings. Feelings are kept under control during the day while at work or in public, and often burst forth at the end of the day, resulting in "evening mourning" or "weekend mourning." Sometimes the process of inhibition of feelings becomes generalized and the capacity for expression is forfeited. This may result in delayed or prolonged mourning.

It is not easy to find permission to mourn for the length of time needed. You need someone to talk to. Ruth related that after her husband died, she found the most comfort and understanding from other widows and widowers who were willing to listen and talk with her.

> No one seemed to understand the turmoil and torment in the way other widows and widowers did. It stirred up memories for others who had already been through it. In that way it helped them to work out more of their feelings. It was an equal opportunity for mourning. Hearing about their problems was not another burden for me, but reassurance that I was normal.

Stewart said:

> I just wanted to talk to someone about my agony. About two months after the death of my wife, I felt my restlessness and pain increasing. I thought "Will this never end? I thought I would feel better by now but I am feeling worse." I had this strong need to ask others: "Did you feel this terrible? Did it last this long? When will I feel better?"
>
> I wanted only to commiserate with others. Finally I called one man, apologetically, asked him to talk and to allow me to share my feelings. I wanted to hear what he could tell me about the duration of this pain. We talked for two hours. He told me how he had agonized. How he would go to work, then get into his car at the end of the day and cry on the way home. The way he shared his grief with me was comforting. Just talking and listening to him made me feel better.

The mutual support among the bereaved has led to the formation of support groups throughout the country sponsored by social service agencies, community centers, mental health centers, churches, and private therapists.

> Betty said she usually kept her feelings to herself. Nevertheless, when the tensions became too great to ignore, she joined a support group. "I was able to share and cry with others and it made me feel stronger."

Betty's reaction is a common one. Since the "Widow to Widow" program was started by Phyllis Silverman in Boston in 1970 thousands of widows and widowers have benefited from sharing their common experience and have regained their equilibrium.[6] Without the opportunity for grieving openly with a person or a group where patience and support are available, your reaction may be to withdraw in order to avoid rejection by people who are not sympathetic to your plight. Ruth offered:

> Another thing I learned quite unexpectedly from other widows and widowers was that my life might still have *joie de vivre*. The strings of my life were gently pulled again and I began to see and imagine possibilities for the future. It was exciting, but I also felt afraid and even guilty at the same time. Jeff was dead but I could still have a life. It wasn't fair. Then my own needs emerged as they will with healthy persons, and that led me to pursue pleasure again.

You learn from others that everything is different, will change and change again, but that life can be good again. It may not be the way you would prefer or the way you had anticipated things would be, but your circumstances will improve.

THE BEREAVED PARENT

The bereaved spouse is left to complete the job of raising children as a single parent. You are confronted with the task of mourning and helping the children to mourn and the parallel task of being a single parent.

Recovering from the loss can be compared to a long convalescence following an illness. It is emotionally and physically exhausting. It becomes even more complicated when there are children whose needs are waiting to be fulfilled. The children's needs may have been a priority in the past, but you feel that you need taking care of also at this time. It is difficult to take care of yourself emotionally and take good emotional care of your children also. You can try to do both and do the best you can. The intensity of need and conflict was expressed by several widows. Bonnie reflected:

I just didn't feel I had the energy to deal with the children. It was too much. I thought if I didn't take care of myself, of my needs, I would die. I wanted to scream at the children, "Who's going to take care of me?" There was a pull for me to do something for myself. I had to be with other adults. I had to find someone to comfort me, someone who was not grieving. I was obsessed with my need for companionship and comfort. I did find it, but the truth was that it took time and energy away from the children. But I felt I wouldn't survive otherwise or be of help to them.

Grief is not only all-consuming, it is also self-consuming and self-centered. You think of yourself, your own pain, your own suffering. That becomes predominant. Within a family the adults often make a choice, consciously or unconsciously, by attending to the others and denying self, or by ignoring others and indulging self. Sometimes there may be a shifting of focus from self to others in an attempt to attend to everyone. This requires juggling feelings around, and is just as precarious and takes as much concentration and effort as performing a physical juggling act. Ruth tells about her juggling in taking care of her own needs while aware of her family's needs and trying to meet those also.

I had so many things to do. I had to gather information for the attorneys and accountants, pay bills, maintain the house and yard, prepare for full-time employment, keep up with "thank you" notes and phone calls, pick out a tombstone, prepare for the holidays, finish my husband's work, and take care of his customers. All this while maintaining some regularity in the house so the children would not feel any additional shaking-up and, most importantly, to keep them talking about their emotions. Even with all these demands and my awareness of the *importance of the continued expression of feelings by the children and that it depended on my direction,* the most dominant thing for me was my own pain and finding some relief and expression for myself.

My husband used to scold me and say, "You're always thinking about the children. You're always concerned about what is right for them." I thought of that many times when all I could think about was my own needs. How everything had changed! I felt selfish.

I just couldn't get it all together. I was late for everything—appointments, the children's music lessons, programs at school, their athletic events. I was late with dinner. I knew what I had to do; I just couldn't do anything very well. It's still hard for me to accept that's how I was the first year and that I really was mixed up. I wish I could have done more for the children. There was so much to do, too much, and I did the best I could at the time. That's all any of us can do. I try to comfort myself with that.

Sally Robbins dreaded facing Thanksgiving and Christmas without her husband. She wanted to take the children away to avoid the contradiction of the "happy holidays" and the sadness and emptiness without his presence. Tom, fourteen years old, objected so strenuously to the idea, she bowed to his wishes and somehow struggled through the weeks of preparation and the actual holiday season. The pressure became almost more than Sally could bear. "I've been through the worst emotional crisis of my life, even worse than when Bob died. I didn't have the energy to reach out and ask for help. I couldn't help the children. I had nothing to give."

It was burdensome for Sally to respond to her son's wishes and deal with her own reactions to the stressful situation. If you express and deal with your feelings, you will be more able to attend to your children. Your own emotional health is necessary for the health and equilibrium of the family. It would be impossible for the parent *consistently* to respond to children's emotional needs at this time. Nevertheless, the adult can be aware of what is happening to the children and try to respond to them. If you use words to tell them how *you* feel, it will help them to understand and will encourage them to do the same. It will still be difficult for all of you, but sharing your feelings will contribute to understanding.

Children may be frightened or upset when a mother or father cries, has to struggle to get out of bed in the morning, or becomes too preoccupied to attend to them. They worry when dinner is not prepared or their clothes are not laundered. They may worry about adequate money for things they need or want, or that emotional support will not be available. When father or mother is late getting home from work, hides behind a newspaper, or is closed off in a room, the children feel uncared for and abandoned. The children feel deprivation on two levels: the loss of one parent through death, the changes in the other through mourning.

It is helpful to have the support of someone outside the family who is not in mourning. Relatives and friends sometimes provide this as in a family where the brother-in-law of a young widow stopped by every day to spend time with her two little boys.

Do not hesitate to call for the help of a family bereavement therapist. Over a period of two years in family therapy, the Robbins have learned to examine and articulate their feelings. The tensions have eased and the arguments among siblings have decreased. The family has gained insight into the effects of grief on each as a person and on the family. They have more understanding of each other.

Single Parenting

Two parents provide balance and division of roles and responsibilities in child rearing. When one parent dies, the other is left to assume the tasks of both. Parental authority becomes a problem because it is so hard to strike a balance between acceptance and discipline. Both the children's behavior and your parental response are complicated by the change in roles, as in the following case:

> Enforcing rules was difficult for me. My husband and I together did a good job. When I tried to be firm and enforce rules, my teen-aged son said: "Don't try to be authoritarian. It doesn't become you." He rebelled against my taking on that role and made it harder for me, and for himself, too, in the long run.

The following quotations typify the feelings of many single parents. Regardless of the age of the parent or the children, there is agreement that raising children is a complex operation better suited to execution by two parents.

Burt, age thirty-four, reported:

> Despite all the support from my family, enough money for competent babysitters, and other help with the children, sometimes I was very angry. I felt cheated. I would yell at my wife: "I don't want to do this alone. We had them together and you left. You should be here helping me."

Forty-five-year-old Lillian, whose children were in their early teens, said:

> Everyone has problems with children and people say it wouldn't be different if David were alive. But it would be different for me because he would support me, buffer me. Although we often differed on how to handle a situation, it was still doing it together.

Learning to be a single parent is a tough process for the parent and is also tough for the children. Edie related:

> When something goes wrong, Mom says, "It wouldn't be this way if your father was here." It makes me feel guilty because she has all the pressures. Two people could handle those pressures. Anyway, I get mad and my sister and I get into fights.

Ruth said:

> Children vent their feelings on a convenient target. I feel as if I took the rap for the misfortune. I tried hard to balance out the roles of two parents and provide as much as I could, materially and emotionally, but even that was resented. The anger the children had at their father for dying came back to me. They behaved angrily toward me. I never got any appreciation. I got a lot of criticism and lack of cooperation.

The expression of feelings about the death is essential in order to avoid the displacement of feelings onto the parent or other siblings. If parents and children share their feelings, many misunderstandings can be eliminated.

THE TRANSITION FROM COUPLE TO SINGLE

One of the difficult things for a widowed person to accept is the role change from being part of a couple to a single person. Couples who have been married 20 years or more can barely remember being single. Most of the things they have planned and done over the years, even their thought processes, have been based on their partnership. This is true even in marriages where the relationship has been challenging or troubled. It takes time to accept the term and concept of *widow* or *widower*. It takes time to think in terms of "I" rather than "we" and to talk of your loved one in the past tense rather than in the present.

Widows and widowers have conflicting feelings about removing their wedding ring. It is the symbol of marriage and being part of a couple. It is difficult to leave these concepts behind and consider yourself a widow or widower, to confront the fact that you are now unmarried, single. It involves giving up the attachment to your deceased mate. Removing your wedding ring is a step forward in accepting your singleness and letting go of the past. This takes many months for some people and years for others.

Some men and women quickly and matter-of-factly remove the ring or have it redesigned or reset. Others replace the wedding band with a decorative ring. For the older widow or widower, the thought never occurs to them to remove the ring. They consider themselves married until their own death. Remarriage feels unlikely, and psychologically the marriage continues. Anniversaries continue to be counted as if the mate were still alive.

Many persons move the ring from the left hand to right hand and continue to wear it that way. This is a good first step. In some cultures the wedding ring is worn on the right hand and switched to the left after the death of the husband. Any change is a step in the process of emotional separation.

Ruth struggled with the notion of removing her ring. It had been worn for 23 years and felt like part of her. She was still very much involved with her grief, even when she started to date. It seemed hypocritical to wear the ring symbolizing her marriage to Jeff.

I got home one night from a date and looked at my ring and decided I had to do something different about it. It was so foreign to think about being without it. I decided I would take it off when I went on a date. At night I put on my gold band with the precious inscription on the inside. This *off-on* routine lasted still another year. Finally, with great resolve, I decided to remove it. I purchased another ring and wore that every day which helped me make the transition. Now I wear no ring at all. I feel single and this symbolizes my singleness.

The ambivalence is apparent throughout the whole process. It illustrates the struggle to accept your new status and put the marriage to rest. There is no rush and, as with other things, the mourner ought to take as much time as he or she needs.

RESUMING SOCIAL ACTIVITIES

Widows and widowers feel ambivalent about resuming social activities. You may not want to go out at first but feel that if you refuse invitations people will not understand or will stop inviting you.

Debby forced herself to go out.

> I really felt my loneliness. I had so many people who loved me, but I felt my loss. I just wanted to be married. I remember being bored to death at a party; I didn't want to be there, but I didn't want to be alone either. I didn't know what to do. After a few tries I decided I was not ready for the social scene.

Don went to his office Christmas party. They were old friends and acquaintances. It was pleasant but on the way home he cried.

> It was no fun to be at a party when I didn't have my wife at my side. I wanted to talk it over with her and say, "Did you see her?" "What did you think of that?"

You may feel uncomfortable about being with other couples, even very old and dear friends. Because you no longer qualify as a part of the couple world, you may feel superfluous in their company. You may want the comfort of the familiar faces, but seeing them together may kindle resentment. Seeing other pairs emphasizes that you are no longer part of a pair and that things are not the way you want them to be.

Eileen Ryan's description of her feelings is typical.

> I hated to even walk the dog in the evening. Every house which I passed had a couple in the garden, or I could see them together through the window. I resented every couple I passed.

It is not that you do not want others to have their togetherness, but seeing other couples and families intact is a reminder of what is missing for you. When you become accustomed to your new status and work out your feelings, your resentment will diminish and disappear.

The change in social relationships is often experienced as another loss. When first resuming social activities, widows and widowers usually go along with old friends who are coupled. This may change as invitations from your previous social contacts decrease. Sometimes single persons feel patronized by others or are uneasy themselves about being unpaired. Some widows and widowers try to continue their social life as if they were still part of a couple. They reject the company of other single persons except for lunches and meetings. You may find that you need to develop new friends who are single also and who have interests similar to yours.

Dating and Relationships

After the death of a mate it seems out of the question to be with another man or woman, but there comes a time when the need for continuity, closeness, and being part of a pair may lead to an overwhelming desire for a relationship. There is a desire to recapture what was lost. Wanting a relationship is also a normal response to the deprivation of both emotional and physiological needs that had been met during your marriage and that now have no outlet. It seems unthinkable to pair up with another person because what you really want is to have your partner back. Loneliness and sexual needs become enmeshed with your love and grief. You may feel conflict between wanting your lost mate and everything the relationship meant to you, and feeling the need for a new relationship. After two or three months, many persons find their longing to be part of a pair again very intense.

Ruth's need to be close to a man coexisted at the same time that her pain over the death of her husband became more acute. The need to be with someone was different for her than the desire to date, dating being defined as going out in public with a man, to dinner or a movie.

> I did not want to date, to go out in public. The idea of this made me very uncomfortable. After my husband's death, I felt so much a part of him and very much married. The idea of being with another man or dating seemed repugnant to me. Somehow, in my mind, I thought I surely wouldn't go out for a year. An old friend called and it was good talking to him. I still was not interested in going out or in being with him but I did want to talk. It was strange, but somehow the idea of contact with another man made me feel there was still a future for me, there was still some hope. Perhaps my

life would not be all sad and lonely. It pulled at a special string in my heart and gave me some hope for the future.

Howard wrote about driving to Florida and how the long hours of solitude helped him sort out a lot of things in his mind.

> I was alone and simply had to come to the realization that my Cynthia was not coming back and I had best make something of the rest of my life and I realized that feminine company was something I needed and craved. The lonesomeness does get me down.

A phenomenon very perplexing to the widow or widower, and probably even more so to others, is the overlap of grieving and the need to be with another person of the opposite sex. The mergence seems strange and confusing but it does exist. The bereaved spouse is at the same time a person with needs. The following lines by the poet Harriet Zinnes captures the meshing of past and present, hurt and hope.

> I am looking inside
> It is a mirror
> I see you and *you* and me
> I see three
>
> I see you and *you* become you
> Then I see you and *you* become you
> You are *you*
> And both of you
> Live with me
> I am three
>
> But you are living
> and *you* are dead
> And I am living-dead
>
> Therefore my head
> my poor head
> it feels like lead
> when I see three
> and am living-dead
> Still, in my head, as Aurelius said,
> I am spinning the thread
> of my being.
>
> There is nothing to dread
> for it is a purple thread

and a flaming red
on the top of my head
that feels like lead
with the three heads
that my heart has bred
out of that spinning thread
of my being.[7]

Harriet Zinnes

For many people, early dating involves sharing the story of the loss with the other person and often creates an immediate pseudointimacy. Persons will relate to each other out of their loss. Ruth recounted:

Toward the end of my first year of mourning, I consented to go out on a date. I got dressed up and looked very well, but I was so jumpy inside and so uncomfortable being with a man, being across from him at dinner. Much of the conversation was about our deceased spouses. My husband kept coming into the forefront of my mind and feelings. I felt ambivalent about talking about him while out with another man, but I was still very much attached to my husband. In fact, I was still wearing my wedding band. It was strange, too, that on the dashboard of the automobile was the name of my date's deceased wife. It was as if the two of them were very much present with both of us.

Eventually you get to the point where you don't want to listen to stories about the other's mate or the anxieties of the person across the dinner table. Mort said:

Everyone wanted to fix me up with their favorite widow or divorcee. After about 10 months I succumbed and called a woman. She was small, thin, and blond and looked like Helen. But all she talked about was her husband. I wasn't interested in her past. My life was new and I wanted to live in the present, not the past.

When you are still mourning, it is difficult to refrain from talking about the past. The past and the present overlap. You are in a period of transition with feelings that do not seem to fit together. A widow related:

When I would go out in public, I really didn't enjoy myself. I wanted to go out, but I felt I was with the wrong person. I felt so uncomfortable about seeing my friends and acquaintances and introducing my date. It just wasn't right. I was with the wrong person.

After she had attended a wedding with a single friend, Dee said:

I missed my husband so. I wanted someone to dance with. And then
I realized what I wanted. I wanted to dance with Don. We knew how to
dance with each other. We didn't step on each other's feet.

Feelings of disloyalty are also stirred up.

Mort shared: I didn't want my friends to think ill of me. I thought, in a way, it was casting a reflection on Helen.

Debbie offered: I was afraid to let his family know because I sensed they would think I was disloyal. Perhaps I thought so.

Even though being a part of a pair again is welcome, the process of dating is often unwelcome and uncomfortable for many men and women. There is a strain to be on your best behavior, to make a good impression, and worry about being attractive and interesting. Ruth said: "I miss being accepted as a whole package, with my strengths and my weaknesses. Now I'm concerned about being accepted and liked." It seems like repeating an adolescent phase of your life. While it is appropriate in adolescence, it is unwelcome in adulthood. Mort said:

I began to realize this was a different situation; something I'd never experienced before. I hadn't dated much as a youngster because I met Helen when I was very young and that was it. In fact, I felt kind of foolish. You look at yourself and think, "It's all kid stuff." You feel this whole dating game is immature. The whole thing was difficult.

You need to start all over again to find someone with common interests, someone with similar views and values. You may want someone who will blend with your life and family in its present form, but you will come to realize that so much will be different.

A growing number of women take the initiative in making a call to a man to invite him to dinner, a concert, or a ball game. After Nancy's death Ken's phone started ringing.

In those first months I had more invitations to dine from widows, divorcees, and unmarried women than I knew how to handle. And in all these years, almost 10 now, it's never stopped. I've just stopped being astounded. I rarely call a woman for a date.

Another man related:

> It was great for my ego but it was not how I grew up. I got a different perspective on women. I had calls from women who were very nice, cultured, and educated. I didn't have to call for a date, they called me.

The desire for social companionship is expressed in the initiative taken by women in seeking out new friends. As age increases, women outnumber men since their life span is generally eight years longer.[8] Statistics rather than personal qualities will deprive many women of the opportunity of another close relationship with a man. Creating new social activities will be another challenge.

Sexuality

Men and women both experience the welling up of sexual feelings and the need for closeness. Sexual expression is the polarity to death. It is an attempt to counteract the burdensome feelings of grief. The desire and need for sexual contact is normal and can be an enjoyable part of a relationship. One woman related her intimate feelings.

> I was surprised at what happened to me several months after my husband's death. I began to have sexual feelings that welled up inside me. For 24 years these sensations had only been experienced in conjunction with my husband. I was surprised that they existed within me in the absence of him as the stimulus. This was confusing. What was I going to do about all this, if anything?
>
> What was most surprising to me was that while I was deeply mourning my husband, I wanted to be with another man. These opposites existed within me at the same time. I knew no one else would understand. I didn't understand myself. I only knew it was true.
>
> My loneliness increased my need for love-making. I was surprised at my own sexual behavior. I had been faithful during all the years of my marriage and had been a virgin at the time of marriage, but values had nothing to do with my behavior now. What was most prominent for me was my need for closeness. Values, previous behavior, and intelligence had little effect on my present behavior.

Sometimes, no matter what your resolve, the need is so great, you do things that may surprise you. As one widower said:

> I didn't believe it was me, it was so out of character, but there I was actually inviting a woman into my bed. She was someone I had known for a long time. Looking back, it's hard to believe I did that. But I so needed to be held, to be intimate.

One source of irritability or restlessness may be the lack of sexual fulfillment. It is better to be aware and acknowledge your needs and take care of yourself in the way that is best for you. This is a very personal matter, and you may do things you have not done. You may find yourself in situations that are very uncharacteristic of you. This is normal behavior during this period of your life when you find yourself without a spouse. There are times, regardless of age, when the heightened sex drive is a reaction to sex problems during the marriage.

> Eileen was sixty-one when her husband died. She was surprised to find herself enjoying a relationship a few months later. "My sexual feelings were and are mixed as Ryan and I hadn't lived together as man and wife for almost 18 years. Life was barren, sexually speaking. Anyway, my sexual feelings are as strong if not stronger, mind you, than when I was a young girl."

Not everyone will find that being intimate with another person is a satisfactory solution, even if a temporary one. You may find taking care of yourself is more comfortable for you or you may direct your energy into physical activities. Often hard work diminishes the sexual drive. Some people find their desire wanes after a period of time.

Sexual encounters are often unsatisfactory and conflict-ridden, especially in the beginning. You may think about your deceased spouse and become sad and emotional. You may feel disloyal or unfaithful because you are still emotionally attached to your spouse. These reactions are also normal and part of your mourning. This will change for you as you move gradually toward separation from the past. Both men and women report that their sexual drive diminished in the first few months after the death or when the spouse was ill for a long time. There are times when a spouse's death leaves the mate feeling the role as a lover is over and desire has died. Mort reported:

> We had practically no sex the last couple years of Helen's life. It ceased to be so important. I honestly believed myself to be impotent. The desire was there for the person, but the act of sex was something I didn't think she could enjoy. It was rare. But I thought I was impotent anyway. It turns out I was wrong: my courtship and remarriage proved that, but I had no desire even after Helen's death.

> Betty had become accustomed to celibacy during her husband's illness. "Once I knew he was not capable, then I just crossed that off my mind." After Roy died, she told her sister-in-law: "I live better without a man than to just pick anyone. At least I have peace of mind."

You will need to decide for yourself what is best for you as you accommodate to your widowhood.

New Relationships

Your emotional and physical needs are different during the first years following the loss of your mate than they will be later. Needs will change as time passes and you integrate your loss. It is therefore, wise to be cautious about making commitments in a new relationship even if you become close to someone. It is important to let go of the past relationship and separate from the mate who has died before entering into an exclusive relationship. Unfinished business from the past intrudes on the present and interferes with new relationships. Some persons seek remarriage to re-establish their social position. Eileen wanted to belong to the couples world. "Walking out of the courthouse in Las Vegas the day I was married I felt: 'Hey, I belong again. Crazy, huh?'" She felt she had been handed a new ticket of admission, the marriage license. It is a sad commentary to think you belong or are worthy only when you are married, or when you rely on marriage to give you self-esteem.

People who remarry *after they have integrated the death of their mate* may still be sad about the death and continue to miss the mate on special occasions, but it is not as prominent as it was during mourning. Many speak of the deceased with tears in their eyes and observe the anniversary of the death and other significant dates. Remarriage does not eradicate all feelings, and usually there are sensitive areas that remain. Although Eileen was thrilled to be married again, she was surprised by her own feelings.

> I *still* miss Ryan as much now as I did the day he died! This surprises me, truly, as I'm married to such a lovely man. He's sweet, kind, and spoils me rotten, which Ryan never did. It's been five years since he died, and I *still* miss him. He was one of a kind, that's for sure.

Some people are fortunate to find another person to form a partnership with again. Howard reported:

> I was married to my Cynthia for 43 years and loved her dearly. Her loss left me so low and despondent I actually felt that I was beginning to just plain feel sorry for myself.
> On a trip I met Mildred...a lovely lady who had a similar experience, a long, loving marriage and several years of suffering at the end. We talked and talked, and I went back and forth to Florida that whole spring. We were married last July, with a wedding party consisting of 25 children.

Neither of us can believe that after so much love with our first spouses we could find such love and happiness again.

Relationships which develop out of loss and mutual empathy should be tested over time and circumstances. When needs are great and two people come together out of painful places and loneliness, the quality of the relationship may be misjudged. Your judgment may be clouded by your grief. The important components of a long-term relationship will often be overlooked as the intense need for connectedness takes precedence. Give yourself time to feel whole and strong. Then you will have a good foundation for a relationship or for living your life as a single person. Many men and women remain single because they do not find the person that would make a satisfactory partner. Many persons choose to remain single and develop other satisfactions in their lives.

6

HELPING CHILDREN AND ADOLESCENTS TO MOURN

THE DEATH OF A PARENT

"Did they wake my mommy up yet?" Lisa's fearfully expectant question burst from her as she entered the house. Grandma reached out her arms, "No, darling," she said, "they couldn't wake up your mommy. Your mommy died." "I knew it, I knew it," the seven-year-old said. "I stepped on her foot and she didn't move. She didn't even say ouch."

At some level she had recognized her mother was dead but needed verification.

Lisa had phoned her grandma early that morning to complain her mommy was sleeping on the living room floor and she couldn't awaken her. When Grandma entered the house a few minutes later, she hurried the child off to school as she phoned the doctor and an ambulance. Now she was faced with the task of helping Lisa, whose father had died when she was an infant, understand the tragic news.

"Will you be my mommy now?" the child asked.

"No, Lisa, I'm your grandmother. You can never have another mommy. But I'll take care of you. I love you."

Typical of a child, Lisa was worried about the fulfillment of her needs.

Lisa sat within Grandma's comforting embrace, crying softly. When her tears dried, she huddled into the corner of a chair. It seemed as if she were mulling over the events, trying to take in the reality of this terrible thing that had happened. After a little while, she began to talk. "I went to say goodnight to Mommy. She's been sick. I made her a get-well card and I made her a Mother's Day card. I gave her a scarf for Mother's Day, and I want that scarf! And I want her jewelry!" she said as if afraid someone would deny her these precious mememtos.

Lisa wanted to hang onto her mother with these symbols and needed to reaffirm the tie to her. She also needed these possessions to identify with her mother and stay part of her.

Her paternal grandmother said, "I have a scarf at home. I'll bring you that scarf," unaware of the message the child was conveying. "Don't cry, Lisa, everything's going to be all right. You'll go back to school and soon you'll forget your sadness." Although well meaning, she denied the magnitude of the loss. "You be a good girl now. Your mommy is watching you. She'll know everything you do." She patted Lisa's head, not realizing the impact of the words she had just uttered.

It is uncomfortable to think that you are not free but are constantly being watched. This does not feel like the protection that the nine-year-old Arnold boy felt mentioned in Chapter 4. He felt as if his brother were "rooting" for him, and was tied in with his own religious belief: a mysterious presence was implied by the grandmother. It can also be interpreted by a child as not really dead.

Friends and family began to gather and Lisa ran to greet each who entered the room. "Did you hear the bad news?" she asked, anxious to talk with everyone about her mother. Each time she said this was an attempt to make it real.

A neighbor came in carrying a shopping bag that caught Lisa's attention. It contained one of her mother's dresses and a pair of shoes to be taken to the undertaker. "I want those shoes," she demanded. "My mommy used to let me wear them to play dress up. I want those shoes." Someone said, "Those things are to dress your mommy for the funeral. There are plenty of shoes around, you can have other shoes to play with."

This was another insensitivity to the symbolic need to keep meaningful possessions. After all, any shoes would do to dress a corpse, but not any shoes were significant to this seven-year-old.

She sat with her aunt in the evening having milk and cookies. "What does dead mean? I don't understand 'dead,'" she kept asking. She was struggling to comprehend the concept of death.

"Do you remember seeing a dead bug?" her aunt asked. "What was it like?" Lisa thought for a moment. "Well, it can't move. It can't walk. It can't see. I still don't understand it." Her aunt tried again. "When you're dead, you don't have feelings." Lisa sat quietly, thinking. "Yes," she replied, "*but I have feelings and I'm sad*." They cried together.

Lisa turned suddenly to her Grandma and asked if she could go to the funeral and was reassured that she could. Grandma, whose energy was drained due to her own devastation because of the death of her daughter and the tasks involved, said "I thought I would tell her what to expect at the funeral while driving to the funeral home." Auntie suggested it would be better if she were prepared ahead of time. She volunteered to talk to Lisa and took her to a quiet room.

She described simply the routine that would be followed the day of the funeral. Lisa was told that when she awakened in the morning she would get dressed and have her breakfast; then a big car would come to drive her, her grandmother, and other relatives to the funeral home. She described the physical setup of the funeral home, the chapel where the family sits, and the coffin and explained that people would come to talk to the family and say they were sorry. Then everyone would sit quietly while the clergy-man said some prayers and talked about what her mommy was like and how everyone loved her. Lisa listened carefully to the explanation of the way the relatives and friends say goodbye to the person who has died and how seeing the visitors helps the family feel better.

Auntie described the drive to the cemetery, prayers at the grave, how the coffin is lowered into the ground, and covered with earth. The child listen-ed, asked a few questions, then sat very still, trying to absorb all she had heard.

Next day, after the clergyman completed the services and people started to leave the chapel, Lisa rose from her chair and started toward the coffin. "I want to see my mother," she stated firmly. Attendants opened the top of the coffin as she walked slowly toward it with her Grandma. The sor-rowful little girl stood there for a moment, half raised her right arm and flexed her fingers in a gesture of farewell. "Goodbye, Mommy," she murmured and turned toward the comfort of her grandma's arms.

On the way to the cemetery, she asked questions adults would not have anticipated. "The coffin looks so long, will it fit into the hearse?" Lisa asked her grandma to have the coffin lowered into the ground and she put a cupful of earth on it. Then the prayers were recited. Grandma stayed next to her. She cried quietly on the way home. Back at grandma's house at the gathering of condolence, Lisa was overwhelmed by the number of people. She sat quietly in a chair sucking her thumb, clutching a stuffed animal. She was comforted by the visits of her teachers and friends.

Lisa stayed with grandma until the end of the summer. Grandma under-stood her need to cry, to have her questions answered, and her need for reassurance. When the house in which she had lived with her mother was sold, Lisa went with grandma to sort through her mother's possessions.

That summer the family gathered to work out the best plan for Lisa's growing up years. The decision was made for her to live with her mother's sister in another city. In her aunt's home the child had cousins near her own age making the adjustment easier for her. Although it was rather soon to remove her from her familiar environment, it worked out well for Lisa. She has made a good adjustment. She now calls her aunt "Mother," although she remembers her own mother, misses her, and talks about her.

The first summer after the death when she visited her Grandma, Lisa was heard explaining to her new friends: "My mother and daddy are really my aunt and uncle, but I call them Mommy and Daddy. My *real* mother died last year." She was matter-of-fact and she *offered* the information. She was not answering questions posed by others. These were continued attempts to deal with reality. Being in her old environment stirred up her feelings. When she came back for the stone setting, it was important to her to let her relatives know that there was a permanent memorial lamp for her mother in her new home town.

Three years after the death, Grandma related: "Her adjustment there is good. They treat her like one of their own, even to disciplining her. We were there in October and everything seemed to be fine." Lisa's new family has given her the stability, care, and love that are essential when a child's parent dies. She is encouraged to express her feelings. On the anniversary of her mother's death, her aunt helped her light a memorial candle. The family went to a restaurant for dinner. Lisa was quiet and morose and her aunt asked what was wrong. "We just lit the candle for my mommy and I'm feeling very sad," she said. "I just can't forget about it."

The prognosis for Lisa's emotional health is good because she is allowed to keep her feelings and memories close to the surface and to express them. For children, mourning continues for many years as they are only able to withstand small amounts of painful feelings. It is important that feelings remain accessible to children so that they are able to mourn in small bits over a long time. Lisa's family supported the expression of her feelings while integrating her into the new family and fulfilling her needs.

Lisa's story is an example of the immense supportive value of guidance from knowing and sensitive adults. Her grandmother and aunt invited help from experienced persons and gave Lisa permission to mourn. This child was allowed to say and do what was helpful for her in dealing with the death of her mother. This illustrates that children can recover from a traumatic event with adequate support and fulfillment of needs even though sadness and other feelings remain a part of them.

Children are deeply affected by loss of any kind: loss of a parent through death, divorce, or separation; loss of a sibling or other close relative or friend through death. Each loss may affect the personality and emotional development of the child. Whatever the loss, children need adult understanding to guide them through mourning. They cannot do it alone. They need a role model, guidance, and permission to grieve openly.

Children who are separated from parents experience profound grief.[1] To hide their pain and confusion, children often assume a detached attitude that is misinterpreted as indifference. People who are unfamiliar with how children respond to grief tend to think they are resilient and somehow magically overcome the trauma. One often hears people say: "They'll get over it"; "they'll forget about it"; "they'll outgrow it." These ideas are prompted by the misunderstanding that only adults are vulnerable to emotional pain. Children are *more* vulnerable because the personality is still forming and they do not have the capability of dealing with grief. They need understanding adults to help them attach language to their feelings.

For a young person the death of a parent is an excruciating experience. Clinical experience underscores the significant impact of this loss. Data exist that link the loss of a parent in childhood to psychological problems later in life.[2] It is important to recognize children's needs and their emotional experience when a parent or other close relative dies and the way adults can help children work through their grief.

TEACHING CHILDREN ABOUT LOSS AND DEATH: A FAMILY ISSUE

Every child faces some losses as he or she grows: developmental losses, a special friend moves away, a favorite toy disappears, a pet dies. Parents can take advantage of the opportunity to teach about separation and endings. Learning about loss and death is an essential part of early childhood education. It is helpful if the concept of death is understood before a child has to experience the death of a significant person.[3] The teaching process can begin when a child is two to three years old, when he or she observes evidence of the life cycle in plants, insects, and animals. Nature presents many teaching opportunities. A child can be shown the difference between an insect on the wing and a dead one on the ground. Sight of a dead bird or animal beside the road is another opening for an explanation of the meaning of "dead."

Most children have pets of one kind or another—goldfish, kittens, puppies, hamsters—and it is inevitable that one of them will die. The child can be encouraged to acknowledge and express his or her feelings about the loss. Adults often hurry to replace the pet in an attempt to avoid hurt in the child. This denies the child the awareness and experience of loss. If the pet is quickly replaced, the child will miss the opportunity of learning about a basic concept of death, its permanence. When a child has the ability to comprehend it can be explained that even though a person's body returns to the earth, their personality lives on in our memories. You need to use your judgment about what to tell them, when and how. Do not thrust more information on them than they are ready to assimilate.

Religious faith can be sustaining but quasi-religious explanations can also be confusing to a child. Children often conjure up their own image of heaven and imagine people and animals walking around in "heaven" (usually in the sky) carrying on daily tasks just as on earth. Children's conceptions and misconceptions are endless. It is up to the adults to clarify these abstract ideas and not use them to avoid dealing with explanations and feelings.

Children struggle with death on two levels, intellectually and emotionally. They try to absorb the concept while dealing with their feelings. They try to understand that dead means the person or pet will not return, that death is permanent and irreversible. The person no longer has senses; does not eat, sleep, run, play, or have feelings of happiness or sadness.[4] That the *survivors* have feelings, needs to be acknowledged. As Lisa said, "*I* have feelings and *I'm* sad."

Children generally acquire the intellectual concept of the meaning of death between five and eight years, depending on their intelligence, education, and experience.[5] They are often creative in finding ways to aid in their understanding of the concept of death.

> The two little Richards boys, aged four and a half and six, were acting out and fighting a lot. The therapist talked openly with them about what a terrible thing it was when their daddy died. It was explained that dead meant their daddy was not coming back. They would reply: "Oh, yes he is, he's coming back. We'll see him again." As a result of using words and play, their understanding gradually changed. They would create new myths: "We're going to invent this magic potion to bring Daddy back and make him alive again. He'll come and stay with us." The older one would say, "I know it can't be, but I still wish it."

They were beginning to understand the reality of his absence and that his return was their wish, but not possible. Children work out their feelings through play and fantasy. Talking with the Richards children helped them bring these fantasies into the open. Thus their misconceptions were rectified and the father's death confronted.

When someone dies, often the family does not know how to relate it to a young child. Stories may be fabricated in an effort to protect. Rather than palliatives, children need to be told the truth in a sensitive and supportive manner. The loss is sensed and exerts tremendous force on the normal growth and development. A toddler has limited verbal ability and only the beginnings of concept development, so there is no way to understand death and no mechanism for mourning. Mourning is expressing and that is dependent on language. It is therefore an especially complex problem and grief work spans the years. The very first step is to provide a loving parent substitute who will care for the young child. This can bring comfort and help ease some of the fear and feeling of abandonment. A sudden death is difficult to explain to a young child, but sometimes unexpected things happen that we have no control over and this aspect must be shared. If the deceased is elderly, it can be explained as part of the life cycle. It is natural for old people to die.

The use of euphemisms is an evasion of the reality and may indicate the adult's difficulty in facing death. Using the phrases "passed away" or "we lost grandma" to tell a child someone has died is not recommended. Children are confused by ambiguous words.

A mother related the death of her infant to her seven-year-old son Sammy: "Walter is with God," she said. Sammy answered, "You mean he died."

One of the fictions that people use to evade the truth is to tell a small child the person has gone away, or gone on a trip, or gone to eternal rest. This kind of avoidance can lead to feelings of abandonment, anxiety, and troubles like those that assailed John.

> His mother died when he was four and he was told she had gone away on a trip. Not until he sought psychiatric help 25 years later was he able to understand why he agonized over saying goodbye to anyone, even for a simple everyday thing like leaving home to go to work or to the post office.

He wasn't helped to understand the difference between gone and dead. When someone is gone, we expect the person to come back. When dead, there is no return.

> When Peggy was two years old, her father died suddenly at home. She often repeats what she had been told: "My Daddy died. He's in heaven with Jesus. He's not coming back." When she looks at her father's picture she recites this. Even after two years she tells her friends, as Lisa did, that her Daddy is dead. She was given a quasi-religious explanation along with the essential meaning of death with the correct words.
>
> One day when she visited the therapist with her aunt and mother, she reenacted the scene of his death with a life-sized doll. It was all done without words. It was a powerful experience for everyone. After leaving the office, she cried all afternoon. She often awakens at night crying. Once she ran to

the window and said: "The green car is gone" (her father's). The way she is struggling to understand and integrate the death is apparent. She has people around her who have given her the appropriate words and permission to express her feelings.

CHILDREN AND ADOLESCENTS NEED GUIDANCE

Adults need to give the words to children to help them express their feelings. They seldom can do it alone. It is a rare child like Lisa who can express herself so well.

Because of the adults' resistance, they may not acknowledge and deal with the children's feelings. They hide their own reluctance and inadequacy with the excuse that since children do not understand death, they do not have feelings about it. The understanding may not be there, but the feelings are and that is just what makes it more difficult.

> Wilma's mother died in childbirth when Wilma was five. No one talked with the little girl about her mother's death. "There was no such thing as help for children in those days. They thought children forgot...were resilient...." The memory of her mother's death so many years before surfaced when a close friend died. "The grief wasn't really articulated back then; it's more feeling than words, and I never thought much to put any words to it."
>
> "You have not been able to put the feelings into words?" the therapist asked. "I have not particularly wanted to," Wilma replied. She said she had not worked on her childhood grief before.
>
> Wilma was asked if she remembered missing her mother: "See, those are words. They have no real meaning. Only feelings remain.
>
> "Maybe that's almost the same kind of thing I'm saying about my friend who just died. *I took it in,* it's always there. I know I had a lot of grief but did not work on it a lot. It happens, I take it in. It stays inside."

No one helped Wilma to attach words to her feelings. She still does not have them. There is a part of her which is reserved and an underlying sadness and seriousness about her. It seems that it is the part of her that is still feeling but not saying.

Most children need constant support and guidance through the trauma to avoid later difficulties. Adults who want to help a child or children through the mourning process must be working to resolve their own feelings about the death so that they are able to respond to the children's needs. Parents and family may not be available to the children when they are absorbed with themselves.

Even though it is burdensome, *it is up to the surviving parent or other close adult to realize that children cannot do grief work without the adult's initiative. It takes many years for children to mourn and integrate a loss because they do not have the emotional strength to endure much pain or the words for expression. Their feelings and memories must be kept available to prevent them from going underground since memories and feelings are needed to mourn.* When grief is repressed, emotional and intellectual development may be hindered. Unresolved grief may stand in the way of forming other healthy relationships and the fear of another loss may linger on.[4]

When the circumstances of the death are unnatural or bizarre, as in an accident, murder, suicide, or drug overdose, there is the added problem of how much information to share. It is a disservice to evade children's questions about the deceased or the circumstances of the death. Their fantasies are often more frightening than the reality. It is not *whether* to tell, but *how much* to tell at one time and in what *manner*. The child's trust and faith have already been assaulted by the fact of the death. Existing relationships help to rebuild trust. Therefore, you must be truthful, but *give the child only as much information as he or she can digest at the time. Use tact and sensitivity.*

Talking with your child will also depend on your ability to face your feelings about the manner of the death. When a child poses a question about the deceased, or about the circumstances of death, it is better to say: "This is all I can talk about right now. Another time, when you are older (or when I am able) we'll talk about it again." This is an honest answer and preferable to distorting the truth. Some answer, however, is necessary.

It is essential to keep an open environment so children can ask questions and talk about how they feel. Invite them to share with you and tell you when they want to talk, even if you are busy. That does not mean you are mandated to answer every question if you believe the child is not emotionally or intellectually able to cope with the answer at the time. Use your judgment, but avoid lying and evasion.

The Funeral

The funeral and memorial service are times to say goodbye and provide a sense of community and caring. Attending this ritual can help a child to mourn. The age of the child, the circumstances of the death, the relationship between the child and the deceased, where the funeral will be held, and the ritual that will be followed will determine whether the child should participate.

If the opportunity presents itself, a child may attend the funeral or wake of someone he or she knew slightly so the experience becomes more educational than traumatic. This, of course, should be done with the support of the parent and only after a complete explanation of funeral and wake customs in general, and what will happen at that particular one. This would not be as traumatic as having to participate in the funeral of a close loved one without prior knowledge of the ceremony and some awareness of its impact on the behavior and the participants. Following is an account of the way in which a sensitive adult introduced this experience to her granddaughter.

> Hallie was four when her great-grandfather died. He lived 450 miles away and visited once or twice a year. At seven, she was upset when visiting great-grandmother to find grand-dad was not there and why. She thought he hadn't visited in three years because he didn't want to come to see the family.
>
> An elderly, sick friend of Hallie's grandparents died. The family felt this would be an opportune situation to help her understand about death, and to help her find answers to some of her questions. She visited with the family and viewed the body with her grandparents. Some of her questions and verbalizing were: "What did he feel like if he wasn't alive?" "Was he soft and warm?" "Could I touch him?" At first she wanted to, then changed her mind, and then decided she would. She felt his hand and commented that the person was "like a doll." Like a doll, there wasn't anything inside that mattered, he could not feel things. She had many questions: "Why was he all dressed up?" "Could I die?"
>
> "Yes," answered Grandmother, "sometimes children get sick or have an accident and can't get well and they die. But that is unusual. Usually people die when they are old."
>
> "If I die, what would I wear?" "Why were so many people sad looking?" "Why all the flowers?" "Why was everybody sort of whispering and quiet?" "What was a funeral? A cemetery?"   "Could you go to a cemetery anytime?"   "Why did the person get put in the ground?"

These questions were all answered truthfully and simply. This seemed to have satisfied Hallie and her concerns about death and customs surrounding it. This is another example, like Lisa, of a child being permitted to follow through to satisfy her curiosity and needs. She used this experience to work through the death of her grandfather in a symbolic way.

Attending the funeral or memorial service is not as difficult as attending the wake and viewing the body. It is usually helpful for a child to attend the service accompanied by an adult and with adequate preparation and explanation. It is helpful in dealing with the separation. When a child is not permitted to attend, fantasies may develop that may be worse than the actual experience might have been. Many adults

remain resentful because they were not permitted, as children, to attend
the funeral of someone they loved.

> "I did not attend the funeral of my father (nor did my sisters) because
> my mother thought we were too young. I know what a mistake that was
> and even then I felt so confused the day of the funeral. As I think about it
> now, I felt doubly abandoned, first by my father, then my mother because
> she went off without me," Tess reported.

When a child is not present at the funeral it might interfere with
acceptance of the reality and integration of the grief.

Viewing the Body

Seeing the deceased may be helpful for a child, just as with adults, in
verifying the reality and finality of the death. If the child is averse to the
idea, he or she *should not be forced*; but not seeing the body can leave
doubts. Sometimes imagination is worse than the reality. Again, the
decision should be based on the relationship of the child to the deceased,
the child's age, the circumstances of the death, and your own religious
and ethnic customs. *The decision also depends on the child's and the
adult's emotional stability. Adults should not insist that they view the
body,* but they can encourage, give the child permission, and stand by
with proper preparation and support. *There are always reactions. This
should be expected and guided by an adult.* The previous examples
illustrate this.

> Ten-year-old Alfreda and her older sisters were led into the bedroom
> where their father's body lay. "He looked like he was sleeping. I was
> scared. Then I saw my father's cousin kiss him and got very upset. I turned
> and ran out of the room right into the arms of another cousin, and she just
> held me. That was probably the warmest thing anybody could have done."
> More than 40 years later when Alfreda related this incident, she was sur-
> prised at the tears evoked by the old memory.

It may have been a shocking experience for a ten-year-old, but she had
a chance to verify the death. An understanding, supportive adult to prepare her and guide her seems to have been missing, even though her
cousin rescued her afterwards. If the child had not seen the body, the
fantasy might have been worse. Even teenagers may indulge in the
fantasy that whoever was buried was not the loved parent. These doubts
accompany the wish that it were not true. Fourteen-year-old Laurel said:
"I really wanted to see him, but then I figured, what if I remembered him

that way? Then I kept wondering if he was really dead. I knew, but I kept wondering.''

There may be extenuating circumstances in the manner of death as in the case of the Blackman family. Mr. Blackman died as the result of an industrial accident. Because of the extreme disfigurement, it was his wife's decision that their two daughters not see him. She felt it was in their best interests that they remember him as he was that morning at breakfast. You can only do what seems right at the time and trust yourself. This is only one aspect of mourning. It is the overall process that is important.

UNDERSTANDING CHILDREN'S AND ADOLESCENTS' FEELINGS

Parents need to be aware of the feelings that their children will inevitably experience. Keeping these emotions in mind is helpful when traces of those feelings are expressed. A child will share his/her feelings at unexpected moments and often with only a phrase or sentence. The opportunity to respond should not be missed. This will help to acknowledge, affirm, and support full expression of those feelings.

The feelings and process described in Chapter 3 are applicable to children with some variation. As explained previously, children tend to have more extreme reactions especially in the shock, denial, and undoing phases. Blocking and denial are more often used by children in an attempt to protect themselves from overwhelming pain. Children and adolescents continue to hope for the return of the deceased, even when they know intellectually this cannot be. They are further limited by their capacity to put feelings into words.

There are other feelings that are prolonged, exaggerated, and often confused for children and teenagers. Guilt and anger may get mixed up. Feelings are often acted out with behavior or displaced onto undeserving persons. To minimize this, they need adults to help them find language for the feelings.

Anger

Children do not escape the feelings of anger that are a part of the mourning process for adults. In fact, anger can overwhelm them. They are angry at the deceased for dying, for abandoning them. They may be angry because they felt the relationship with the parent was not all it could have been and because there will never be an opportunity to work out misunderstandings. Displaced anger is an ambush from which the unwary victim is attacked. An angry person looks for an outlet and may provoke a confrontation.

> Sixteen-year-old Tom Robbins was angry. He admitted the feelings are still there three years after his father's death. "I think it is more of a long anger....having it so long sort of imbedded in me." He continues to blame his father for his death and turns the anger against his mother.
>
> The therapist confronted Tom with the idea that he was transferring anger at his father to his mother. "Why would I be angry at her?" he denied. "I'm not angry at anybody except him a little because he could have saved himself by taking better care of himself."
>
> Then he admitted he deliberately incites family dissension as an outlet for his own feelings: "Why do I elbow her [his young sister]? Because she's there. Why do people climb mountains; because they're there. Why do I hit Rene, because she's there. It gives me a sense of accomplishment. I get back at her. It starts a whole chain of events—Rene crying, Mom reacting, a round-robin anger." His teasing is an indication of his underlying hostility and an attempt to hide the inner seething. *Tom converts his sadness to anger so there is an exaggerated dose of anger. Many youngsters and adults mix these feelings.* Sadness seems to be just below the anger.

Because there is an expectation that parents will take care of everything, when a parent does not have the power to make everything all right, especially over matters of life and death, children become angry. These expectations are unrealistic; but, these feelings often exist. When these ideas and feelings are verbalized so they can be dealt with, matters can be clarified. When they are not verbalized and the adult does not have any idea what is going on, relations between parent and children can deteriorate. The child's testing of reality cannot be supported when the adult is unaware.

Guilt

Guilt is one of the many feelings mourners confront. Young children often find the cycle of guilt and anger confusing. They do not have the ability to differentiate between fact and fantasy. They confuse thoughts with results, often nurturing the belief that their thoughts or behavior caused the death. They may have become angry and perhaps wished their daddy would go away and not come home again after a severe reprimand. Then, if Daddy dies even months later, the child may think himself responsible. Unless someone can elicit this, help the child put his fantasy into words, the unresolved guilt and grief can color his life.

Another source of guilt that roils emotions is the oedipal conflict. Children ages four to six normally wish to have the opposite-sex parent all to themselves. If the same-sex parent dies, it may stir a recurrence of these oedipal feelings of "Now I'll have Mommy (Daddy) all to myself," followed by guilt for even thinking such thoughts. Children need to be reassured that thoughts do not make things happen and these feelings are normal.

A difficulty for a child of any age arises when there has been an uneasy relationship, anger and conflict between the child and parent. There may be guilt due to a sense of relief that the source of conflict is gone. There may have been times during arguments when the child felt the extreme of anger, wishing to be rid of the cause of the discord. The feelings of guilt may alternate with disappointment and sorrow that, now that the parent is dead, the conflicts can never be resolved. The child will have to work to conquer the feeling of unfinished business and will have to work out these feelings with a third party.

Even though there was no serious conflict between parent and child they may feel guilty over not having behaved better.

> "I remember when we were home that night after he died," Edie, sixteen, told the therapist. "I wished that I had said 'I love you' before he died. I felt guilty that I'd ever upset him."

It is normal to have regrets when a relationship ends in an unnatural abrupt way. These regrets fade during the course of mourning.

Idealizing

Idealizing and remembering only good things about the deceased are common after a death, but after awhile other memories begin to emerge. It cannot be emphasized enough that it is essential to look at the whole person and the whole relationship, the satisfying and the unsatisfying parts, to successfully integrate the loss.

> Three years after Gary's father died, he was still talking about him every day in only complimentary terms. Twenty-two-year-old Gary, his mother, sister, and brothers always talked about Mr. Gold as though he had been a saint. When Gary was twenty-seven, he began psychotherapy. One of the notions scrutinized was his relationship with his father and the true nature of his character.
> What emerged was the fact that Gary's father was not always exemplary in his behavior toward his wife and children. As myths were stripped away

Gary was able to remember his father without the burden of worshipping a nonexistent idol. His relationship with others changed as a result of his insights, and working through his grief.

> When Jeff died, he became the focus of his daughter's worship. Cari idealized her father and the marital relationship of her parents. It has taken six years for her to begin to accept the fact that Jeff was human, with human foibles. The rest of the family were able to accept the realities, and even joke about the disagreements that Cari had forgotten. It took her a long time to admit that Daddy did not belong on a pedestal and that her parents' marriage, like all good marriages, had periods of conflict.

There are times when the surviving parent colludes in the exaltation of the deceased because of an inability on his or her part to come to terms with mixed feelings about the deceased. That presents an unrealistic role model for a child to try to emulate. There are dangers in a child's idealization of a parent and the relationship between the parents as it is not good preparation for other relationships. It results in the setting up of unrealistic goals for oneself.

"I Didn't Know Him (or Her)"

Many people whose parents died during their childhood or adolescent years say: "I feel I didn't know him, I wish he could have known me while I was growing up; I would like to be able to tell Dad (Mom) about how well I'm doing in my job. I've needed his/her advice about so many things." Children feel cheated, and justifiably so.

> Although Danny spent more time alone with his dad than many boys during their lifetime, he often says: "I didn't know him." He wonders how they would relate to each other today. "I wish he were here."

> Donnie Roth was seven when his father died; his sister Charlotte was thirteen. Six years later when they talked about their father, Donnie remarked: "I didn't really know him." Charlotte, always mature for her years, tried to explain. "You knew him better than you realize. You've forgotten a lot, but we'll be talking and telling stories and then you'll remember." He can only remember his father as he was when he was seven.

Memories are lost along with the attempt to shield the pain. Talking and telling stories as Charlotte suggested will help him "know" his father.

Children will always miss the lost relationship. As children mature perceptions of their parents change and ways of relating change. When a parent dies, the relationship that existed is frozen in time. The child whose parent died years before is saying: "Right now, we don't know each other. I don't know what it would be like to have a relationship with my father (mother) at the age I am now." In the context of the present the child wonders what it would be like if the parent were alive. It is painful to be deprived of a parent. It's also a way of saying, " I miss him/her."

Fear of Another Loss

It is natural for children whose universe has been turned upside down to fear that another terrible thing will befall them, that someone else close to them will die. They become oversensitized to loss and fearful everyone important to them will somehow disappear. They often ask, as Hallie did, if they, too, will die. The need for reassurance is being expressed along with the fear.

Children have difficulty separating from their parents or surviving parent after a death in the family. They want to stay close to those who are important. Adolescents also remain fearful of impending disaster. Mac said: "I wondered who would be next." These fears are often apparent in dreams. Steven, when fifteen, came into the kitchen one morning looking very upset. "I dreamt that something happened to you, too, Mom. It was awful. I'm so glad you are here." These fears are normal. Adequate reassurance over a period of time will reduce the fears, and they will eventually fade. Encourage your children to relate their dreams to you. They reveal important feelings.

The same dynamic may enter into the forming and ending of adolescent relationships. The inability or unwillingness to form close or lasting relationships may be due to the fear of losing someone important again. It appears to be self-protective, but the individual loses by giving up the chance for intimacy and joy. A teen-age relationship may come to a natural ending, but the loss may be too difficult to bear. Feelings similar to those following the death will be reexperienced. Sometimes it seems easier to stay in an unsatisfying relationship rather than bear the ending.

Seeking New Relationships

Sometimes it is easier for young children to accept new relationships because of their needs. They may seek a substitute to fill the emptiness and longing for the deceased. A child's need for love and attention may seem excessive to a parent who is bereaved and also very needy. If another member of the family can fill in the gap, it can be supportive for all. An uncle visited his two orphaned nephews every day for years after their father's death.

Although no one can replace another person, there is room in everyone's life for other relationships. Children can continue activities once shared with the deceased or they can try new things. If they went fishing, riding, walking with Dad or played tennis, went shopping or swam with Mom, they can do the same things with another adult. When a boy or girl continues the activity, it helps them realize that life's routines and pleasures do continue. It is an opportunity to talk because it stirs up feeling about the deceased and the way in which life changed. The accompanying adult needs to encourage the child to talk. The expression makes room for continued enjoyment.

Young children may actively seek to recover what has been lost. It is not uncommon to hear a young child ask: "Won't you be my Daddy?" or "Won't you be my Mommy?" They want a whole family again and are too young to understand what having a new daddy or mommy entails in the way of adult relationships.

As children enter the preadolescent and adolescent stages, their horizons broaden and different things come into focus for them. They begin to deal with identity issues. The loss of the same-sex parent is especially troubling. It interrupts the process of identification and leaves the child without a role model. The teen years are a time of wondering about the meaning of life and the direction lives should take. The death of a parent during the crucial years between twelve and eighteen, when problems of separation and identity have to be worked out, is an assault to the total emotional development. When an adolescent is trying to figure out the meaning of life, life suddenly seems meaningless.

At this age, the death of the parent is traumatic. Children lose their moorings; a vague sense of identity in an adolescent becomes even more vague and it is even more difficult to achieve clarity. There is tremendous confusion over values and confusion over what behavior will bring the desired results. Faith in the future is lost. Everything seems useless and not worth the trouble. What meaning can be found in life when your most important person is snatched away? The meaning of life becomes incomprehensible.

Adolescents may consciously or unconsciously seek someone to assume the parental role. They will look for a teacher, scout leader, relative, or friend of the family to whom they can turn for companionship, counseling, and as a role model to help them formulate and reinforce ideas about their role in the family and society. They need two adults to supply guidance and direction for future choices regarding a job or education. When the same-sex parent is no longer available as a guide and the sex role model is missing, identity problems increase. The adolescent is often disappointed however because the substitute relationship does not measure up to the parent relationship. The level of caring, attachment and commitment is different and rarely measures up to what was lost.

Sometimes teen-agers act out their wish for replacement and need to belong to someone through sexual activity. The search for someone to alleviate the deprivation may lead to pregnancy or early marriage.[6]

Changes in Parents

Children observe changes in their parents if a sibling has died, or in the surviving parent if one parent has died. In addition to experiencing the death, they also experience a change in the parent or parents. The parent is a *mourning* parent and is not the same. What the child formerly perceived as strength and being in control is supplanted by tears and remorse. This does not necessarily mean the children will not be taken care of, but they may become anxious and angry and experience the change as a loss.

> Edie, at fourteen, admits that she would be very angry when her mother could not stop crying: "I was mad 'cause she'd sit there. I'd just get so mad I'd like to punch her in the nose. She'd carry this on day and night and a couple of times we wondered if she were competent enough to take care of me and Laurel.
>
> "One night when she was sitting there, I remember thinking of whether she'd be able to take care of me or not. She was thinking of maybe sending us down to Pennsylvania to our aunt. I said, 'You'd better not.' I really got mad at her and then I felt guilty too because I thought it was my fault she was crying, 'cause she'd bring our fighting into it. I didn't feel like I was doing anything wrong but all of a sudden, she'd start crying. *I knew it was related to my Dad's death. I didn't realize that it would be related that strongly* and so I thought it was something Laurel and I were doing and I didn't know what it was. That made me really mad."

It is appropriate and natural for a parent to mourn openly and be honest in expressing grief. At the same time, children require the parent to give words to the experience and to their tears, and to reassure them. They need to know that their father or sibling is missed and that sadness is prominent. They also need to know that even though you are distressed, you still love them and will take care of them. The household and routine may not run as smoothly as before the death, but somehow you will all get through it together. They need to know you are not afraid of your feelings and that you will manage, even if it does not seem that way sometimes; otherwise confusion may result.

> A nine-year-old said after the suicide of her father: "I found mother crying a couple times when she was making breakfast for us. I felt respon-

sible for her and worried that she would leave us too. So I tried to be good and to make her happy.''

The eighteen-year-old sister saw her mother differently. ''I couldn't tell my mother of my needs. Then I would have disappointed her. I thought I had to go on and act strong. I modeled myself after her. That was how I perceived her.''

Children of all ages react so differently. You need to keep talking to each other; otherwise misunderstandings may be created that take years to undo. Steve was sixteen when his father died. He shared this years after his father's death:

> My mother's intense emotionalism and constant tears was not only irrational to me but also frightening. In addition to my fear of painful feelings, I rebelled against my mother's seeming overreaction. I didn't want to believe that was the way to mourn and if it was, I didn't want that. She thought I was underreacting and I thought she was overreacting, so began a sequence of misunderstandings that continued for nearly five years. I felt that not only had I just lost a father to a heart attack, but also lost a mother to extremism.

Steve was unwilling to share his feelings, but he surely had them. He related:

> ''In the few months after Dad's death, my brother and I would take turns consoling each other, climbing into bed together and crying in the darkness. My brother and I were taking care of each other.''

> In the Breen family the mother walked in on her daughters one day and found them crying, the nine-year-old sitting on the eleven-year-old's lap.

It is apparent that adults and children have similar needs for expression and comfort during mourning. Although children become confused, angry, or frightened, they need to see an honest *expression of emotions from adults accompanied by explanations and reassurance*. They are thus provided with a model for mourning.

There are times when as a parent doing what you know is right will not bring the results you want. If an adolescent is in the stage of rebellion, communication and cooperation are limited.

> My mother, who was so consciously trying to make up for the loss of our father, lost the congruity of being a mother to me by attempting to be something she wasn't: both parents. Our relationship which had always been close began to disintegrate.

> One day Steve said to his mother: ''Don't try to be authoritarian. It doesn't become you.'' He was not cooperative. He said, years later: ''I

couldn't take care of my own feelings on the matter. Now I question whether my rebellion prevented me from supporting my family at all."

It took years for Steve to be able to say: "I was holding back in fear of feeling."

Preadolescence and adolescence are important periods for emotional development. Ordinarily, they are years of gradual separation from the parent. When a parent dies during childhood or adolescence, the separation is sudden and beyond control. This makes the natural and timely separation from family more difficult. The adolescent may try to take control by initiating separation before emotionally ready to do so, or may delay leaving home. He may end relationships prematurely in an attempt to control the end rather than risk a loss.

> Steve said: "Suddenly, I felt it was time to take care of myself. Like many young people I toughened up on the outside. I would tell myself, 'You can handle it,' whenever a new situation would arise or if I needed support. I refused any help from my family to the extent of moving miles away—a complete disassociation with all that I was dependent on. It took me a few years to discover that physical independence has little effect on self-reliance and being responsible."

Steve had to learn that geographical separation is not synonymous with emotional separation. In his family there was shared grief, open expression of feelings, and emotional support available from many sources. Steve was part of many, many hours of family sharing, but the depth of pain was more than he could share or bear.

Another adolescent was able to express himself through poetry.

> In Truth
> I know more than you my friend,
> For I can see the space beyond every man's soul.
> I know beyond wonder, each thing has its end,
> Worth, choice, and valor mix not into physical being.
>
> In the natural world there is no reason nor fault.
> Like lightning that strikes, and the tree lays withered.
> I stand in despair, staring coldly into naught:
> For my mother has died, and the world died with her.
>
> David Kesler

MODELS AND MEMORIES ARE NEEDED TO MOURN

Children need help from adults to do their mourning. Adolescents as well as young children need permission to mourn, a model, and guidance. Mourning continues at a very slow pace, in ministeps throughout the years. It is very gradual. Adults can work on only one little piece of grief at a time. Children are even more sensitive and vulnerable and have less capacity for dealing with large chunks of pain. It is important, therefore, that they have help to keep the memories and feelings available to be recalled for grief work over the years. Many memories must be recalled and reexperienced before children can separate themselves emotionally from the deceased. They have to understand that articulating their own grief is acceptable. They need prompting to keep their feelings and memories in their consciousness .

It is tempting to adults to evade the subject in an attempt to avoid their own grief and avoid the additional responsibility of helping the children. It is easier to fool oneself into believing the children are not thinking about the loss when they do not talk about it. Too often, adults collude in this silence by not responding to their children or not taking charge in guiding them through the mourning process. Parents need to take responsibility by providing an environment where sharing of feelings can take place. Sometimes the parent's own overwhelming emotions stand in the way of that realization.

> Catherine Blackman said it was important for her to know what Edie, sixteen, and Laurel, fourteen, were feeling after their father died. "But," she said, "they won't talk about their father or the accident." When the girls participated in a family session they revealed a different version. They felt their mother evaded the subject whenever they tried to talk to her.

After Catherine realized she was "holding her feelings at bay" and overcame some of the horror of her husband's death, she recognized that she had missed opportunities to talk about the death with her daughters. She was unable to respond to them and to their clues. Being unable to acknowledge her own feelings cut short the children's opportunity to mourn. As she mourned more fully, she was able to support the girls.

There are things the parent can do to facilitate the process and keep the memories alive: expressing one's own feelings, explaining and labeling them, asking children what they are feeling. There are various ways to maintain links to the deceased: keeping pictures in prominent places around the house, looking at the photo album together at special times like birthdays or anniversaries, allowing the child to have a favorite possession of the deceased, talking about everyday things they did together such as going marketing, to the zoo, or fishing. It is helpful to remind children of the love the deceased had for them and to continue to bring the deceased up naturally and casually in conversation: "Remember when?" Continue to check on the feelings aroused when recalling the deceased. Memories need to be cultivated and cherished.

Memories are essential for the mourning process because the individual needs to experience the attachment to the deceased and then separate gradually. The ego, especially a child's, does need protection. Letting in too much pain at one time would be overwhelming. In an attempt to lessen their pain, children and adolescents lose the memory of the deceased. A void exists and adds to the feeling that they did not know the parent. As Danny and Donnie Roth both said: "I didn't know him." The pain is not really gone; it is submerged, but it must again be felt before the loss can be integrated.

The death of a parent is always a significant event. The effect of the loss on the child's personality is related to the support and guidance at the time of the death and throughout the ensuing years. The child who is not helped to mourn may be haunted all of his or her life by an underlying sadness or anger.

> Alfreda said: "Actually, my whole life has been colored because of the fact that I never really overcame the death of my father. I did horribly in school, was a juvenile delinquent. I really thought I was dumb . . . but I was angry and didn't know it. . . . My mother prided herself on being a good soldier and never cried. She was not going to fall apart in front of her children. I looked to her for guidance and couldn't get it."

> Tess related: "I spent my childhood and teen years feeling disconnected. My father was dead, my mother was incapable of dealing with it, and the rest of the family had their own problems. No one talked about or discussed their feelings unless they were feelings of anger. My mother created an atmosphere of rule by fear, and I bought the whole package. I grew up in a home where I could not really complain or express my fear or negative feelings without fearing that mother would annihilate me."

Neither of these women had support or guidance during their childhood mourning. The family also missed the opportunity to prepare them for the loss that was clearly inevitable.

Tess continued: "When he died, I felt a cruel joke had been played on me, that everyone knew he was dying but nobody told me."

Alfreda said she knew her father was ill. He had been confined to his bed since returning from the hospital, but her mother sent the girls off to the movies; when they returned, their father was dead. Even then, at first, their mother said only that their father wasn't feeling well. The truth came out quickly though, because the relatives were gathered and crying and they could not hide the fact from the children.

When there is illness, it is essential that children be informed of the nature of the illness and the prognosis. When a child knows there is illness but is lulled by assurances that "Daddy will soon be better," the impact of the death is frightening and overwhelming and causes mistrust of others as well as mistrust of one's own perceptions.

The parents or parent has to take the leadership and say to children, "Look, this is what we need to do. No matter how hard it is for you, we need to talk. We need to keep our feelings going." No matter how much adolescents balk and protest and say "I can handle it," it is up to the parents to take charge, the hardship notwithstanding. If you need someone to support you, find help. The task may be too difficult to do single-handedly.

Retrieving Memories

A child or adolescent has to get to the point at which he or she feels strong enough to bear the pain of mourning. With support and encouragement the memories can emerge even years after the loss occurred. Memories may remain submerged, but they exist in the recesses of the mind. Memories may have been blocked along with unpleasant feelings, but they are there and you can get them back if you allow yourself to feel again. Danny related his process:

"I didn't think I could recall many chummy-type instances with Dad. But I have been starting to remember more things, just all of a sudden, something brings it out, and Wow!

"I can remember running up and jumping in his arms and kissing him when he came home. I can remember sitting with him on the couch or the chair and rubbing my head against his like a cat."

Danny finally opened his feelings and found a full range. He is an insightful person: "It takes energy to hold all those feelings down. That's where all my energy has gone. But I haven't been able to make any huge, fantastic breakthroughs. It's taken awhile."

There is seldom such a thing as a "fantastic breakthrough." There are only slow ministeps. Nina, twenty-two years old, describes her steps seven years after her father's death:

> I felt very safe, like I had it all figured out and in a nicely wrapped package that I could show you, "See it's all nice and together." But I know I have to get inside and find out what's underneath. I have to stop pretending. All of a sudden (this had been sparking on a few occasions) I thought of how much I missed not sharing the new breakthroughs that are happening in my music with my father. I felt my heart fall. It hurt. How much we shared as mutual appreciators of art, music, dance, etc. I began remembering all the performances he attended of mine; how he truly reached out to me, especially then. The pride he felt and made me feel. I remembered the times he sat down with me and tried to teach me how to speak publicly, with diction (and I'd be so frustrated because of course I thought he was criticizing me). I have his picture on my desk that I haven't *really* looked at in years. I studied it *AND CRIED, CRIED, CRIED.* And flooded my heart with the warmest memories that any girl could be lucky enough to have. I stayed with it. And I know that this is just the beginning. Much more is yet to come and maybe some not so pleasant memories, but I just wanted to take one small step at a time.

Another young woman released a flood of feelings and memories when visiting her mother's grave. She had avoided it for 10 years.

> I was crying hard and began talking out loud, telling my mother how much I miss her and then I became angry. I said, "How could you have left me when I was little and needed you? How could you have gotten sick and abandoned me?"
> I was then able to recall our relationship. I began remembering things I had put away long ago. She became clear again as a person, as my mother. I could remember her love and concern and things we did together. Even though it hurt because I was aware of missing her, it was good to have her back with me, through my memories.

Sixteen years after the death of his father, a young adult wrote this on Father's Day, finally able to retrieve his memories:

> Dad showed me how to look at the clouds and make animals out of them,
> so calm and relaxed, lying on our backs laughing.
> He told us stories at night to help us sleep, in the heat,
> and to pretend that a beautiful tree was a cool lake and we were
> swimming in it.
> He gathered us together during that big tornado one night so we
> wouldn't be afraid, and showed us the size of the hailstones so that
> we would understand and respect the storm.

He told me a story that helped me learn to fight my own battles.
He tipped his hat, smiled, and said "hello" to all women.
He left me brothers and sisters.
He said goodbye to me.
He lives in me.

Steffie was ten when her father died. A void abided within her as she had forgotten so much about him. She "worked" for many hours on her feelings about his death. After she was helped to re-create some childhood experiences, she gradually retrieved memories of him. At the end of the session she made this moving comment: "Thank you for giving me back my father."

Faith in the strength to endure some pain will loosen up memories. Then the pain subsides and remembering becomes spontaneous. Comforting memories will emerge naturally. This will support mourning to the point of integration.

Surrogate Parenting

Children, adolescents, and young adults need help in retrieving memories. If both parents have died, as in Lisa's case, the surrogate parents may pay more attention to fulfilling immediate needs and daily adjustment than to keeping memories of the parents alive. A lack of dialogue about the deceased may abort the mourning process.

The example given earlier about Lisa, and Paulette's case which follows, are examples of adequate care supplied by caring surrogates. Although Paulette was taken care of, no guidance was given for the mourning process and no help in retaining memories.

Thirty-eight-year-old Paulette was born in Paris, France. Her father died when she was seven and her mother a year later. She related:

"It's a hard part of your life, losing both of them in the same year. Nobody wanted to talk about it. Uncles, aunts wouldn't talk about the deaths in front of us."

After the summer at her uncle's country house, Paulette and her sister were enrolled in a Catholic boarding school for orphaned girls. Her brother worked and continued his studies at the university but still "found time to visit us and sometimes took us to the zoo." The children spent Easter day and Christmas day at their uncle's home. The girls lived under the loving protection of the nuns. "It's another way of life. They were so kind. I don't remember thinking about my mother or father. Those years with the nuns were very, very important in my life. There was no physical show of affection, but we did not seem to need hugging. We felt secure."

During those years Paulette cannot remember speaking with anyone about her mother or father. "Maybe because we did not miss them. We were so well taken care of and the nuns were so kind. We didn't think there was anything missing. We were all alike. I was no different from the others.

"But when I went home to live like a family seven years later, then it was felt." At fifteen, Paulette went to live with her brother and sister. She moved from the protective environment of the orphanage where all the girls were in the same parentless circumstance to living with her siblings. Her brother supported the family, sister kept the house, and she enrolled in a nearby school. She was struck by the reality of her parentless existence. She met girls who talked about their mothers and fathers and family activities, and she realized her family was different. Then she started to miss her parents. "I miss not having that period of growing up, between fifteen and eighteen, with my mother. I remember her physically. In a sense I knew something about her, but mostly in my imagination. I remember her picture." She has some vague memories of her parents but cannot recall details.

She cried about it, but always alone. She never shared her sadness with anyone until years later in a distant country when she met the man she eventually married. She has little recollection of talking with her sister or brother about their parents.

After this discussion she said: "I have never talked with anyone like this before. I learned there is something missing. I think there is so much I have to remember. I discovered the blackout, but the feelings are still there. A person who has experienced death realizes how terrible it is. You're stronger when you are older and you know you can take care of yourself; but you also realize how vulnerable you are. It doesn't go away. It's 30 years, and I'm happy; but it's still there. Even if you look happy, if you have lost a part of you, you can't forget it inside. You have to go through life; you can't sit in the house and cry all day. But you do keep the sadness.

"I recently took the children to church and when I came home I told Pete: 'I think I have never prayed like this day. I don't know why I have remembered more and more of my parents today. Especially my mother. I prayed for both of my parents. I couldn't hold back my tears, it was such a strong feeling.' When I feel like crying I tell myself: 'Don't be afraid to cry' and I do it, and it helps a lot."

Paulette was urged to talk about her parents with her brother and sister, now forty-six and forty-one. They were eating lunch together. Her brother got up from the table in tears. He had kept the sadness too.

Adequate surrogate care made a difference in Paulette's later adjustment. She did not feel singled out and different from other children. There was time to grow and develop her character. Her mourning was delayed until the time she lived with her brother and sister, then the deprivation became more apparent. Her brother and sister became surrogate parents, and they had a semblance of family life. Education became focal for her and took up most of her energy. She continued to function adequately.

Then she suffered another set of losses: her native country, her sister, a relationship. She made another difficult adjustment and continued to pursue her career. She fell in love, married, had two children and a medical practice. The effects of the multiple losses she suffered emerge in her recurring periods of depression, and an abiding sadness within her. Mourning was abridged because of circumstances and an absence of memories. Although she has arduous periods of adjustment, she has not been disabled by her losses. She is a warm person with satisfying relationships.

BEREAVED CHILDREN AND SCHOOL

If an open letter were to be written to schools, it would incorporate the following ideas in an attempt to enlist understanding and patience from teachers of children who are bereaved.

Mourning is a very gradual agonizing process. A well-adjusted adult would need approximately three years to integrate and adjust to the sudden death of a loved one. This would of course vary according to individual differences. Although the resolution of grief results in accepting the reality of death of the loved one and reinvesting oneself in new interests and relationships, the sadness remains forever and becomes part of the person.

For children, the resolution of death takes longer than it does for adults. They can only deal with the loss in small segments. They do not have the ego strength to deal with the pain in its full intensity. Therefore, much of the pain and sadness goes inward and takes its toll on the individual. It is often expressed in a way that does not seem to an observer to be related to the loss. *Children often act out by misbehaving, seeking attention, talking back, by a loss of concentration and motivation, or an overall decrease in school performance.* So much energy is expended in grieving or fighting painful feelings that not much may be available for productive functioning.

Most families do a good job in dealing with their loss and functioning in a world which does not understand the impact of death and the changes it forces on individuals. They need to deal with people who want to maintain distance from the threatening issue of mortality. There is no *set* time in which one should be "over it and back to normal." There is no status quo for children or adolescents whose father or mother is dead. Their "normal" consists of a penetrating feeling of sadness and deprivation as they go about doing the things other boys and girls their ages do, and doing the best they can even though they are often depressed and unmotivated and unable to explain why. Although it is always in their hearts, it is seldom on their lips.

It is hoped that understanding the impact of a death on a child will engender patience and understanding, as well as an understanding of reduced school performance. A mother related the way in which her children's teachers reacted to the death of their father.

> Many teachers were very sympathetic and kind in extending their concern in the months after my husband died. There were many visits, warm personal notes, and gifts extended to all of us. The principal offered help in whatever way he could.
>
> Others were very insensitive and caused unnecessary hurt. One teacher asked my daughter in front of the whole class the nature of her father's work. "My father died," she answered. A teacher should have unusual data about students so that painful and embarrassing situations like this can be avoided. It was a small suburban school so information like this could easily have been shared.
>
> Four months after the death, my son's teacher selected a song for a musical program that was about "things dads and sons did together." Tony rehearsed this song repeatedly and performed it for the program with the other boys. It was unbearable for me to hear once. Can you imagine his reaction to practicing the song every day?
>
> Later he disclosed the appalling lack of understanding on the teacher's part. He told me that not only did he have to sing this heartbreaking song with the class, he had also been assigned a solo. During rehearsal he started to cry and couldn't sing. "Now just stop crying!" the teacher ordered. "Stop that right now. If you can't, you'll get a demerit. So just sing it." When Tony could not control his crying, the teacher sent him to the infirmary "to calm down." He stayed in the infirmary for awhile, then returned to the room. The homeroom teacher talked to Tony about gardening, a subject he knew interested him. However, the well-meaning teacher avoided talking about what had taken place in music class and why Tony was sad and upset.
>
> The mother continued: "I felt my son was unnecessarily hurt by the lack of sensitivity by those two teachers. The homeroom teacher didn't acknowledge his loss, but at least he was gentle with him. At the time I was vulnerable myself and couldn't take on the school and educate them about grief.
>
> "Eventually we learned to cope with these things, but some sensitivity in the early months of grieving would have been so appreciated."

The experience these children had in two different schools was unfortunate. Even years after the death, children might remain sensitive to situations like the one above. It is hard to accept such insensitive reactions from teachers only months after the event. Gentleness, consideration, and acceptance of feelings by teachers are called for in dealing with bereaved children.

> After Joel Arnold's sixteen-year-old brother died suddenly, you will remember that his schoolwork declined, and he developed an extraneous motion which was distracting to all. Out of concern for him the nuns at the school realized the source of these reactions and tried to get help for him. They were aware of his distress and contacted the family and the school psychologist to help in alleviating his tension.

Many principals and teachers respond with understanding and a willingness to help. They know grief is pervasive for a youngster, that it is difficult to talk about, that mourning lasts for years and can be expressed in deviant behavior. The overwhelming feelings interfere with concentration. Sadness and anger keep intruding on thoughts. A decline in schoolwork is an expected reaction to the death of a loved one. The decline may not take place immediately. Good students like Edie and Tom went from A's to D's the year after their father's death. Sometimes the fight to keep thoughts and feelings away does not succeed. Tony said that he had often cried in school. "It creeps up at times I don't expect," he admitted. "I tried to hold back the tears but sometimes I couldn't help it."

It is very distracting and takes considerable energy to keep feelings pushed inside. Energy used in suppression is not available for reading lessons or algebra. It is supportive for children if teachers understand that it will take time to function and perform as they did previously.

Children and adolescents are disturbed because they are different. They feel that everyone has two parents except them. After returning from her friend's house one Sunday afternoon, Sharon cried: "Everyone has a daddy to be with on Sunday except me." Some children feel damaged and stigmatized. The difference in a single-parent family from a two-parent family seems to be underscored when children are at school. They become aware of this loss and are sensitive to conversations.

> Tony said: "I heard the boys talking about their fathers and what they did over the weekend. I realized I didn't have a father and everybody else did and everybody talked about it. How could I forget about it?"

> A teen-age boy related: "I hear my friends talk about disagreements they've had with their fathers and how angry they are at them. I wish I had a father to argue with."

Awareness of a loss intrudes at times that often cannot be controlled. As Tony put it: "It just creeps up on you." When teachers are understanding of the mourning process and the effect of a loss on the personality and on functioning, an additional stress on the youngster is reduced and personal growth is supported. Acknowledging the loss honestly and in private is helpful. Allowances need to be made for children, and patience is necessary from teachers to see the children through a burdensome experience.

Integration and assimilation of the death is a slow process for children. They will come through it and develop an added dimension to their personality with guidance and emotional support from adults. Danny, when fourteen, put it in these words: "You get to a point where you can put away your feelings; *put away not push away.*" Cari wrote these words:

Even though my father is dead,
I still believe in life.
Daddy taught me to believe in life.

7

DEATH OF A CHILD

Even before a child is born there are dreams and expectations for a joyful future. When these hopes are shattered by death, pain and a multitude of memories remain.

> Whenever I see a seashell I think of Lanny. We had been going over her school project on seashells the night before she died. I came across this book that has her handwriting in it. I treasure even the misspelled words: "I am prtey. I way 63." I want to remember.

It is unnatural for a child, whether a youngster or an adult, to die before a parent. It is an assault on our understanding of the life cycle and a corruption and interruption of the emotional investment made by parents. A child is the link to continuity and immortality.

The death of a young child is an excruciating experience for a parent. The death of any loved one is a loss of part of ourselves, but the death of a child intensifies the feeling that a crucial part of you is missing. One of the tasks of child rearing is effecting a healthy and gradual separation and loosening of the bond which is initially established for survival. The death of a child does not permit a natural separation. Although the emotional bond continues, the relationship has ended in an unnatural way. Your parenting role with this child has been severed. You feel as if your responsibility as a parent is unfulfilled. The work of mourning involves the shedding of the relationship.

The age of the child invokes different kinds of emptiness. Death of a newborn infant leaves a parent grasping at a fantasy because there was no time for a relationship to develop. This is also true for miscarriages and stillbirths. The separation is complicated by the absence of the relationship. The maternal-infant bond is one of the strongest human attachments. Loss of that attachment when a young child dies can be devastating, leaving the mother particularly with no focus for her love and energy. The pleasure of watching the maturation of a teen-ager is short-circuited when life ends before the growth is completed, leaving only the big, unanswered question: "Why?" Although your child's image remains the same, he or she travels through life with you in absentia, and you continue to count birthdays, graduations and other milestones their contemporaries celebrate. The untimely death of an adult child can leave the older parent bitter, asking: "Why not me?"

Regardless of age, the death of a child is a shocking event. The child's death exerts unexpected stresses on family relationships. These must be dealt with in order to rebuild family stability and provide support during the mourning process.

The Feelings of Grief

The poet can capture the acute and pervasive pain after the death of a child.

> Grief fills the room up of my absent child
> Lies in his bed, walks up and down with me,
> Puts on his pretty looks, repeats his words,
> Remembers me of all his gracious parts,
> Stuffs out his vacant garments with his form.[1]

William Shakespeare

Although the physical and psychological symptoms of the mourning process are similar to all losses, the death of a child may intensify certain feelings. The loss permeates all aspects of your life and all relationships. One parent may blame the other when seeking a target to project the pain brought to them through their child's death. This can wreak havoc with the marital relationship. The tragedy is no one's fault but the result of unfortunate circumstances. Recognizing this can reduce conflict between parents.

You may become overprotective of your other children, denying them the normal pursuits of their age group. This stems from fear of another disaster. Nancy is not aware of being over-protective of her children, but she admits she reminds them to be careful whenever they leave the house.

> Somewhere at the back of my mind I think God couldn't let anything happen to one of my other kids. Things don't happen like that. But I do think of Peter crossing in that crosswalk every day. I wonder if I should ask him, "When you cross the street, do you think about it?"

The Breens just could not allow their nine and eleven-year-old daughters to sleep overnight at a friend's even though they had always enjoyed spending the night at a friend's home. Their older daughter met with disaster at a girl friend's house.

A father remembers a time when they were concerned about their twenty-year-old son and his behavior.

> We had been at a family wedding and it had begun to snow heavily. We insisted my son drive home with us because we did not think he should drive by himself. He was so mad! "We are afraid you might have an accident in this weather." We talked about his brother who had been killed when the car he was driving skidded and crashed. I told him, "Mom and I could never go through losing another child. Just think about it from that standpoint. We love you so much."

It is best to talk with the children and explain your concerns. Open discussion will ease the pressure and their negative reactions. Guilt and undoing phases are painful after the death of a child. Parents feel that it is their job and responsibility to nurture and protect their children from harm. It feels like failing at the job of parenting. Mr. Shuman believed that if he had been there, he could have saved his daughter. "I would have known what to do." You may wish decisions made about doctors and treatment could be reversed. "We should have tried a different doctor, another hospital, a new medication." Many parents wish they had not given permission to participate in the event which led to the death. They keep saying, "I should have said no." Of course, then the child would still be alive and no one would be suffering. Mr. Breen said, "I go over this again and again in my mind. In my fantasies, I can make everything come out all right." This is part of the process of attempting to undo what has happened.

You may berate yourself for having been harsh with the child, for not having fulfilled a promise or for things left undone. You may have regrets about unresolved conflicts between you and not having a chance to work these out.

Sometimes parents try to avoid their feelings by keeping busy but, in the end, the feelings emerge regardless of the barriers raised.

"We have been trying to keep busy with conventions, confirmations, weddings, and, of course, the other children," wrote the father of the drowned boy, "but at night without fail, he comes before me every day since his passing. I always told others that time is a great healer, but I'm beginning to wonder if that's true."

It is not the passage of time itself that is healing. It is the expression of grief over a period of time that leads to the healing of painful memories.

SHARING YOUR GRIEF

It is essential for mourning and the preservation of the family system to share your feelings and tears with each other. It is not an easy task. Each one in the family may be in a different phase of grief at a given time, each feels very needy, and there may be no precedent for sharing feelings in the family.[8]

Grace, whose fourteen-year-old daughter had been killed in a highway accident, said: "We certainly had plenty of moments when we all really took our hair down and talked, got it all out. But we still retreated into excessive politeness. As for being supportive of each other, I can only view it from my point of view. Yes, I felt that my children were extremely supportive of me and that the two older ones had the ability to express themselves and feel no restraint, particularly my oldest. How much help we gave them I'm not sure, but they were very helpful."

Leslie's son, Dennis, age eighteen, died following a long illness. In her family, emotions were tightly controlled.

We have four other boys. We *had* five boys. You know boys, crying is just taboo. I couldn't express any emotion, not in front of them. That was really out. If I had cried, I couldn't have handled it. Emotion is just not part of their macho.

After Denny died, I kept trying to get them to talk, but they had trouble. I had trouble myself, verbalizing or pulling the emotions together so that they could be articulated, and they have that same problem. They talk about him but not about feelings. It just isn't their way. I suggested journals and one of them kept a journal and that's a good outlet. They try, but as far as giving that kind of support to each other, no.

Tears are a natural response to news of the death of a loved one, but not everyone is able to cry. When in shock, tears often do not come. Grace shared:

> I can remember wandering through the house most of the night and there was somebody on every bed and everybody was crying and it just struck me as being such a lonely situation. I would go from person to person and I was the only one that wasn't crying. My son, husband, everybody but me, as soon as they got the message they started to cry. I have never been able to do that, you know, spontaneously weep over something that really warrants it.
>
> "I guess I really have been to that point where I would like to have a good cry when they sing my daughter's favorite hymn or something," Grace said. "There are several I am still absolutely unable to sing. I'd like to really sit down in the pew and have a good cry but I can't really do that. And when I'm by myself, I can't will myself to cry, will myself to feel bad, I just can't."

It is hard to recapture your feelings after they have been driven inside. People have the need to comfort and be comforted. It would be less lonely if some inhibitions were abandoned.

Sometimes there is a fear that if you give in to your emotions, if you cry or talk too much, it will cause a chain reaction among the family members.

> Margery felt it was her responsibility to remain "strong." "I really was so concerned for all the kids. I was dying to cry, but I was so concerned for all of them. I figured they'd all break down, everybody would get hysterical, and they just wouldn't be able to control themselves. I showed them that I could make it. I just wanted them to know that you can get through whether you want to or not."

You *can* get through whether you want to or not; that does take *real strength. In actuality, it is easier to get through when you give spontaneous vent to your feelings and share them within the family. Strength is not measured in self-control.* Margery's self-control carried her through only until the children went off to school.

> After everybody got off to school I cried. And I think I cried every day thereafter for...I don't remember when I stopped. I cried at least for a year, but I haven't cried an awful lot since. In fact, I crawled into his bed, lay on the pillow, and just cried. And then it wouldn't get any better; and I'd get mad at God and I'd tell Him off because He did this to me...I did most of my crying alone.

Margery was isolated with her feelings much of the day, but could share them with her husband at the end of the day.

> Matt would come home in the evening from work, the kids were down-stairs, and he'd put his arm around me, and I'd cry some days and other days I wouldn't. There was always that special time, kind of reaffirming I got through the day and he got through the day, and there was another day coming. A couple of times he cried with me, just quietly, a few tears, or he'd hold my hand and I'd hold his. I would never have made it through without him.

Many parents find it more difficult to share with their children. This may be experienced as a lack of permission or avoidance by the children. They need to be helped and gently confronted.

There is a common feeling that prevails with parents and siblings. On some level the deceased child remains part of the family. It is hard to reply to others when asked: "How many children do you have, or how many brothers or sisters?" As Margery said: "I could not answer two children when I had three. It's true that I now only have two living, but I feel Ronnie is still part of our family. It is hard to explain this. Sometimes I hope I will not be asked. A lot of emotion wells up in me every time. When I feel up to it I say I have two and one is deceased. Other times I say two."

People often hesitate to share their sorrow with others. Friends or other family may be uncomfortable with your tears, but you need not let others dictate your behavior. If you swallow your sadness and keep it inside, it is harder for you to function. Others also get a distorted idea about what mourning actually is. They may not know you want to talk and wait for a signal from you. Nancy reported a luncheon date with a friend.

> As we were talking, I said to her, "I miss Lanny so much. I want to hug her." My friend was surprised by my openness. "You know," she told me, "I could never talk to you. I didn't think you wanted to talk." I admitted I love to talk, but I don't want to burden anyone. So we talked and talked. And she talked about her mother who had died four years before. She had never talked with anyone about her feelings about her mother's death. So it was good for both of us.

Mourners are comforted to know that others remember the child and are sad and tearful too. Nancy spoke about how thankful she is when people talk openly about her little girl.

> Some are afraid to say anything, even when I verbalize a memory of Lanny, but *the people who are the most helpful are the people who talk about her.* My neighbor brings up little anecdotes about her that I never knew. It's so great because I'm learning new things about Lanny. I like remembering her. That's how she stays with me.

Being able to talk, cry, remember with a sympathetic person is a balm for the aching spirit. There are times when the deceased and your pain are not so prominent. They fade into the background and give you temporary relief. Other times you will be reminded. A mother shared that she longed to hear her son's voice say "Mom" with his voice rising. Nancy said:

> All I have left are my memories, and I am sad. Then I conjure up seeing her doing something, riding her bike down the street, and I see her. I'm losing the sound of her voice a little bit, but I can always hear her call me. She always accented the "mee"—you know how kids call when they come in, even before the door is all the way open, as if to confirm you're home. She'd call "Mom-*my*," always with the accent on the "mee."
>
> It's like finding things in the house that were hers. I found a sock she and I had looked for. I held it and said, "Lanny, I found the sock," and I cried. Then I have to take a deep breath and go on with whatever I have to do. She's gone.

As time goes on, the periods of relief will increase, and it will become easier for you to go on.

Death Following a Long Illness

When the illness has been prolonged you have the chance to prepare emotionally for the death by doing anticipatory mourning. A lengthy illness often entails changing the focus of one's life, regardless of the age of the child. The parents' involvement in caring for the patient will be all-consuming.

When the child dies, the emotional and physical dependency suddenly disappears and the part of the mother and father that was invested in caring for the child has no avenue for expression. The emptiness is magnified in cases where the child has been ill for a long time, perhaps years, and family life has revolved around the needs of the sick one.

Taking care of a young child who is ill can become a way of life, even when the parents try to maintain a "normal" life for the child and the rest of the family. The emotional life of the family is tied to the child's physical condition. There are periods of elation and hope when the child has "good" periods, can attend school, play with others, and is alert and active. Feelings of helplessness and anger surge again when the disease, whatever its nature, recurs. The family routine is again in upheaval with additional pressures on relationships as parents became preoccupied with caring for the child at home or spending a lot of time at the hospital, often unable to meet the needs of the other children. The other children also need time and reassurance. They may be frightened by the illness and impending death. Regardless of age, they need opportunities to talk about their feelings and to be reassured of your love.

Parents are often thrown into conflict about whether or not the sick child should be told the nature of his or her illness, especially when the prognosis is death. Failure to communicate the truth to a chronically ill child or siblings can lead to lack of confidence in the parents. Children sense when something is wrong and read the clues given out by everyone. What one imagines is often worse than the truth. A sick person knows when he or she is ill. Thinking that you are protecting the person by pretending places an extra emotional burden on everyone and lowers the quality of the remaining relationship by depriving it of honesty. However, honesty is no excuse for the lack of sensitivity as the impact of the truth can be devastating. The child needs to be given emotional support and information in a *sensitive* manner. Parents and other adults must be available for emotional support and to encourage expression of feelings. Honesty, with sensitivity and continued devotion, will build mutual support and strength. Then energy can be directed to daily living and enjoyment.

Whether or not you have been able to share the facts about the illness with your child, you have done what was right for you. You have the consolation of knowing that you have done everything medically possible to try to save the life. You had the opportunity to care for your child and, through your ministrations, reaffirm your love.

Sudden Death

When death comes suddenly and unexpectedly, the shock is devastating, and it takes longer to work through that first phase of grief. There has been no forewarning, no time to prepare for the trauma. The emotional impact is more acute when there has not been a preparatory mourning period, as there is in a prolonged illness. Sudden infant death syndrome strikes without warning and leaves the parents stunned. In any sudden death, the guilt, and confusion are hard for parents to deal with. You will find that you are haunted by the circumstances of the death. You may find yourself wondering whether or not your child suffered.

> Margery said: "I wondered how much pain he had, what went through his mind, did he wish we were there? Finally I could accept the fact he was dead and the pain was over for him. So why should *I* be suffering, worrying about the pain he *might* have had?"

> Nancy said when Lanny was killed, the only thing that kept them from falling apart was they were assured she was killed instantly and did not suffer. But when Nancy drives by the corner where the accident happened, she can't help thinking: "Was she looking in that direction?" And I pray to God she wasn't.

This is another way of staying involved with the deceased. This happens often after the death of a child, because of the nature of the attachment between parent and child. Sometimes parents hang onto the pain of grief fearing that if they do not feel that pain they will not remember the child. You need to give yourself permission for relief of that pain and allow the gentler sadness that comes with remembering.

In the event you did not view the body, you may fantasize about it. It is usually better to see the body even if there has been mutilation. Very often the fantasizing is far worse than the reality. It depends on the circumstances.

> Nancy felt Lanny was hit so badly that perhaps it would be too difficult. "Maybe if a person is hurt too bad you don't look at them. I never asked my friend who identified her. I haven't satisfied myself with that yet. I know I wanted to see her, but they wouldn't let me."

When a loved one dies, there is sometimes a feeling of the continuing "presence" of the person. Margery's experience is typical:

> Everybody looked like him, a young man in the coffee shop, other places. When we came home after the funeral, I felt he was there, that he was in the house, his spirit. I knew he wasn't but when we came home I felt it. He was in my heart.

Margery continued:

> I feel that my anger has now subsided. One can only be angry so long. It almost seems as though my anger has prolonged a substantial amount of my acceptance.

When I think of Ronnie being dead for eight years, it doesn't seem that long ago. If I think of having him for 22 years, again time becomes an elusive thing. If he had never been born to us, how empty our lives would have been. I should just thank God we had him for the time we did, but I can't be that generous yet—I do thank Him for having him.

STRESS ON THE MARRIAGE AND FAMILY

Many people believe that the death of a child can draw the parents closer together because of the mutual need for comfort. The loss exerts inordinate stress on the relationship. If the marriage has a history of commitment and mutual support, the relationship has a good chance of withstanding the stress. The fact that each may have different coping mechanisms, and each goes through the phases of grief at a different pace, may disrupt the marriage. Although you can mourn together, your mate cannot bear your pain for you. Understanding the other person is hurting too and being able to talk and cry together does soften the hurt and preserve your closeness, even if you do not have the same emotion simultaneously.

Hank held a position in a large corporation so he had to be under control most of the time. Nancy was able to spend more time at home, talking and crying as the demands on her emotions dictated. "If Hank would walk in with tears streaming down, I would almost feel guilty because I wasn't feeling the grief the way he was at that moment; almost as if I should be, because he was. And then I would remember he'd been holding back all day."

Margery and Matt talked about Ronnie, their feelings about their other children, and about themselves.

I wouldn't have survived without Matt. Of the two of us, he has always been the stronger person. He always kids me and says it's not so. Without him, I don't know how I would have gotten through. There's just nobody else that would have been able to help. He was extremely attentive. I even feel now that he probably hid a lot of his own feelings or made them secondary to mine without ever saying. I just knew by the things that he did, like bringing roses, coming in and putting his arms around me, or holding my hand that he just knew what I was going through. We are so fortunate we have each other, I know.

Sometimes couples try to protect each other, but by doing so they deprive self and other of comfort. It is comforting to cry in someone's arms. Margery continued:

I've heard of other people who have lost children and ended up being divorced or almost divorced over it. At the time we were mourning Ronnie's death, Matt happened to be in a group where a woman talked about her son being killed. Her husband wouldn't talk about it. It was just awful. She was trying so hard to relate to him, but he wouldn't respond. Matt was able to talk with her and kind of help her. When he came home he said, "It has to be terrible when one feels such anger at the other person, almost like he was blaming her."

We had suffered this terrible loss together. Between us, this is what we suffered, and I could feel for him and he could feel for me. We never lost touch. I feel I would never have made it through without Matt's support.

Husband and wife must help each other express grief. It is a reciprocal process. A member of the family may fall into a pattern of stoic behavior because of social cultural expectations or to appear strong and reliable to their spouse. Sometimes it is their own inability or unwillingness to express emotion. This behavior may be perceived as unfeeling and uncaring. Rather than being supportive it is distancing behavior. The partner feels as if the other does not hurt as deeply and feels isolated. It is more loving and binding to cry together rather than putting on a facade of being "strong for him (or her)."

When a couple suffers the loss of a child, there is often a breakdown in the relationship between the grieving parents. Gail and Mickey had problems which began almost immediately after their loss. She had a miscarriage. Her grief manifested itself in a refusal to admit her feelings.

"I kept the loss inside. Instead of sharing feelings, I hid them and that was wrong but I was so depressed," Gail said.

Mickey continued: "She was sick and very depressed. For the next eight months we had not one meaningful conversation. When I would approach the subject, Gail didn't want a long conversation about it. Before we could talk about it, Gail would turn off. She had two ways she'd do that: she would just not hear or she would become aggressive and that would start an argument. Every day we would get farther away. We weren't hostile to one another after a while, just growing apart."

Gail continued: "I buried myself and my feelings at work. My output increased, I worked late, made trips I didn't have to. I realize now it was subterfuge to stay away from Mickey and hide my real feelings."

"I didn't know what to do," Mickey said, "I felt angry when she abandoned me, frustrated. I knew she would have to go through all the mental and emotional gyrations before it would get better. At some point there was something I said or something Gail thought about and we started to grow back together. We didn't want to be apart. It just started to turn around."

"I learned I wasn't even aware of how he felt. He told me later, he was in tears after I had the miscarriage. And I had no idea it affected him as badly as it affected me. I had always felt he couldn't understand how I felt because I felt totally responsible for the miscarriage. I knew he had surface feelings, but I didn't know how deep they were.''

This couple's experience illustrates many dynamics operating between couples during the mourning process. They grieved separately as Gail would not share her feelings. This increased her isolation and decreased the chance for support and understanding, even when it was readily available. Her unwarranted guilt expressed as anger also created distance between them. She thought she was the only one who was hurt and did not realize her husband's depth of feeling. They were reunited emotionally when they were able to share their feelings.

When there is an absence of understanding and of a real desire to preserve the marriage, the death of a child may weaken the relationship to the breaking point. The shared tragedy does not automatically mean shared emotions. Without the empathy, a chasm may develop between husband and wife because of the inability to give support. Each may expect too much from the other and receive too little when it is needed most.

Other pressures may work against keeping the marriage stable: being physically and emotionally overloaded, financial burdens, guilt, or blame. When a child has committed suicide, guilt and blame run high. This is a complicated bereavement, and the stress is terrible on the family. The couple may continue the vicious cycle of blame and guilt, and the marriage may deteriorate.

Problems will often develop in the sexual relationship. Even when a couple is close, there may be a shutting off of feelings. A woman shared:

> My husband would put his arm around me. I guess I must have frozen, because he finally said he had the feeling I was turning him off. It was only that I had no sexual feelings, I just had *no feeling* except pain.

Like many bereaved parents, she was able to feel only the great pain and a tremendous tightness. There was no room for any other feelings. A young woman said: "Our sex life was disastrous. I figured if he didn't touch me, I wouldn't have to get pregnant again and risk another loss."

Other couples seek the closeness of the sexual encounter. A young woman related the emotions that would arise within her after a sexual encounter.

> A reaction that I had for a long time, was that after we would make love, I would start to cry. . . . The only thing I could ever figure out was that making love or making life (reproduction) was so beautiful and natural and pure, that somehow my sadness and mourning would come out after doing this very beautiful thing. . . .

Her emotions were deep. Making love is a bonding experience, and you feel less isolated. It gets you in touch with your aliveness when you have been so immersed in feelings about death. It has a rejuvenating effect.

Children are affected deeply by the death of a sibling. It is very threatening when someone close to one's own age dies, especially a young person. They are frightened by this in addition to mourning for the deceased. They see their parents in mourning and feel a loss because of the changes they observe. Mourning is the focus of the emotional life for a while, and the deceased may seem to demand more attention than when he or she was alive. The other children may begin to wonder if they are still loved and if they will get the attention and recognition they need. They feel, "What about me? I am alive. Am I important?" This is the emotional experience of children of any age. It does not necessarily indicate the parents' neglect. It is the nature of mourning that thoughts and feelings about the deceased are all-consuming until some balance is reached between grief and maintaining other important relationships. Parents need to consider these feelings in their children.

There is a growing goodness about a person who has died, especially a child. They tend to become angels. One day when they were talking about Lanny, Jerry said: "She wasn't always an angel, you know." And they talked about some things she did or did not do. Nancy told of one incident when Hank spanked her. There were not many spankings in the family. Brother described a couple of other incidents of misbehavior, one in great detail. Nancy said, "It was a childish misbehavior. After all, she was only nine. How bad could she be?" It is important to remember the total person and not make him or her into an angel. Siblings will usually help keep these memories alive if no one else takes this responsibility.

OTHER LOSSES

There are other losses suffered by parents that precipitate a mourning reaction. The birth of a handicapped child, miscarriages, prenatal (stillbirth), and neonatal (newborn) deaths are serious losses. An abortion is also an emotionally-laden experience for a woman. In all these losses, mourning is necessary to work through the feelings and to be free to form healthy attachments. The importance of mourning may not be recognized and a superficial cure or cause is often suggested such as: "It was meant to be; have another baby quickly; it was your decision." Openly mourning these losses are not socially sanctioned which makes it more difficult to give oneself permission to mourn.

Feelings of guilt are prominent in these losses. The woman may blame herself or look for a cause for the misfortune. Sometimes women feel defective if the pregnancy or child is not perfect. There is rarely any real cause or blame. Some things happen that are not within our control, and we have no explanations for them. The couple is usually on its own after consultation with the physician.

> Natalie suffered three miscarriages within three years, although her doctor could find no physical cause. "People told me I should be glad it happened, that the fetus was probably defective. I thought something was wrong with me because I was not glad. I was sad. I had lost my baby. No one understood my sadness."

Miscarriage, prenatal and neonatal death are seldom mourned adequately. A young woman related: "People tried to tell us, in their awkward way, to have another baby right away. It was very much like them wanting to do away with our grief by having something good happen right away."

These losses also require the individuals involved to grieve thoroughly. A young mother whose daughter was born with birth defects related:

> We certainly experienced a great deal of bereavement when our daughter was born, although it didn't hit us until a while afterwards. So much of our deep sadness was in mourning for the normal baby that we had planned for and expected and didn't get. I think we also went through the stages of sadness, anger, etc., as if there were a death of some sort. I cried a little every day, some days more so, for almost a year.
>
> I rarely cry now and feel that is because the mourning is over, and on some level I have accepted Bonnie for who she is and whatever defects she has. . . .
>
> Of course, it is different from a death. We still have Bonnie with all the love and pain it takes to raise a child like her.

These young parents had unusual support from their friends and family to help them with their acceptance and adjustment.

MUTUAL SUPPORT

You may be convinced that no one else can possibly feel the same agony you do. Comfort comes when it is spoken by someone who has experienced the death of a child. Out of mutual sharing the bereaved finds solace from words or gestures from others who have been through it and have somehow survived. Margery and Nancy found this to be true:

Margery shared: My sister-in-law, whose child had died four years before, just hugged me and said, "It will be all right; it will be all right." That's all she said, and it *is* eventually all right.

The same kind of solace was given by her mother-in-law: "I knew that she knew how I felt because she had lost two children. I got out of the car, and she just hugged me. There really was nothing to say."

Nancy Hickock said that many of the hundreds of condolence messages they received when Lanny was killed, "were from people we didn't know. They, too, had lost a child, and we found their words most comforting. Now Hank and I clip out stories when we read that a child has died, especially accidentally. Perhaps through our own agony we can reach out to solace others."

Andrea wrote after the sudden unexpected death of her teen-age son:

"Vinny and I talk constantly, almost a litany, but it keeps us sane. I think it's nonsense that one must plunge into something all-consuming in order to side-step grief. I think it's disastrous to find shortcuts. Of course we need to focus on the other things and we need our work, but we are also very vulnerable at this time, easily hurt, and disoriented. The key is that feelings must be verbalized. My precious seventeen-year-old has yet to cry for his brother.

"Death is a vast learning experience about ourselves. I find new insight each day almost in wonderment that out of this horror can come some sense of order."

Nancy said that her life is so changed. "The sadness hits you. It's so changed. Even with all the fun, the 'busyness' of our lives and the joy of our children, there's always a heaviness. I guess you just learn to live differently: I guess you learn to accept that."

Years after her son's death, Margery shared: "I have come to the conclusion my loved ones are not really gone. Bodily yes, but I feel Ronnie is still with me because he is in my thoughts. The love is still here. I have finally figured out he is alive in my thoughts and in my heart."

8

DEATH OF AN ADULT'S PARENT

The death of a parent marks the end of the first significant relationship formed in a lifetime. There are differences in the intensity and duration of mourning depending on the age of the adult child and the age of the parent, the quality of the relationship between parent and child, and the circumstances of the death. Young adults miss the milestones in life that will no longer be shared with parents, like a wedding, the birth of children, family celebrations, and other important occasions. When an aged parent dies, feelings are tempered by the blessing of long life. It is not an insult to the life cycle as it is when an untimely death occurs. However, the appreciation for a long life and the expectation of death do not eliminate experiencing emotions after the death of a significant person.

The death of a parent when you are an independent adult is not usually a tragedy unless the circumstances of the death itself are tragic. Sarah's father shared these thoughts as he anticipated his own death: "I don't have much longer, but it's not a tragedy. After all, I'm not a young man and I don't have small children." Nevertheless, acceptance is not automatic, and there are feelings to be expressed, memories to be explored.

MOURNING HAS MANY ASPECTS

The course and duration of mourning will be affected by many dynamics. The emotional preparation for the final separation, that is, anticipatory grieving, facilitates mourning after the death. It eases the shock and the first phase of grief. It is helpful to take the opportunity provided by aging or illness to do preparatory mourning.

Another aspect of mourning to be dealt with includes emotions that are stirred up about the quality of the total relationship throughout the years. The successful emotional separation from parents, the resolution of the conflicts in the parent-child relationship, the extent of dependency or the development of independence and outside attachments are all important issues that affect the course of mourning.

The adjustment after the death will depend partially on the extent to which your daily life changes. If your parent required attention or care due to illness or the limitations imposed by aging, you may have devoted time and emotional energy to frequent visiting and caretaking. You may have assumed the role of parenting your parent. After the death you may feel relieved of the responsibilities but at the same time may miss the role and function of caretaking. It takes a while to restructure the time and energy previously invested in these tasks. You may feel lost until you use the available time to do things you may have postponed. When there is little or no change or disruption of daily activities, the loss requires less readjustment.

Old hurts and deprivations are re-experienced. The interaction of various family members and siblings is increased and heightened during the parent's illness and death and early dynamics and conflicts often resurface. These factors all add to the tasks of mourning the parent and are part of the process when an adult's parent dies.

THE ABSENCE IS FELT

When the parent who dies is young and vital, it is a blow to a child's understanding of the universe. It is further complicated by a child's dependence. When the parent is older and the child an adult, there is an awareness and understanding of death as part of the life cycle. An adult is also better able to verbalize feelings. Nevertheless, a parent's death involves many emotions because of the intensity and uniqueness of a parent-child relationship. A twenty-six year-old woman acknowledged: "I felt as if things would never be right again. Important things will have a shadow over them, like when my baby is born and mother won't be there to hold and cuddle it."

Sarah felt her loss deeply. She said, two months after her father's death:

Dad died after his ninetieth birthday. I missed him and felt his absence. Sometimes I felt as if I were not entitled to feel bad because he had a long life and I was lucky to have him part of my life for so many years. But I know what I felt and that was sadness and lonesomeness.

When the death is sudden, there is often a feeling of something left undone.

> Robert phoned his eighty-five-year-old father every day when he was home, but he and his wife were vacationing when the news of his father's death came. Disbelief was the first reaction, then tears. He missed his daily phone conversations with his father. Years after the death memories evoke sadness and tears.

Margaret is a thirty-eight-year-old business executive. She related:

> I have tremendous joy in my life because I did have my good friend, my father, and my life is enriched by that. He was very supportive of my career ambitions. He didn't meddle but was helpful when I did seek his advice. Many beautiful memories often recur to remind me of our relationship.

No matter what our age, in some part of us we maintain the fantasy that when we have a parent we will be taken care of and loved in a special way. We feel we belong to someone. When a parent dies, the insulation and protection are gone. Witnessing the debilitation of a parent and reversing roles help us gradually to dispel our fantasies. A special bond still remains between parent and child that is ended only at death.

COMPLICATED MOURNING

It is important for the bereaved to recall all kinds of memories of the deceased. When a person clings only to the good memories, there is a denial that *every* relationship involves some conflict. Pleasant memories soften the unhappy ones.

Mourning may be complicated by a dependent or domineering relationship between parent and child, by many unresolved conflicts, or because the relationship was basically an unhappy one. When a parent has left behind memories of a difficult relationship, the mourning process is arduous. Mourning occurs for the disappointments in the relationship in addition to mourning the death.

Difficult Relationships

> May struggled through an unhappy childhood. When she graduated from a local college, she moved to her own apartment. All her life she had been secretive about her mother's alcoholism. It caused strife between her parents and embarassment to her in front of her friends. She experienced

verbal abuse. Nevertheless, she never gave up hope that the situation would somehow be rectified and that her mother would get help.

Even though her mother's death was related to her alcoholism, May had an unwarranted feeling of responsibility for the death. She also had the usual feelings of anger: anger at her mother for dying, anger because her mother did not take care of herself, and anger because she believed if she had been a better daughter her mother would not have died.

She still wished, and wanted to believe, that she could have prevented the death. She was stuck in the phase of undoing.

It is usual to have some regrets after a person has died. It may seem that if another course of action had been taken the death would have been reversed. Although other courses of action might have been possible, they can not reverse the fact of death.

> May continued to mourn. There were some good memories of her mother, too. She had been an excellent cook. Months after the death, May decided to make a family dinner for Thanksgiving. She did all the planning, shopping, and cooking for a holiday dinner for 12. "My mother was with me. I remembered how she did things. I wished mother could see me. I wanted to say: 'Look Ma, I made it all myself.'"
>
> May's conflicting emotions were resolved as she moved through the phases of mourning.

Following is another example of adults struggling with their feelings after their father's death.

> A family of adults mourned the death of their father in his midseventies. He had been known to show open favoritism among the children and grandchildren. Joan, the thirty-seven year-old daughter said: "It hurts me to think of the kind of person he was. I suffered because of him. I don't like those memories."
>
> Joan also recalled her father's hobbies, his meticulous grooming and the workshop with all his fine tools kept in perfect order. She kept as a fond remembrance things he had made for her.

It is sometimes hard to recall good memories but this is essential. It is always necessary to deal with the total relationship in order to integrate the loss.

Dependent Relationships

The relationship between parents and children normally undergoes a metamorphosis as a person matures. Mourning the death of a parent can be more difficult when the ties are exceptionally strong and the normal separation and independence have not occurred in adolescence and young adulthood.

Frances' attachment to her mother was so strong neither marriage nor motherhood diminished it. Many of her decisions about what to do, where to go, and where to live were based on her perception of her mother's wishes. "I was moved by what I knew would please my mother...I automatically did what I knew would please her." At sixty-eight, two years after her ninety-three-year-old mother's death, Frances reports:

> There isn't a day in my life now, not a day, when I don't think of her 20 times. I travel a lot, and there isn't a time when I come into the airport when my first instinct isn't to go to the phone and say, "Mom, I'm back and I'm okay." We were very close. She was a wonderful dame, terribly intelligent. I realize now, as I didn't during her lifetime, that she had me under very firm control.

Even after two years she was plagued by ill health and often curtailed social activities because of her deep grief. Instead of exploring feelings and understanding the nature of the bond between them, Frances continued to view the relationship in an idealized way. "I never, ever had a quarrel with my mother all my life, never! Not that I wasn't hurt, but how do you quarrel with a woman like that?" Eventually, Frances overcame her depression, and her sorrow became the minor theme of her life. Mourning her mother is no longer interfering with other activities.

A dependent relationship is not confined to mother/daughter. Sometimes the dependency is on the father or can occur in any combination. Following is an illustration of a man's emotional tie to his mother that was so powerful her death precipitated ill health for him and increased tensions between him and his family. Fifty-two-year-old Harlan's mother lived with him, his wife, and three daughters. Since her death three years ago, he has become more and more withdrawn. His wife Cora said,

> He's a tortured man, and I can't reach him. He talks all the time as if his mother had only gone around the corner and will be back soon. He just sits and complains about his mother being gone. He forgets that she was a very critical person. No matter what you did for her she wasn't happy. All he can remember is how much he loved her and wants her back.

Harlan continues to deny the finality of his mother's death and cannot get past the myth that she was perfect. He needs to examine and understand the whole relationship between himself and his mother, in order to work through the loss.

Even when a person does not marry, it is the norm nowadays to move out of the parental home and build a career and new friendships. It is part of the evolution to a mature adult. There are, however, people who never leave home until the parents have died.

> Stan was a devoted son whose father died when he was twenty-four. He remembered the day his father died. "I felt sad. I cleaned him up as best I could, held him and hugged him until the ambulance arrived."
>
> Stan did not move from his parents' home. He believed that his mother was his total responsibility. He talked about the ensuing years: "I took her here and I took her there and we were always together except when I had to travel for my job. Mother died after a long illness 15 years after Dad, but it was not as debilitating and painful as my father's death had been. When I was informed that mother had passed away I went to the room. I touched her arm. I didn't feel a thing."
>
> Three years after his mother's death, it was still difficult for him to talk about it. He did not say died but "passed away." Stan was stoic in his recitation and never gave any indication he felt like crying. Although he could not separate from his parents, he was separated from his feelings about them.

Stan eventually went into psychotherapy to work out his feelings about his parents' deaths and to understand the dynamics of his relationship with them. This is recommended in cases where the mourning is complicated by overdependency, problems in the relationship, prolonged mourning, or inhibition of the expression of feelings.

EFFECT ON FAMILY RELATIONSHIPS

Sometimes the death of a parent exacerbates feelings of jealousy, envy, or anger between siblings. Increased family contact stirs up feelings and early family dynamics. Roles in the family system, feelings of being favored or unfavored, and sibling rivalry are reawakened and come to the fore.

There is often resentment when one child has assumed more responsibility than the others or is the chief caregiver for an aging or ill parent. Even when the financial burden and caregiving have been shared, the perceptions of each one's role may be colored by the individual's own emotions resulting from the unique experience in the family.

Money and possessions become symbolic and children make a last attempt to hold onto something from the parent. Material objects may serve as a displacement for feelings or a substitute for the caring parent. Family relationships can be ruptured by a parent's last will and testament which unequally assigns money or possessions indicating the parent's preference for one child over another. Anger toward the parent as a result of such actions may be directed onto a sibling and may divert the focus from the loss of the parent into conflict with each other. Often there will be eruptions over otherwise easily resolved matters because everyone's feelings are raw. These disagreements serve as a distraction from the real business at hand, mourning the death, with all of its implications from the past.

It is normal to want mementos of a deceased loved one. When there has been conflict and unhappiness in the family, the desire for mementos becomes overcharged. They become symbolic of the parent's caring, or a substitute for it.

If a parent has been unfair by showing favoritism or by unequally dividing possessions without known reasons, it would be best for the siblings to talk this over together and share their feelings. You need to be cautious not to direct your anger at sisters and brothers when you are actually angry at your parent. Since you no longer have the parent to deal with, it is not unusual to displace the feelings onto another relative. Often young children displace their anger and frustration by fighting and taunting each other when the conflict is with a parent, and adults do it in a more disguised fashion. It is helpful to understand these dynamics and be aware of your feelings. Then you can approach your family with some objectivity.

There are times when the death of a parent will free up relations between children. This may happen if the parent has consciously or unwittingly played one child against the other, creating and perpetuating estrangement through criticism of one and praise of another. When the source of the irritation is removed by the death of the parent, the adult children may come to realize the source of the conflict. Then they can rebuild their own relationship.

AGING OR PROLONGED ILLNESS: OPPORTUNITY TO SAY GOODBYE

It is painful to witness the day-by-day physical and mental changes wrought by the aging process or illness. However, this period of your parent's life provides an opportunity to say goodbye by sharing feelings, resolving old rifts, remembering and talking about the highlights of the person's life and your life together. This is a last chance to take care of the person through physical care and emotional caring. People who have had this qualitative time with a parent, or other loved one who is terminally ill or aged, have experienced feelings of closure and satisfaction rather than feelings of something left unsaid or undone, or feelings of guilt or lingering hurt. Some moving examples have been shared in the pages that follow.

Erica, whose father died when she was a young adult had come from college to help care for him because her mother was going to a daily job.

> Mom wanted me to check with Dad regarding my return to school. I went and talked to him, and he said, "I want you to stay two weeks because in two weeks you will know about me one way or the other." Evidently my face just dropped because two weeks seemed like an eternity. He said, "I know it sounds like a long time but I wish you would stay." That's when he talked to me about death, that death was a part of life. He told me he was proud of me and that he loved me and wanted me to do what I wanted to do with my life. I was very upset and crying through the whole thing.
>
> It was always hard for me to be with him. I always got myself bolstered up before going in and then, when he started talking like this, I cried and cried. Amazingly, he never cried. I had seen him cry before but then he was very calm and peaceful. But he always let me cry and was very comforting to me. I was very moved inside that he could talk about dying and I couldn't. I always felt he loved me and that he was reaffirming that love.

The fact that her father urged her to do what she felt was important to her, helped her make an important decision about her future. It was a gift he had not been able to give her earlier. After his death, she learned he had spoken with each of her brothers and sisters, too, leaving them all with a special joy that he had cared enough to speak openly with them.

The doctor had reported to Margaret and her family that her father had a fatal disease in an advanced stage.

> The first time he mentioned malignancy was on my thirty-first birthday. He said: "I hope they got all the malignancy." I looked at him and said: "I was wondering when you would say that. I'd been dreading it, but Daddy, it's not nearly as painful as I thought it would be to talk about it." He said: "Well, I know what the score is." "How do you know?" "Because nobody told me how healthy I was." I said: "They did the best they could, that's why you're having the therapy." He said: "I know that. I also know what the odds are. I figure whatever time I have is borrowed time. But I'm not going to give up my life."

Then I told him about an article I'd read in a newspaper. It said something about not shutting somebody out of your life. *When you've shared everything else in life, it's not right to shut them out from your death.* So he and mother talked about it that week. The interesting thing was *there was far less tension afterwards, far less tension.*

He was brave and I told him so and I started to cry. I was so embarrassed and I was mad at myself because I thought I should be strong, not show my grief or anger with him. Daddy understood. He said, "I've shed my tears, too. It just makes me very sad."

It is agonizing to witness helplessly the illness and debilitation of a parent. However, it offers a chance to review and finish up a relationship. Elaine related the way she said goodbye to her mother.

Probably the best example in my life of what my mother gave to me was the "full circle" her death completed for me. I had a call from my aunt that my mother wasn't going to last much longer. Consequently, I made my reservations for San Diego. I almost missed the plane. My reluctance at this awful task was so mixed with so many other emotions. I remember waking up the next morning with a boulder in my stomach knowing I had to go. I had to go and say goodbye literally forever to someone who had meant so much to me, who now meant so little in my daily life.

My aunt led me into the "home." The stench of urine was the last straw at holding my equilibrium. I felt terror now. We went into my mom's room and I burst into tears. Propped up in a wheelchair with only one arm rest sat a human being in her last moments on earth. Sat me. Sat you. Sat my mother. Sat God. Sat Jesus or Buddha—and my life reeled before me like an unfinished symphony of things I hadn't said in better days because I forgot, because I was angry, because I was doing something else. I decided then that the only thing I could possibly do now was to be real.

So I held her in my arms kneeling on the floor the best I could. And yet I felt the fear of her "disease" killing me, too, if I breathed her breath or let my mouth kiss hers. I allowed myself this very natural fear, although I was ashamed of it. And I cried and cried in her arms feeling again like a little girl, helpless, afraid, and needing mommy's love. Only then could I look deep in her eyes and tell her how much I loved her. At that moment we were equals. We could have reversed roles we were so equal.

As I pulled myself together, I realized I could only bring little momentary pleasures—a touch, looking into her eyes, and telling her that I was glad she was my mom.

I fed her, as she had me. I watched her wipe her gravied bread on her head, so bald, as she had me. I watched her diapered. I found a flower for her to play with, as I'm sure she had done in years so long ago for me. I took my keys off my silver heart key ring so she could amuse herself by running it through her fingers, dropping it again and again, only so she could pick it up.

And then I knew that she was me. And I was her. And the circle was complete, and nothing else mattered. When I said goodbye it was forever. I had let go by embracing. I had closed the scene by opening my soul. I was the child of the mother and the mother of the child. And it was too perfect for me to say it just right.

Sarah shared a series of farewells she had with her aged father.

It was quite clear that we were talking about his death but the words "die," "dying," or "death" were not used. He cried and he said that he "felt that the end was coming." When the nurse who was ending her shift came in to say goodbye to him, she said, "I'll see you on Monday." He said, "I don't know if I will be here on Monday," and I said to him, "Well, you might not be, it's possible that you won't be, but I hope you will be. I hope you will be here Monday." I wanted to be truthful but not hurtful.

Dad cried; he put his head on my shoulder and he cried. I said, "I'll miss you. Will you miss me?" He said, "No. I won't be here for the birth of your daughter's child. I won't be here for Fred's wedding. But how can I miss you? I'm just flesh. That will be the end of it. It won't be me. I won't miss anything." And I said, "But I will miss you." He nodded his head.

In anticipation of one's own death, the dying person may be aware of the forthcoming separation from loved ones and verbalize this. They sometimes say they will miss those they love; they will miss being a part of future celebrations and events.

I asked him if there was something he wanted to tell me or something he wanted me to do or a request he wanted to make of me. He made an association to his funeral. He said, "Well, I'm just a plain person. I won't have any kind of a fancy funeral. I'm just an ordinary person." I said, "Well you are a loved person. You are loved by a lot of people and you are important to many people," and I named them. He agreed.

I listed the relatives who would miss him and who loved him. He said, "I know. I'm a plain person. I started as a carpenter. But I was in business for 65 years, and no one ever said a bad word about me." I said, "I know, you are an honest man and have integrity." I asked again if there was anything special he wanted to ask or request. He said, no. He said he was proud of his children. I asked if he was proud of me. He said yes, he was very proud of me. (I had waited a long time to hear that). He acknowledged my education and that I was making use of it. He spoke in metaphors and used phrases like "I'm a goner," "My goose is cooked," "I won't last." He cried again and put his head on my shoulder.

Another day he said he didn't think many fathers and daughters had conversations like ours. "I talked to you with feelings—*heart by heart*." I cried and said, "Friday you were crying and today I'm crying." I put my head on his shoulder and he patted me.

He faded into death peacefully, not without pain, not without a struggle, but finally with peace. For two and a half weeks he was surrounded by those he loved. He had thousands of pats on the head, hundreds of kisses, dozens of "I love you."

Conversations and experiences like the preceding examples are cherished by survivors. The opportunity to say goodbye and separate from your parent facilitates mourning. The relationship is ended in a loving way and the dying person feels valued and feels that his or her life has been meaningful.

UNFINISHED BUSINESS

There is often an afterthought or something left unresolved. It is not possible to anticipate all the feelings that may follow or to address all issues in the relationship.

Sarah reflected two months after her father's death:

I spent the last two years of his life when he was so ill and close to death numerous times, preparing myself and him for the final separation his death would bring. But I realize now that there were parts of our relationship we did not resolve. After his death some old wounds festered again. They were issues I did not think to talk to him about. I wish I had. Some things still hurt. I tried hard to do it all but perhaps it's not possible.

It seems that no matter how old the adult is at the time of a parent's death, how much emotional preparation and anticipatory grief, or how many goodbye conversations are held, there is still unfinished business or questions that arise that could not have been predicted. Knowing this, it is important to take every opportunity to talk about feelings, old and new, to prepare for the separation of death. It is helpful for the bereaved.

MISSING AND REMEMBERING: VALUES ENDURE

The death of a parent focuses primarily on one unique relationship between parent and child. Rachel had the unusual experience of having an intimate relationship with two women, her mother and her aunt who lived with the family. Unfortunately, they both died within two years, each one after a period of illness. She kept a journal of her feelings part of which is shared here:

> I can't bear to write it. It hurts so to see another person so defeated, so vulnerable. A gray skeleton and no one talks about it. "Ma is dying," I scream out, but to deaf ears. What could I say to my mother? I kissed her, gently held her frail body and touched her head with my hand. Why was it so difficult to communicate during the past 15 years, though at times we did and most meaningfully. I'm in a quagmire. I can feel it pulling at me, the quicksand contagion of depression. I can fully understand and accept the roots of Auntie's devotion, of the endless days and nights in the hospital. Does it have to be so futile? I am afraid.
>
> I am sorry that Ma and I could never completely reconcile our differences regarding life-style. However, I've mellowed and learned a lot over the past three years without her. Now I would like her possessions, beautiful in their own right, but as symbols for the love and care that was put into the choice of each one.
>
> At the end Ma accepted me, though she never fully understood who I was.
>
> Auntie's illness was detected accidentally, peripherally, 18 months after the death of her beloved sister, my mother. An aura of denial pervaded reality just as with Ma's illness and death. Again, I was overwhelmed by futility, and the need to pretend with her, for her. She knew she was sick, but never asked for a time frame, although I knew the limited time frame in which we were working.
>
> In a letter to Auntie I told her of all the things I wanted to share, parts of me. I wrote of life, death, questioning her as to what aging meant to her, what her dreams were, and what she felt like at thirty-seven, my age. I wrote to her, "You taught me how to learn to seek wisdom from those who can give it, never to stagnate, to value life and its essence, above all."
>
> On New Year's Day Auntie awoke and *knew* she was going to die. We had six goodbye conversations within the next four weeks. I know how deeply Auntie has loved me and how much I've meant to her. She told me she wasn't afraid to die and that she has *been* with Ma for the past several weeks. Her death will be an *absolutely* tremendous loss for me.
>
> Auntie spoke in metaphors thus acknowledging her awareness of imminent death and separation from those she loved. She said, "I'll hold it off for a couple of minutes. We should pull the shade. Whatever they choose will be done, the people who pull the blind. I want the alarm to go off."
>
> As I was flying to her apartment to see her, she died. To two beloved sisters, to my two beloved mothers, I say thank you. I love you both so dearly.

Rachel's account of her emotional experience during her mother's and aunt's illness and death is very moving. She expressed great depth of emotion. Rachel shared her feelings with her mother and aunt during their illness and possessed acute self-awareness. It was still not possible to resolve all the rifts of the past. She took the opportunities she had to communicate with them and finish the relationships. Relationships differ and depth of feelings differ for various individuals. In the following paragraphs, Pat describes her experience after the death of her parents.

My mother died when I was forty-one years old. Although I had loved her very much and we had a good relationship (not that we didn't have our disagreements—but, then, that's inevitable when two strong-willed women are involved) her death was not a traumatic experience for me. My life was so full of so many things that epitomized the middle-class suburban housewife of that era. So even though I was saddened by mother's death I had no time for grief. The only tears I remember shedding were when my tearful father phoned me early that limpid April morning only two weeks after mother's sixty-ninth birthday and very briefly during the funeral service the next day.

But, except for the ceremony of the unveiling of the gravestone a year later, it was many years before I returned to the cemetery. I always made an excuse to avoid the cemetery where mother was buried. I always said I didn't have to visit there because she was always with me. Years later my youngest son said to me: "You never really buried your mother." I guess he was right. But I was too. Even now, 22 years later, my mother is still with me as a lovely presence. She is with me but not here, and I'm saddened by her absence when something nice happens in the family that I would like to tell her about, or when I have difficulty working out a problem.

My father died at 86. He was buried alongside my mother, and I cried a little for him because I loved him and he'd been a good father, although sometimes a very difficult and stubborn man. I carry my sadness with me. My solace is in my memories and the values and precepts both parents instilled in me.

Pat related that her parents' deaths were not traumatic for her. However, the denial of her feelings is evident in having "no time for grief" for her mother, absence of crying, and her avoidance of the cemetery. She herself acknowledged that maybe "she never buried her." She seems more aware of her sadness, her memories, and her parents' values as she herself ages than she was at the time of their deaths.

Jane, aged thirty-two, shared her reactions after her father's death. He died at the age of sixty-two.

I realize just how difficult it is for me to confront my feelings about my father. They get all jumbled up together amid anger and resentment and guilt and longing and sadness and joy. To concentrate on the sadness is easy and hard because of all the other overtones.

I deeply, deeply miss my father's emotional support, his "everything will work out," and his help in working it out. I miss the fun he added to all of our events. My friends miss him too. My father was a buddy to my friends. We reminisce a lot. Before we moved, a friend asked if I would like her to go to visit my father's grave when she goes to her father's. I was very moved. In fact, I'm crying right now because I don't have that outward symbolic place where I can go to leave a stone. I only went to the cemetery twice in the past year, but there is some small comfort in being able to pay homage at a specific dedicated spot.

I guess even in death his memory is a refuge to me. Sometimes, when I get very, very lonely for him, I feel a sense of guilt for not having been able to help him. I feel guilty also on another level because of my longing for him, to be dependent on him again. I wish I had had the chance to work out my relationship with him before he died.

He had a way of easing the way even if it was hard. I especially miss him when I watch and marvel at the growth of my sons. There's a practical aspect of what I miss. My father provided me with relief from my children. He took a lot of time with my husband explaining and teaching things to him. Sometimes it seems inconceivable that he is dead. He is so alive in my mind. He is also so absent in my life.

Margaret remembers her father often. She recalls the things he taught her.

I talk to him periodically. I say: "Thanks a lot for starting me out right." I still feel very close to him. I don't pray to him, but there are times when I say; "Wish you were here to help me out, so if you can do anything. . ." I don't think of it as prayer but maybe it is. I still feel Dad's presence and I don't mean that to sound supernatural or anything. I still feel his presence in my life and his influence, from the standpoint of standards and quality of life, dealing with people, dealing with family, responsibility for action, because I feel very much a product of my upbringing. I still step back and say when I take a course of action: "What would your father say to that?" I try to make decisions that I can face tomorrow. This is the way I was raised.

No matter what the age of the parent or the circumstances of death, it is nurturing to hold onto the values and ideals by which he or she lived. That is a way of making the person's life meaningful and a way to give meaning to your own life. It is a way children of any age can continue to be nourished by their parents' love and beliefs. Remembering the wisdom and errors of the parenting that brought you to maturity may bring laughter as well as tears when you recall the qualities that characterized your parents and influenced your development.

The next chapter addresses the planning and writing of an ethical will.

Through an ethical will you can bequeath to your children the values and wisdom gleaned from *your* parents and from other people who have been important in your own life.

9

ETHICAL WILL

A Legacy of Love

One way to be remembered and to reach beyond one's life span is to write an ethical will. This is a letter left behind for loved ones which shares wisdom and feelings, makes requests, and gives advice. Such letters of love often crystallize the meaning of the life of the writer and transmit the hope that the writer's values will be preserved and continued through the heirs. It is a summary of what the writer has learned from life and what the writer wants most for his or her loved ones. An ethical will is a legacy of love from the deceased which is treasured by the family.

BACKGROUND

There is an old tradition that a person writes two wills. One will is to dispose of worldly possessions: house, business, belongings, and money. The second will, the ethical will, leaves to one's heirs a legacy of at least equal importance: a statement of values, beliefs, the philosophy with which one's life was conducted, and how he or she wishes to be remembered by children and significant others. The document includes the wish that the values set forth be upheld by the heirs. Early wills also contained directions for care during illness and for burial but were usually opened by the family after the death of the loved one.

This tradition has a long history that began with the Patriarchs of the Bible: the blessings of Jacob, the exhortations of Moses and Joshua to the people of Israel, and David's advice to his son Solomon. The oldest known ethical will is dated in the eleventh century when oral tradition evolved into written testament. "Show honor to the poor...Be careful to offer your gift in secret, not in the public gaze. Give him food and drink in your house." This excerpt from a will written about 1050, simply and clearly bequeathed a lesson of modesty and charity.[1]

The following will was written in Spain around 1190. In lovely poetic fashion this father expressed and passed on his values of education, books, and sharing.

> Make thy books thy companions, let thy cases and shelves be thy pleasure grounds and gardens. Bask in their paradise, gather their fruit, pluck their roses, take their spices and their myrrh. If thy soul be satiate and weary, change from garden to garden, from furrow to furrow, from prospect to prospect. Then will thy soul be filled with delight!
>
> Never refuse to lend books to anyone who has not the means to purchase books for himself, but only act thus to those who can be trusted to return the volumes.
>
> Behold a small cloud rising from the sea of science and learning, carried by the breeze of wisdom and understanding.[1]

Although the custom of ethical wills originated in Jewish culture, it was not used exclusively by Jewish people. In the early centuries of Christianity, bishops left letters of direction and advice for their monks. Ethical wills were found in the Apocrypha, the Roman Catholic biblical canon. Testaments can be found in the literature of the Middle Ages, the Renaissance, and the twentieth century.[2]

> A woman who lived in Egypt during the Middle Ages addressed a letter to her sister. In this letter she entreats her sister to care for the daughter she leaves behind. The writer begs her sister to see to it that the young girl receives an education even though she realizes how poor the family is and how difficult their struggle is to survive.[2]

The rabbis of old spoke with lyrical voice, often of spiritual things, but in later days they addressed themselves more to morality and the realities of life. The will that follows written by a Chicago rabbi in the early twentieth century, sets forth his desires and reinforces his children at the same time. There is a call to religion. As in many traditional wills, there is special mention of the mother and wishes expressed that they respect and care for her. His simple goodbye is touching.

> The small saving which I leave will come to you only after the death of the mother. I know you; I may trust that you will not meet in an unfilial

way about possession and disposition. The heritage which is already yours is a good name and as good an education as I could afford to give. Remain strictly honest, truthful, industrious and frugal. Throw your whole energy into the pursuance of the calling you have chosen. Serve the Lord and keep Him always before you; toward man be amiable, accommodating and modest, and you will fare well even without riches. My last word to you is: Honor your mother. Help her bear her dreary widowhood. Leave her undisturbed in the use of the small estate, and assist if there should be want.

Farewell, wife and children![1]

CONTEMPORARY ETHICAL WILLS

There is a contrast between the traditional ethical wills where fathers were prone to loftiness and sermonizing and the earthiness of contemporary wills. Although recent ones include values and guidance, there is also an expression of love, appreciation and validation for children. In many wills the intergenerational values continue to be underscored. Children are asked to continue traditions, and nourish family relationships. Sam Levenson, the late American humorist and humanist, was blessed with an ability to transmit his convictions with poetic language. Through publishing his will, he left something special to all of us. For many of us there are people other than family who have left a philosophy or a way of behaving which is an ethical legacy. He passes on respect for his origins, loyalties and social values to his grandchildren and to children everywhere.

I leave you my unpaid debts. They are my greatest assets. Everything I own, I owe:

1. To America I owe a debt for the opportunity it gave me to be free and to be me.
2. To my parents I owe America. They gave it to me and I leave it to you. Take good care of it.
3. To the biblical tradition I owe the belief that man does not live by bread alone, nor does he live alone at all. This is also the democratic tradition. Preserve it.
4. To the six million of my people and to the thirty million other humans who died because of man's inhumanity to man, I owe a vow that it must never happen again.
5. I leave you not everything I never had, but everything I had in my lifetime: a good family, respect for learning, compassion for my fellow man and some four-letter words for all occasions: words like help, give, care, feel and love.

Love, my dear grandchildren, is easier to recommend than to define. I can tell you only that like those who came before you, you will surely know when love ain't; you will also know when mercy ain't and brotherhood ain't.

The millennium will come when all the "ain'ts" shall have become "ises" and all the "ises" shall be for all, even for those you don't like.

Finally, I leave you the years I should like to have lived so that I might possibly see whether *your* generation will bring more love and peace to the world than ours did. I not only hope you will, I pray that you will.

Grandpa Sam Levenson[4]

One need not be a poet or a great essayist to counsel one's children to be honorable and to live by moral and religious principles. The will can be simply written. "Words that come from the heart enter the heart," says the Talmud, the body of Jewish civil and canonical law. Simple statements scribbled on a scrap of paper and letters written at the moment thoughts occurred, are very precious.

With all my heart I want all my children to live constantly in perfect harmony, not to allow family ties to loosen, to avoid all disputes and unpleasantness and to exercise tolerance to one another. Let my children set an example for their children for these qualities have always insured happiness and prosperity. And I hope my children will never forget my wish.

With all my love,
Ma
Lottie Tobin (Mrs. David)

This elderly woman expressed with directness and simplicity her desire for her children to stay connected and close and to pass this on to the succeeding generation. Her son cherished this ethical will and shared it with pride and affection. It was left in a strong box and discovered after her death a few years ago.

The following letter was found after the mother's death. She reiterated her religious beliefs, the importance of her family, and expressed her abiding love.

My Dear Daughter,

Today is an exceptionally happy one for me. My family and I are on our way to a happy religious experience and my heart is joyful. My main prayer is for a renewal of faith and with faith a new experience in loving and joyful living—being able to express our love to the other just a little easier.

We each know our inner feelings best and I want to express my deep love and respect for you. Sometimes I am not able to show affection as I desire to do so—nevertheless my love is always with you. My family is my only love.

At this time let me apologize for the mistakes I've made and I offer no excuse as I acted according to my best judgments. If errors were made as I'm sure there were, let us try to leave them here in the hands and heart of our eternal mother. May she guide you long after I'm gone and so some day we should all meet again.

Your father would have been proud of you as I am also. You are as beautiful to me today as the day I first looked at "a daughter." You have always been sweet when I needed you. That is why I had to kiss you in church last Sunday. Let us try to be more friendly and display the affection I've held back through all these years. I was afraid to love openly while all the time I only kidded myself. God knows how much I love you; but I was afraid even to have you love me lest the sorrow would be too great in parting. I never believed I'd be here with you today.

May this be a new beginning for us.

> As ever,
> Your Mother
> Elizabeth Thompson

This precious document was treasured by the daughter when she discovered it. She regretted that her mother never shared the letter or her feelings because it would have made a great difference in their relationship.

An immigrant with little formal education but a great deal of innate business acumen and an unshakable belief in acts of charity, left this letter to his children and grandchildren. Although he had accumulated great wealth, his most significant and prized bequest was the short letter found amongst his papers. In his own inimitable language, he set forth the philosophy that had governed his life.

To my family, and Grandchildren

This is my last letter and when you read it, I will only be a memory.

I don't think that I have to write you much, as thank God you are educated and smart enough to understand that this world is not easy. I am sure you will endure it and you will continue to follow in the footsteps of Mother as she was one of the greatest women who ever lived.

The luckiest thing for me was meeting your mother, and she to some extent, was responsible for the accomplishment of many of the successes in our life, as she was not only looking for herself but what can be done for the family and others. To some extent she copied our Grandparents. I am sure that you will continue the kind of life and keep close with all our families and try to do as much as you can for each other.

Don't forget your seats at the Park Synagogue.

Stay well and keep up your good work.

Your Father, Grandfather
Leonard
Leonard Ratner

This will was written about seven years ago and was intended as a traditional ethical will. In it Mr. Ratner gives his children the gift of his faith in them. He stresses intergenerational values, the importance of family and maintaining religious ties. His wife is remembered and extolled in his loving letter.

IMPROVISING AN ETHICAL WILL

The continuity and influence of one generation upon another is a basic concept in an ethical will. Usually it is written by parents addressed to children and grandchildren. Sometimes we are strongly influenced by foster parents, aunts and uncles, siblings, friends, teachers, clergy, and mentors. If your parents or other significant persons have not left you a written document or letter, imagine you are a scribe writing one for them. Step back and explore the character and values your parents or other significant person professed. If your parents are living, you can do more than think about it; you can discuss it with them. People who have had these discussions with their parents or other significant persons have reported these to be meaningful contacts. Constructing your parents' ethical wills can be an exciting project for three generations to share (grandparents, parents, grandchildren) and adds a significant dimension to the construction of a family tree.

If your parents are deceased, try to imagine a conversation with them about the things they believed in. Imagine you hear them trying to get ideas across to you, and talk to other relatives who knew them. Even if your memories are blurred, with searching you can recall statements, deeds, and incidents that illustrate the keystones of your parents' character. Reviewing photographs will help you jog the memory. The recollections can then be a guide for constructing an ethical will your parents might have written had they thought or known to do so or anticipated its value to you.

Below are portions of the wills Elaine Shuman Kittredge wrote for her parents while they were both alive:

My father's legacy to me:

He gave me the openness to be generous to strangers and friends and not use money as a tool to control people.
He gave me the knowledge that to be proud of my achievements is not vanity but a part of human joy.
He gave me the knowledge that to give all of my love does not deplete my resources. That to give everything I know and believe is worthwhile to others, is the meaning of life.

My mother's legacy to me:

She taught me how to laugh loudly and to cry without shame.
She taught me that I am responsible for myself no matter what age I am.
She taught me to be proud and strong as a woman in an unliberated day and age.

Every important relationship has problems and conflicts that are a part of it. There may be a particular characteristic of your parents that you do not want to imitate. Perhaps your relationship with your parents held more conflict than stability. There may have been problems because of an unstable personality, an uncontrollable temper, alcoholism, violence, or other negative factors. Unpleasant memories and feelings may be the most prominent for you, or you may have blocked out all memories—the good along with the bad. However, there are certain to be some good memories and you can, if you work at it, retrieve them. It is possible to learn from negative characteristics and turn them into positive guidelines. There is always something to be learned from your parents' example and your relationship with them. Your awareness of their mistakes and weaknesses can also be a bridge to compassion and understanding.

After you have created an ethical will that your parents or other significant person could have written, examine your way of living. You may discover the ways in which you reflect your parents' values and beliefs. Perhaps you have used their standards as a foundation and have creatively evolved your own values. At first it may appear you are different but with a closer look you may find similarities.

Outwardly it often appears that a child has rejected parents' values but on close examination the similarities become clear. Paula's mother had

an upper middle-class home, tastefully furnished with exquisite possessions she had planned to bequeath to her daughter. Paula lived on a farm
in New England, raised her own food, and used a wood burning stove for
heat. The exterior trappings of their lives were in contrast. After her
mother's death Paula sobbed:

> I hope she knew I do hold her values, the most important ones she worked
> so hard to make real for me. She taught me to be empathetic, compas-
> sionate, sensitive, honest; how to be well organized, competent, depend-
> able and authentic—to always be the best kind of person I could possibly
> be—and to have no regrets. I value my education, but most importantly I
> value the *process* of learning, of stretching to comprehend and acting on
> that knowledge. I appreciate my musical and dance training. I love music
> and dance. It surrounds me in so many diverse forms: lambing season,
> maple sugaring, the night sounds and smells of spring, the slow unfolding
> of the light green leaves which become larger and more deeply colored as
> they mature through the season and grow to the crescendo of fall.
>
> My family is most important to me. My husband and I share chores and
> decisions just as my parents did. Essentially she taught me her values and I
> augmented and personalized them. I do hope she knew.

VARIATIONS

Telling or writing your parents or another significant person what he
or she means to you, how your life has been influenced by your contact,
and remembering special times together is a way of writing an ethical will
for them or with them. It is an ethical will in reverse. This is a way of
helping the person to recognize the significance of his or her life and the
importance the relationship has had for you.

> Sarah's dear friend, thirty years her senior, has enriched her life and has
> been a major influence on her. Sarah related: "Esther's relationship with
> her husband, the form of her creative talent, and her attention to social
> issues have provided a powerful model for me. The influence of her values
> and principles and the importance of the relationship have been acknowl-
> edged in letters as well as in conversations in which we were both deeply
> moved."

Many times statements have not been made either orally or in writing
because the idea has never occurred to the individual. Family members
can encourage and lead a conversation that will allow opportunities for
recounting the high points, special events, and relationships that

motivated and gave value to the person's life. This may include the trials and tribulations and the mastery of those hard times. It is comforting for the person to be reminded of the role he or she played in molding the character of children, grandchildren, and other relatives and friends, and how that wisdom and influence will continue to guide them throughout their lives. Even though the phrase "ethical will" is never used, there is a reciprocal process of comfort and bequest between the special person and loved ones. This variation of the ethical will is valuable with the elderly, the chronically ill, or terminally ill relative, friend, or patient. These things can be talked about and the discussion continued from time to time. You may suggest writing it down for the person, but do what is appropriate and meaningful for the situation.

A variation of an ethical will can be created through a letter to a significant person motivated by a special occasion or crisis in the family. Two years had passed since the traumatic death of Belle's husband. She was feeling better and stronger and giving new direction to her life. She reflected on this one day and realized there was a strength within her that came from her relationship with her mother. This was shared in the following letter:

Dear Mama,

I want to thank you for being my mother and helping me to become the person I am today. You have been a source of strength and courage to me. I don't know exactly how you did it, all I know is whatever you instilled in me in my formative years has helped to sustain me, particularly in the past few years.

I think what I love most about you is your great zest for life and your willingness to meet new challenges. Could one ask for more than such a guiding force?

I love you Mama and always will. Thank you for giving me life and teaching me how to live, think and feel, and how to give and receive love. You have been the single most important person in my life.

Love,
Your loving daughter
Bella
Belle Savransky

Her mother called her immediately after reading the letter and said: "Thank you. It was the most beautiful letter I ever got."

The following letter from a young man to his grandfather brought tears to the old man's eyes and lifted his heart:

Dear Grandpa,

I am rushed by thoughts of you. Going to Highlands was such an emotional experience. I stood in the back of the store where you used to have the jeans stacked and cried and cried and cried. I cried for the frailty of my Grandpa's body—and for mine which has grown bigger and older than I ever thought it would.

I know that you are very frustrated with your frail condition but perhaps there is a purpose to it. Many men might have died from what you have already suffered. Perhaps God has given you this time for a reason. Perhaps He wants you to sit back, to remember, to feel, to ponder your life. Perhaps He wants you to open your arms and gather up the love that has come back to you in this life from family and friends. And this will take some time—to grasp your life, its deficits and riches—because it has been a long life and a complex one and a blessed one.

And when you are ready you will go to God with your arms full of the goodness and the love and you will say: "I am Sam Silberblatt. Behold the wonder of your work. I bring you much love and a bloodline vibrant and true to you." And I know God will embrace my Grandpa. I know this.

Love,
Bob
Robert Kamm

Bob is a sensitive and articulate young man, generous in sharing his innermost feelings. Grandpa's illness is recognized, not denied, and is addressed honestly as well as with sympathy. He is given credit for his strength and for surviving. Bob validates his grandfather as an individual and underscores the importance of his life. The letter was cherished by the old man.

More Variations on the Theme

Another variation of the form of an ethical will is transcribing a message on audio tapes. Dr. Moses Joel Eisenberg, the father of Rabbi Frederick Eisenberg of Fairmount Temple, Cleveland, Ohio, and Mr. Samuel Bernstein, the father of the composer and conductor Leonard Bernstein, recorded 12 hours of conversation together on tapes over a four year period.[5] This was done about 10 years before their deaths. These men had pride in their knowledge, their ideas, and their accomplishments. These conversations were meant specifically as an inheritance for the family and were designated as ethical wills. It was a creative and lively way to record their ideas and precious for the families to be able to hear their fathers' or grandfathers' voices. These conversations included their understanding of religion, the meaning of life, how they felt about the world and even some stories from the old country. Each conversation was seriously thought out. Dr. Eisenberg's grandson recently heard a tape and was able to glean an aspect of his grandfather that he had never known.

An ethical will may take the form of a discussion of ideas and principles among members of a family; it can be a philosophy and ideals inculcated by words and example over the years. Madeline's memory of her father is his ethical bequest to her:

> The song "Do It My Way" brings tears to my eyes. It unmistakably sums up my Dad. His work was centered on standing up for what he believed and fighting for it for himself and others. His position was often unpopular and people were angry at him. I remember his example when I have to stand up for something I think should be done at work. It gives me courage to know that's the way Dad would have done it, and it gives me strength to do what I need to do. I know he would have been behind me.

We can learn from children, too. One mother remembers her daughter's lovely disposition and her ability to reach out to others. She often thinks, "My daughter would have done it this way. That's what I will do."

DO IT YOURSELF

Constructing your own ethical will is a difficult task and can be a deeply moving experience. The death of a loved one jolts you into acknowledging your own mortality. It means realizing that you will not always be around to say things to your children or others who are important. It involves confronting yourself, clarifying your values, reviewing the significance of your life, and evaluating your important relationships in an attempt to insure a clear legacy of your values that may sometimes seem ambiguous. In a way you are saying to your loved ones: "I want to be sure you know what I believe in and what my life is about." You have to know this for yourself before you can convey it to anyone else. An inventory of your own standards is taken as you also face your own mistakes, failures, and regrets. This will give you an opportunity to see if your values match your everyday actions. Ask yourself, "Am I doing what I want to be doing; is my behavior synchronized with my beliefs; does the way I put in my time demonstrate what and who is important to me?" You can use your will for yourself as well, and make every effort to translate what is important to you into your behavior. You can talk to the people to whom you have something special to say. Following is part of Elaine's legacy to her daughter:

What my legacy to Nancy will be:

> To fully appreciate each thing for itself and to accept and love people as they wish to be known at their best.
> To forgive people their small faults when it doesn't hurt anyone.
> To be kind and affectionate to people when they are tired and crabby rather than blaming them, remembering similar moments of her own.
> To let herself "crack up" or be "taken care of" when she feels weak, knowing that if she does, she can get up again stronger, weakness and strength being two poles of one concept.
> To have a good time in life and play a lot.
> To do experiments like this one just to see what happens.

Writing an ethical will can start a new tradition in your family that may bind the generations together in common values and love. Your family may also revel in the wealth of their memories.

10

HELPING THE BEREAVED

THE DEATH OF A RIGHTEOUS ONE
Expiation and Irony

All you have to do is say
    that someone died
      some one
    and people will be nice
      to one another.
Petty arguments will dissipate
and all you have to do is say
    Phil dropped dead
      waiting to cash a check
      at the bank.
If he was forty-four
    it is better.
If he left five orphans
    and a wife
      so much more the tragedy
      so much more
    the conversations switch
      to moderates,
    to neutral subjects,
      to Phil's family.
Think of the Kennedys—
    how we all watched together,

227

the boots turned back
  in the stirrups
    and the caisson's pull
  to Arlington
  and eulogies.
No man slapped his son that day.
No sister screamed or hit her little brother.
Everywhere there was a sense
  of peace on earth
    good will towards men.[1]

                         Danny Siegel

The poet's words describe with pathos, the suspension of pettiness often evident for a short time after a death. All are affected by a death. Too soon, the hushed voices and special concern for the bereaved are dissipated as friends and family disperse to their own involvements.

The communal gathering, although short-lived, is a concentrated demonstration of concern for the bereaved. Mourners feel supported and cared about and feelings of isolation are reduced. The death causes ripples in the lives of anyone connected to the deceased or to the family. The world stops for a while to pay tribute to the deceased and to show concern for the bereaved.

There is a realistic aspect as to how much time others can allot to this demonstration. It may appear harsh or unfeeling, but of necessity the community must get back to work, back to their own daily lives. They come together only to disperse again leaving the bereaved on their own.

The mourner looks in wonderment at the rest of the world which apparently goes on as if nothing happened. For the mourner, the whole world has stopped, surely the whole world has changed. Life goes on for the community, and mourning goes on for the mourner.

The fact that life goes on or daily maintenance tasks are continued by most people is not an indication to the bereaved that mourning should be put aside. You, the mourner, need to pay attention to your own feelings and do what is best to express them. Follow your own inclination to support yourself during the process of mourning. Do not be thwarted by misinterpreting messages from others or having unrealistic expectations of yourself.

Disharmony persists throughout the mourning process as movement is made from chaos to clarity. You need to be able to tolerate the emotional chaos and stay with the experience as it unfolds in its own natural way. There are many changes to accommodate. If changes and endings cannot be assimilated, the unfinished business of mourning, that is, the prominence of the deceased and the grievous feelings, will continue to intrude upon the present. It will interfere with involvement in your daily life and in relationships.

A natural completion of the relationship is not possible when death forces an ending and there may be a sense of unfinished business. Closure is desired and it is natural to repeat over and over again in an attempt to gain completion. You need to be in touch with your feelings, your own needs, and allow your own expression. The mourner needs support in order to reach beyond the familiar means of coping.

The way to express your feelings is through *permission*: the permission you give yourself and the permission you receive from others. Restraint and suppression of feeling can be harmful. There are people who face the crisis by denial, self-imposed or societally imposed. Any barrier raised between you and your feelings merely prevents integration and the ability to clear the way for rebuilding your life.

The avoidance is fostered by clichés offered to the bereaved by well-meaning friends who do not realize they are invalidating the person's normal feelings, leading the mourner to believe there must be something wrong because he or she continues to feel badly. "If everyone tells me it's time to forget, why do I still feel so pained and sad?" The bereaved need someone to help with their grief; not discount it; someone to mourn with them. It is supportive to accept the expression of feelings and be non-judgmental.

Sometimes well-intentioned friends, not knowing what to say or how to be helpful, repeat clichés that foreclose expression of grief and make mourners feel they are not understood. They are verbal rituals that are relied on when feeling helpless and wordless: "It's God's will; you must be strong; the children need you; you must keep busy; you have to go on living; be glad his suffering is over; things will get back to normal soon; time heals all wounds."

"It's God's will" implies you are not supposed to feel badly about it. This is an unfair position to put God in. God does not will misfortune on anyone. Believing in God does not remove sadness. No matter what your religious belief, when a loved one dies it is normal to have the feelings concomitant to bereavement.

"You must be strong" usually means: "Don't cry; I can't bear to see you cry." Tears are a physiological as well as emotional release for grief. Crying has nothing to do with strength; it is an expression of feelings.

"The children need you" implies you would be incapable of caring for them if you show your emotions. Actually, the children need you to be real, to give expression to your feelings, and to be a model for them. Showing your grief openly does not mean you will not be able to go on with your daily life and take care of the children.

"You must keep busy" is a suggestion for the denial of the reality of the death. It suggests a flurry of activity will stop you from thinking and feeling. Contrary to the implication that "busy" makes it better, keeping overly occupied inhibits the mourning process. People need to take time to pay attention to their feelings; that is the only way they can be worked through.

"You have to go on living," you don't really have any choice about that. You do go on living, except the living is difficult. Some people have fantasies about how they would react if their loved one died. They think: "If this happened to me I couldn't go on, or you look so sad, as if you're not going to make it. So stop looking so sad." The implication is that you should go on as if nothing has happened. That, of course, is impossible. Your life has changed, but it will go on.

"Be glad his suffering is over." After a painful or debilitating illness, it is natural to feel relieved that your loved one is no longer suffering. That does not mean you do not have other feelings that accompany the relief.

"Things will get back to normal soon." There is no such thing as "getting back to normal." Life has been changed and the transition will be painful but maturing. You will take up some of the strands of your past life, but many things will be different.

"Time heals all wounds." It is not just the passage of time that heals, but the use of time to do your mourning that heals and leads to integration.

You must be allowed and allow yourself to go through the mourning process. It takes a long time, and unless the mourner permits all feelings, no matter how often they recur, and expresses them through tears and words, the intensity of grief will not subside. It may be tamped down, but will inevitably flare up at some time in the future.

Recovery from the trauma of bereavement does not mean forgetting. Sadness and memories remain, but the integration of the loss allows you to appreciate your life again. Sadness and enjoyment can coexist. You can laugh again, form new attachments, and turn toward new directions, and even be able to find pleasure doing some of the things you had once shared with the loved one who died.

HOW OTHERS CAN HELP

Mourning is long and arduous and moves from foreground, the major focus in one's life, to background, after the feelings have been felt, the memories relived and repeated, and the tears shed. Repetition is an important aspect of the mourning process. So repeated here are a few salient points to be remembered by those who want to help their loved ones through the experience.

It is most important for family and friends to understand the mourning process and to give open permission to share feelings. Encourage the bereaved to talk about the deceased, talk about their pain, anger, sorrow, and let the tears flow unashamedly. Avoid clichés. Do not preach the three sermons too many people utter: "Be strong; keep busy; things will get back to normal." What was "normal" before the death or illness is no longer possible. Everything becomes different, difficult, and a challenge. A new *normal* evolves.

Be mindful of the things that are hard for the bereaved: working, daily chores, making decisions, having no one to talk to, weekends, holidays, birthdays, and anniversaries of the death. Even seemingly simple things like sleeping through a night and getting out of bed in the morning are troublesome. It is painful to see the unoccupied chair, the constant reminder of the missing person. Staying home alone without the companion of many years is as difficult as going out in public. Making small talk is terribly taxing, and staying alone is lonely. Friends and family can help by lending a hand with everyday tasks, running errands, *being available to talk when the mourner desires.* It is helpful to offer to accompany the person on those first excursions such as shopping at the supermarket, taking a walk around the block, returning to work or socializing.

From the time of the first condolence call until the death is integrated many months or years later, others need to encourage the bereaved to talk about feelings. They should share their own sense of loss. Do not hesitate to talk about the deceased, recalling fond memories and amusing incidents.

It is very important that friends and family not expect a quick recovery. Do not let the bereaved be saddled with unattainable expectations. Do not rush them. Be patient with each one's own time schedule for mourning and reentry into activities. If you are concerned about the bereaved and believe, despite your support and interest, there is no movement through the phases of grief, you might suggest broadening the support base by encouraging the person to investigate community programs for the bereaved. Many family and social service agencies, churches, and hospitals offer support groups for the bereaved. Some persons may prefer individual help from a psychologist, social worker, or psychiatrist; some find comfort from reading about others who have suffered a similar loss. We urge the bereaved to follow their hearts to the sources of support they believe will help them through this sad and painful time.

Above all, be loving, be patient, be there. Remember that the mere presence of a caring and concerned person is very comforting; it attests to your love and concern and makes the loss a little easier to bear.

It is not easy to be a good friend to the bereaved, to become emotionally involved and feel some of the pain of loss. Nevertheless helping someone else through the traumatic time can illuminate your own life. Being close to death can change your perspective and priorities and help you make decisions about your life you might otherwise have avoided.

> For the first time in my life TIME, now, in great big capital letters, is of paramount importance. It's closing in on me as if I have to do everything now. Right now! I felt if I was going to make changes in my life, now is the time to do it. Life has become more precious.

Your perception of life and time changes, following the death of anyone dear to you. Having matured from the experience, you grow strong and able to face the future, realizing how precious time and life are.

WHIRLPOOL

Nighttime swims in a whirlpool of
Confusing tenses.
Truth turns in a blur.
All questions spin to the surface,
blinking with astral reflections.
   Then everything stops.
   A star is falling.
Morning runs on the mountaintop
Gravel crunches under every step.
Sunrise fills the hills with new color,
Soothes the ripples in the pond
Warms the sense of life.

David Weizman

REFERENCES

CHAPTER 1

1. Becker, Ernest. *The Denial of Death*. New York: The Free Press, A Division of Macmillan Publishing Co., Inc., 1973.
2. Worden, J.W. & Proctor, W. *Personal death awareness*. Englewood Cliffs, N.J.: Prentiss Hall, 1976.
3. Parkes, C.M. *Bereavement. Studies of grief in adult life*. New York: International Universities Presss, 1972.
4. Lindemann, E., Symptomatology and management of acute grief, *American Journal of Psychiatry*, 1942, *101*, 141–148.
5. Caplan, G. *Principles of preventive psychiatry*. New York: Basic Books, 1964, pp. 62–63, 82–85.

CHAPTER 2

1. Rosenblatt, P.C., Walsh, R. & P., Jackson, D.A. *Death, grief and mourning in cross cultural perceptions*. New Haven, Ct.: HRAF Press, 1968, p. 41.
2. Aries, P. The hour of our death. New York: Alfred A. Knopf, 1981.
3. Steel, R.L. Dying, death, and bereavement among the Maya Indians of Mesoamerica. *American Psychologist*, 1977, 1060–1067.
4. Pasachoff, J.M., Cohen, R.F., & Pasachoff, N.W. Belief in the supernatural among Harvard and West African University students. *Nature*, 1970, 227, 471.
5. Gorer, G. *Death, grief and mourning*. Garden City, N.Y.: Doubleday, 1965, p. 127.
6. Klein, I. *A time to be born, a time to die* (Ecclesiastes 3:2). New York: Youth Commission, United Synagogue of America, 1976.
7. Salzberger, R. Death: Beliefs, activities and reactions of the bereaved: Some psychological and anthropological observations, *Human Context*, 1975, 7, 103–116.
8. Schwab, J.J. Bereavement, studies in grief, a preliminary report, part II. In B. Schoenberg, I. Gerber, A. Wiener, A.H. Kutscher, & D. Peretz (Eds.). New York and London: Columbia University Press, 1975, p. 78.
9. Glick, I.O., Weiss, R.S., & Parkes, C.M. *The first year of bereavement*. New York: London, Sydney, Toronto: Wiley, 1974.
10. Lamm, M. *The Jewish way on death and mourning*. New York: Jonathan David Publishers, 1969.

CHAPTER 3

1. Furman, E. *A child's parent dies*. New Haven and London: Yale University Press, 1974.
2. *Websters new world dictionary* (2nd college edit.). New York: Simon & Shuster, 1980.

3. Kübler-Ross, E. *On death and dying.* New York: MacMillan, 1970, 1969, 1974.
4. Parkes, C. M. *Bereavement, studies of grief in adult life.* New York: International Universities Press, Inc., 1972, p. 71.
5. Rees, W.D. The bereaved and their hallucinations. In B. Schoenberg, I. Gerber, A. Wiener, A.H. Kutscher, D. Peretz. *Bereavement, its psychosocial aspects.* New York and London: Columbia University Press, 1975, p. 66.
6. Clayton, P.J. Weight loss and sleep disturbance in bereavement. In B. Schoenberg, I. Gerber, A. Wiener, A.H. Kutscher, & D. Peretz. *Bereavement, its pyschosocial aspects.* New York and London: Columbia University Press, 1975, p. 72.
7. Winfrey, C. "Harlem firehouse cries for two who fell in duty," N.Y. Times, June 29, 1980, p. 18.
8. Bowlby, J., Processes of mourning. *The International Journal of Psycho-Analysis,* 1961, *42,* 317–340.
9. Dohrenwend, B.S. & Dohrenwend, B.P. A brief historical introduction to research on stressful life events. In *Stressful life events: Their nature and effects.* New York: Wiley, 1974.
10. Bartrop, R.W., Lazarus, L., Luckhurst, E., Kiloh, L.G., & Penny, R. Depressed lymphocyte function after bereavement. *The Lancet,* 1977, Vol. I, No. 8016, pp. 834–836.
11. Leshan, L. Cancer mortality rate: Some statistical evidence of the effect of psychological factors. *Archives of General Psychiatry,* 1962, *6,* 333–335.
12. Leshan, L., & Worthington, R.E. Personality as a factor in the pathogenesis of cancer: A review of the literature. *British Journal of Medical Psychology,* 1956, *29,* 40, 49–56.
13. Parkes, C. Effects of bereavement on physical and mental health—A study of the medical records of widows. *British Medical Journal,* 1964, *2,* 274–279.
14. Rosch, P.J. Stress and illness. *Journal of the American Medical Association,* 1979, *242,* 427, 428.
15. Schleifer, S.J., Keller, S.E., Camerino, M., Thornton, J.C., Stein, M. Suppression of lymphocyte stimulation following bereavement. *Journal of American Medical Association,* July 15, 1983, Vol. 250, No. 3.
16 Holmes, T.H., & Rahe, R.H. The social readjustment rating scale. *Journal of Psychosomatic Research,* 1967, *11,* 213–218.
17. Rahe, R.H., Ryman, D.H., & Ward, H. Simplified scaling for life change events. *Journal of Human Stress,* 1980, 22–26, Vol. VI, No. 4.
18. Rahe, R.H., Meyer, M., Smith, M., Kjaer, G., & Holmes, T.H. Social stress and illness onset. *Journal of Psychosomatic Research,* 1964, *8,* 35–44.
19. Lynch, J.J. *The broken heart.* New York: Basic Books, 1979, p. 36.
20. Carr, A.C., & Schoenberg, B. Object loss and somatic symptom formation. In B. Schoenberg, A.C. Carr, D. Peretz, and A.H. Kutscher, (Eds.), *Loss and grief: Psychological management in medical practice.* New York: Columbia University Press, 1970.

21. LeShan, L. An emotional life-history pattern associated with neoplastic disease, *Annals of the New York Academy of Sciences, 125,* 780–793, 1965/1966.
22. Simonton, O.C., & Simonton, S.S. Belief systems and management of the emotional aspects of malignancy. *Journal of Transpersonal Psychology,* 1975, *7* (1), 29–47.
23. Dohrenwend, B.S., and Dohrenwend, B.P. "Life Change & Illness Susceptibility," In *Stressful Life Events: Their Nature and Effects.* Chapter III, p. 45, New York: John Wiley & Sons, 1974.
24. Frey, W.H., III. Not-so-idle tears, lab report. *Psychology Today,* 1980, *13,* pp. 91–92.
25. Frey, W.H., III. Personal telephone interview. January 30, 1981.
26. Selye, H. *The stress of life,* New York: McGraw-Hill, 1956.
27. Selye, H. Have a good cry. *Prevention,* 1980, 126–130, Vol. 32, No. 8.
28. Clayton, P.J., Halikas, J.A., & Maurice, W.L. The depression of widowhood. *British Journal of Psychiatry,* 1972, *120.* 75, 76.
29. Gorer, G. *Death, grief and mourning.* Garden City, N.Y.: Doubleday, 1965.
30. Pincus, L. *Death and the family.* New York: Vintage Books, 1976.

CHAPTER 4

1. Personal Interview with Mathise Jacob Malosioa, from Johannesburg, South Africa, October, 1977, Cleveland, Ohio.

CHAPTER 5

1. Holmes & Rahe. *Social readjustment scale. Journal of Psychomatic Research,* 1967, *11.*
2. Parkes, C.M. *Bereavement studies in grief in adult life.* New York: International Universities Press, Inc., 1979.
3. Holmes, T.H., & Masuda, M. "Life change & illness susceptibility." In B.S. Dohrenwend & B.P. Dohrenwend (Eds.), *Stressful Life Events: Their Nature and Effects.* Chapter 3, p. 68, New York: John Wiley and Sons, 1974.
4. Leshan, L.L., & Worthington, R.E. Personality as a factor in the pathogenesis of cancer: A review of the literature. *British Medical Journal Psychology,* 1956, *29,* 40, 49–56.
5. Schleifer. S.J., Keller, S.E., Camerino, M. Thornton, J.C., Stein, M. Suppression of lymphocyte stimulation following bereavement. *Journal of American Medical Association,* July 15, 1983, Vol. 250, No. 3.
6. Jacobs, S., Ostfeld, A. An epidemiological review of the mortality of bereavement. *Psychosom Med.* 1977:39:344–357.
7. Helsing, K.J., Szklo, M., Comstock, G.W. Factors associated with mortality after widowhood. *American Journal Public Health,* 1981:71, 802–809.
8. Rees, W. "The Bereaved and Their Hallucinations." In B. Schoenberg, I. Gerber, A. Wiener, A. H. Kutscher, & D. Peretz.*Bereavement, Its*

Psychosocial Aspects. Part II, Chapter 7, p. 66, New York and London: Columbia University Press, 1975.

9. Silverman, P. In *Helping each other in widowhood.* D. MacKinzle, M. Pettipas, & E. Wilson. New York: Health Sciences Publishing Corp., 1974, pp. 1–172.

10. Marcus Aurelius Antonius, *Meditations, X.5.*

11. *U.S. Census Report, 1980. Statistical Abstract. U.S. Department of Commerce, Bureau of Census, from Statistics of U.S. Department of HEW Social Security Administration, July 1970.*

CHAPTER 6

1. Bowlby, J. *Attachment and loss, Vol. II, Separation,* New York: Basic Books, 1973.

2. Bowlby, J. Processes of mourning. *The International Journal of Psycho-Analysis,* 1961, *42,* 317–340.

3. Dunton, D.H. The child's concept of grief. In B. Schoenberg, A.C. Carr, D. Peretz, & A.H. Kutscher (Eds.). *Loss and grief: Psychological management in medical practice,* New York: Columbia University Press, 1970, p. 355.

4. Furman, R.A. Reaction to loss. In B. Schoenberg, A.C. Carr, D. Peretz, & A.H. Kutscher (Eds.). *Loss and grief: Psychological management in medical practice.* New York: Columbia University Press, 1970.

5. Terman, L.M., & Merrill, M.A. *Stanford-Binet intelligence scale.* Boston: Houghton Mifflin, 1960.

6. Rahe, R.H., Meyer, M., Smith, M., Kjaer, G., & Holmes, T.H. Social stress and illness onset. *Journal of Psychosomatic Research,* 1964, *8,* 35–44.

CHAPTER 7

1. Shakespeare, Wm., *King John, Act III,* Methuen & Co., London, 1967 Edition.

CHAPTER 9

1. Abrahams, I. *Hebrew ethical wills, Pt. I.* Philadelphia: The Jewish Publication Society of America, 1948.

2. Reimer, J. *Moment,* 1975, 88–91, Reaccess Two Ethical Wills, Vol. I, No. 1.

3. Reimer, J. *Hadassah,* What will you leave your children? 1979, 8–11, Vol. 60, No. 8.

4. Levinson, S. *Women's Day,* 1977, 40th yr., 9th issue.

5. Eisenberg, F. Personal Interview, January 12, 1981.

CHAPTER 10

1. Siegel, D., *And God Braided Eve's Hair,* United Synagogue of America, New York, 1976.

INDEX